CULTURAL PROFICIENCY

THIRD EDITION

Dedication

To Terry L. Cross, Barbara L. Bazron, Karl W. Dennis, & Mareasa R. Isaacs for their seminal work, Toward a Culturally Competent System of Care *(1989, 1993), which serves as a major source of inspiration to us.*

CULTURAL PROFICIENCY

A Manual for School Leaders

Randall B. Lindsey
Kikanza Nuri Robins
Raymond D. Terrell
Foreword by Darline P. Robles

THIRD EDITION

CORWIN
A SAGE Company

For information:

Corwin
A SAGE Company
2455 Teller Road
Thousand Oaks, CA 91320
(800) 233-9936
Fax: (800) 417-2466
www.corwinpress.com

SAGE India Pvt. Ltd.
B 1/I 1 Mohan Cooperative
   Industrial Area
Mathura Road, New Delhi 110 044
India

SAGE Ltd.
1 Oliver's Yard
55 City Road
London EC1Y 1SP
United Kingdom

SAGE Asia-Pacific Pte. Ltd.
33 Pekin Street #02-01
Far East Square
Singapore 048763

Printed in the United States of America.

Library of Congress Cataloging-in-Publication Data

Lindsey, Randall B.
Cultural proficiency: A manual for school leaders / Randall B. Lindsey, Kikanza Nuri Robins, Raymond D. Terrell.—3rd ed.
    p. cm.
Includes bibliographical references and index.
ISBN 978-1-4129-6362-6 (cloth)
ISBN 978-1-4129-6363-3 (pbk.)

   1. Multicultural education—United States. 2. Education—Political aspects—United States. 3. Academic achievement—United States. I. Robins, Kikanza Nuri, 1950- II. Terrell, Raymond D. III. Title.

LC1099.3.C844 2009
370.117--dc22   2009010944

This book is printed on acid-free paper.

15 16 17 18 12 11 10 9

Acquisitions Editor:	Dan Alpert
Associate Editor:	Megan Bedell
Production Editor:	Eric Garner
Copy Editor:	Paula L. Fleming
Typesetter:	C&M Digitals (P) Ltd.
Proofreader:	Susan Schon
Indexer:	Sheila Bodell
Cover Designer:	Rose Storey

Contents

Foreword to the Third Edition

"So, what do you want your students to be able to do when they graduate from your schools?" When I heard this question, I was with a small group of educators and university students at a conference in San Francisco in the mid-1980s. Almost a challenge, the question was posed by Seymour Sarason, a professor emeritus from Yale University.

As a new school site administrator, I was impressed by the thoughtful responses of my colleagues in the room. Many of the responses were similar: mission and vision statements from their school districts. After we spoke, we all looked expectantly to Professor Sarason. He responded with a look of boredom and a sigh. Although you could see in his eyes that he clearly understood our answers, he also knew the statements rang hollow. Did our mission and vision statements really translate to educating the whole child? Did they encompass preparing our students for a future quite different from our childhood?

I recall Professor Sarason's response as if it were yesterday: "Would it not be easier to simply state that we want our students to leave our schools wanting to know more about themselves, others, and the world?" More effectively than all of our words in those mission and vision phrases, he clearly articulated all our hopes and dreams for our students in one sentence. Imagine every student having a deep desire to be self-reflective, to care and know and learn about their neighbors—neighbors not just next door but also in faraway places around the world. With Professor Sarason's words as a catalyst, I began in earnest my journey toward cultural proficiency.

Wanting to learn more about ourselves, others, and the world! A simple statement that was very difficult to put into action. Since the 1980s, my journey toward becoming culturally proficient through self-reflection has guided both my personal and my professional growth. Begin with the inside first and learn more about ourselves.

The third edition of *Cultural Proficiency: A Manual for School Leaders* starts with that premise: a commitment to examining your own values, assumptions, and behaviors to ensure that we serve the needs of all our students. The text provides the reader with effective tools to develop introspective skills and become fully aware of one's strengths as well as barriers to becoming culturally proficient. It is not a quick recipe book or a text for those looking for an easy road to becoming culturally proficient. It does fully engage you in the guiding principles, the language, and the behaviors necessary to celebrate and value diversity.

The text provides illustrative examples of district leaders looking inward to make the changes required to be responsive to their community; it outlines a process for individuals to identify their strengths and areas for improvement along a continuum of cultural proficiency and provides the same framework for the community and the organization. The reader will come to face the historical barriers each of us must overcome to become aware of our behaviors and beliefs that stop us from truly engaging our community and our organization to be culturally proficient.

There is no more visible symbol of change and new leadership in America than the election of the first African American president of the United States. We can take this as testimony to the strength of diversity in its broadest definition. Another president, John Quincy Adams, said it best: "If your actions inspire others to dream more, learn more, do more, and become more, you are a leader." The challenge to be such leaders is upon us. True leadership in the 21st century is built upon the foundation of cultural proficiency. We cannot settle for less—our children and our country depend on it.

—Darline P. Robles

Superintendent
Los Angeles County Office of Education

Foreword to the Second Edition

In the fall of 1968, I left a Roman Catholic seminary and walked into Dominguez High School in Compton, California. As a rookie schoolteacher, I knew nothing about the forces of cultural diversity shaping the school and the history of inequitable school policies and practices in that district that had caused all manner of chaos, including racial tension, riots, bomb threats, and assaults. What I did know is that students, teachers, administrators, and parents couldn't get along and that their disagreements were impeding both teaching and learning.

Thirty-four years later, as I retire this fall as the longest-serving urban superintendent in the country, it's a real pleasure to discover a book for school leaders that offers a systematic approach to addressing problems and challenges that have impeded teaching and learning in so many classrooms, schools, and districts for such a long period of time. I would add that the problems and challenges today are not as obvious as those I encountered as an emergency permit teacher in that tumultuous year of that tumultuous decade. They are, in fact, much more subtle and below the surface, but their ability to impede is in some ways much stronger and more problematic.

This is a book that is grounded first and foremost in respect for people and institutions as they struggle with the important issues of diversity, equity, and fairness. It provides leaders with a profound understanding of the importance of cultural proficiency as a guide to long-term improvement in schools and classrooms, where differences should never be ignored in our haste as school administrators to maintain positive public relations at all costs. It challenges school leaders with a moral imperative and a bias for action that puts the importance of leading the change process as the defining factor in their daily work lives.

Those who are looking for quick fixes, magical cures, and short-term spikes in student achievement will be disappointed by this second edition.

The case studies are rich, the practical applications are relevant, and the exercises are designed to force thinking in new ways that profoundly challenge the status quo. Such activities provide a real guide to longterm thinking about new policies, programs, and practices that offer genuine hope in creating a bright future for all those students who have been left behind in school systems everywhere.

This is the beauty of the moral imperative and urgency that these authors capture better than most in the literature on this subject. It goes without saying that our failure to act and to understand the importance of these concepts will lead to continued handwringing about an achievement gap that couldn't be closed in 1968 and won't be closed in this new century.

—Carl A. Cohn
University of Southern California

Foreword to the First Edition

For years, education work that went under the label *multicultural* was well intentioned and appropriate in orientation but superficial. *Culture* was undefined. Rarely was there any grounding in the study of culture. Even as anthropologists were brought into the picture, our understanding of diversity was not enhanced much given the extremely wide range of cultures that are a part of the American mosaic.

Not only was cultural understanding superficial, but our understanding of pedagogy (especially valid pedagogy) was not much better. Even now, it is hard to have a coherent dialogue about valid pedagogy. It is hard to separate the trivial from the substantial. It is hard to see how valid pedagogy makes a difference in everyday work. Yet powerful general approaches to teaching and learning exist and are well documented, and many demonstrations can be seen (e.g., Eakin & Backler, 1993; Ladson-Billings, 1994; Sizemore, 1983; Suzuki, 1987).

Valid pedagogy shows that, given a high quality of teaching and nurture, all children succeed in spite of IQ, poverty, crime- and drug-ridden neighborhoods, and other issues. Simply put, ordinary teachers who are well prepared, motivated, and dedicated produce high-achieving students. This production is not rocket science. With reasonably hard work and an appropriate focus, success is certain for all children (e.g., Sparks, 1997).

Culture can be understood, and powerful pedagogy is within the grasp of well-prepared teachers. So why does success elude us, especially for so many poor minority students? Simply put, a third factor complicates and obscures our view of both culture and pedagogy. It is politics. Teaching and learning in schools are the sites for power struggles. These sites are the places where hegemonic agendas are played out (e.g., Freire, 1970; Kohn, 1998; Kozol, 1991; Oakes, 1985). The intersection of these three things is the context within which teaching and learning take place. No understanding of school success and failure is possible in ignorance of how these things interact.

A sophisticated understanding of each of these three components separately and in interaction with each other is necessary to raise the level of professional dialogue, analysis, and professional practice.

This book is one in a small number that presents clear voices on these matters. These authors plumb the deep structure of the diversity issue in education. They provide precise definitions of such things as culture and oppression. Moreover, they offer a wide array of anecdotal examples that have the ring of authenticity to them. The anecdotes alone are a rich source of stimulating materials guaranteed to launch meaningful dialogue. The anecdotes bring to life what would otherwise be dry and perhaps irrelevant talk about abstract things, things that are also likely to be decontextualized. Yet the authors weave these anecdotes skillfully into the text, giving it a robustness seldom found in educational literature.

As if this were not enough, the authors provide many activities suitable for staff development. Even veteran staff development leaders will find activities here to enrich their repertoires of best practice.

Culture is real and is a major element in all human interactions. Those who are blind to cultural diversity are blind to reality. Teaching power is also real. Those who are blind to that must improve their own competency. Above all, power and hegemony, the desire by some to dominate vulnerable groups, are alive and well. The ugly history of American apartheid (segregation) is but one example of how hegemony plays out in education and becomes embedded in structures of schooling, root and branch, from ideology to methodology to curriculum to assessment.

The theory and practice described and presented here challenge all to offer at least as much quality as the authors have shown.

This book is a major contribution to the education literature on diversity and pluralism in education. Cultural proficiency, as discussed here, contributes to the language of empowerment.

—Asa G. Hilliard, III
Georgia State University

Preface to the Third Edition

This edition of *Cultural Proficiency* has provided us with the opportunity to write together again and to share with you what we are learning about cultural proficiency. We are most appreciative that Corwin continues to be supportive of our writing and advancing the notion of culturally proficient practices. The third edition incorporates our learning from two sources: (a) our work with schools, educational agencies, and organizations engaged in educating their staffs and clients and (b) colleagues, like you, who have used previous editions to deepen their own understanding of cultural proficiency in the service of their organizations.

Since the publication of the first edition in 1999, we have been pleased with three consistent responses to both previous editions of *Cultural Proficiency.* First, we have had numerous experiences with educators and community partners approaching us after having read vignettes and indicating that we must have modeled the case story on their school/community. In most instances, we had never visited their school or community. We began to see the pervasiveness and timeliness of the issues addressed in our writing. Second, we receive very supportive comments about the design and presentation of the activities. Users of the activities are appreciative that the activities support the content of the book and are leveled to take advantage of the experience of the facilitator and the readiness of the group. Third, we get very positive feedback that we have fused practical, on-site applications with the prevalent theoretical and research literature that addresses issues of oppression, education, and leadership in an integrated approach.

While we've worked hard to retain the integrity of prior editions, we've made the following improvements to this edition:

- A conceptual framework for cultural proficiency is presented in Table 4.2.
- The content and vignettes are updated and expanded.

- Several new activities are added in the Resources section at the back of the book.
- The format has been reorganized to facilitate ease of reading and use of activities.
- A matrix has been added that describes how to use other Cultural Proficiency books.

CONCEPTUAL FRAMEWORK

In ongoing discussions with our coauthors and colleagues, Franklin CampbellJones brought to our attention that our actions imply an underlying conceptual framework to cultural proficiency that needs to be explicated. Developing the conceptual framework shaped our thinking about the book and led to the other revisions designed to make the work more relevant, accessible, and effective. The conceptual framework demonstrates the interrelationship of the tools of cultural proficiency. Chapter 4 presents and describes the conceptual framework, and Chapters 5 through 8 provide detailed descriptions of the tools of cultural proficiency.

UPDATED CONTENT AND VIGNETTES

The world has continued to change since the first and second editions were issued, and we have endeavored to keep the content and vignettes relevant and forward-looking. We pride ourselves on our continuous involvement with P–12 schools, educational agencies, and organizations engaged in educating their staffs and clients. In this edition, we continue to base the behavior of the characters in the vignettes on our experiences and use the vignettes to present issues relevant to today's schools and agencies. The content that surrounds the vignettes reflects what we are learning about personal values and behaviors and organizational policies and practices that support being successful in our schools and agencies. In the case of the vignettes and the content of the text, care is taken to support the material with relevant academic and research citations.

NEW ACTIVITIES

We have added new activities, dropped some activities, and streamlined a few of the activities. This edition has about 25 percent new activities, some developed by us and some by colleagues (duly noted, of course). For ease of reading, all activities have been moved to the Resources section and are presented in the same sequence as the chapters they support.

REVISED FORMAT

The format of this third edition is designed to make the text easier to read. Part I provides the opportunity to develop an understanding of cultural proficiency. Part II takes you deeper into understanding the tools of cultural proficiency with historical, systemic, and personal applications. Part III recaps the case story to inspire a commitment to culturally proficient practices.

The Resources section of the book presents structured activities for you to use in your own personal learning and in professional development with colleagues. Each of the activities correlates with a chapter in the book, and each activity is rated for the expertise of the facilitator and the readiness of the group. *Caution*: Be sure to read the "Introduction to Resource Activities" prior to using the activities with colleagues: this brief essay provides tips to ensure that your experiences will be successful.

MATRIX

Much to our amazement, 10 books on cultural proficiency are now either available or in production. We use the word *amazement* deliberately, because when we began writing the first edition of this book in the early 1990s, we *never* anticipated that the work would be this well received. Obviously, we are gratified to be able to support the work of culturally proficient educators and those who aspire to exhibit culturally proficient practices.

Each of the Cultural Proficiency titles offers a distinct application of the tools of cultural proficiency, and the matrix is organized to inform you which book(s) may be appropriate for your use.

We are most appreciative to those who have contributed to the improvement of this edition of *Cultural Proficiency*. Educators in P–12 schools, colleges/universities, educational organizations, and agencies engaged in educating their staffs and clients throughout Canada and the United States have been generous in describing how they use the content and activities from this book to enrich their own learning and in professional development with colleagues. We are very grateful to Corwin for its ongoing interest in and support for our work. In particular, we are very fortunate to have the collegial guidance of Dan Alpert, our editor and advisor, and the support of Megan Bedell, our associate editor, who keep us focused and on track. The production team at Corwin is most impressive in their commitment to high standards throughout all phases of turning the manuscript into a book. Finally, we appreciate you for your interest in this book and trust that it will serve you well in your professional endeavors.

Randall B. Lindsey, *Escondido, California*
Kikanza Nuri Robins, *Los Angeles, California*
Raymond D. Terrell, *Woodlawn, Ohio*

About the Authors

Randall B. Lindsey, PhD, is Emeritus Professor, California State University, Los Angeles, and has a practice centered on educational consulting and issues related to diversity. Currently, he is coordinator of an EdD cohort in Los Angeles for the School of Education, California Lutheran University, where he served as Interim Dean. He has served as teacher, administrator, executive director of a nonprofit corporation, Distinguished Educator in Residence at Pepperdine University, and Chair of the Education Department at the University of Redlands. All of Randy's experiences have been in working with diverse populations, and his area of study is the behavior of white people in multicultural settings. It is his belief and experience that too often people are observers of multicultural issues rather than personally involved with them. To that end, he designs and implements interventions that address the roles of all sectors of the society.

Randy and his wife and frequent coauthor, Delores Lindsey, are enjoying their current phase of life as grandparents, as educators, and in support of just causes.

Kikanza Nuri Robins, MDiv, EdD, has been an Organization Development Consultant for 27 years, helping people and organizations that are in transition—or ought to be. She specializes in the areas of leadership, change, spirituality, and diversity. Kikanza facilitates groups as they wrestle with and reconcile their conflicts, coaches managers as they make the internal shift to become leaders, serves as a change agent for people and organizations that seek to transform themselves from the inside out, and mentors institutions that are adjusting their systems and structures to improve their effectiveness. She has worked in school districts from New York to California; taught in schools of education; and consulted with corporations such as IBM and Baskin-Robbins, government agencies, and large and small not-for-profit organizations, helping them to close the gap between who they are and who they want to be.

Raymond D. Terrell, EdD, is the Assistant Dean, Research and Diversity and a member of the Department of Educational Leadership at Miami University in Oxford, Ohio. He has served as a high school and junior high school English teacher, an elementary school principal, and an assistant superintendent in public schools in Ohio. He spent one year as a faculty member at Texas A&M University in the Department of Educational Administration. He spent 19 years at California State University, 14 years in the Department of Educational Administration, and for 5 years he was the Dean of the School of Education. Ray has 35 years of professional experience with diversity and equity issues. He has served school districts in California, Arizona, Nevada, Michigan, Ohio, Pennsylvania, and Indiana. Ray writes about issues of diversity, inclusion, and equity.

Ray lives in Woodlawn, Ohio, with his wife Eloise. They have two adult children, Dina and William.

Contact us.

We would love to hear from you. If you would like to talk with us about your work, share an activity, or ask a question, send us a note. We appreciate knowing how our readers use this work.

culturalproficiency@earthlink.net

PART I

Understanding Cultural Proficiency

1

Cultural Proficiency

Any student who emerges into our culturally diverse society speaking only one language and with a monocultural perspective on the world can legitimately be considered educationally ill-prepared.

—Sonia Nieto (2004, p. xv)

Rolling Meadows Unified School District has been getting some bad media coverage. In the past month, local newspaper feature articles about the school district have blared:

"RUSD Misses AYP Target for 2nd Straight Year"

"Local Attorney Alleges Racism at High School"

"Once Proud District, Now Troubled?"

Superintendent Hermon Watson is concerned and privately incensed. He has provided leadership for this district for the past 20 years, and he is not happy to have this kind of press coverage. One of the reasons people live in this bedroom community is that, historically, it has been a stable, safe, family-oriented neighborhood in which to raise kids. It has been a place where people move because the schools are good and people don't have to deal with the issues caused by integrated schools and neighborhoods.

At the same time, Superintendent Watson knows there is basis in fact for the news coverage. First, two of the schools in the district have missed their AYP targets. Second, one of the few black parents in the district, Barbara Latimer, an attorney, has accused some of the high school teachers of racism. However, he reacts strongly to any suggestion that the district is "troubled."

Although Rolling Meadows has its own business and civic center, the majority of the population makes a long commute into the urban center for work. The trade-off is a community that is not fraught with problems associated with larger, urban areas. Today, the paper is quoting parents as saying, "We came out here to get away from these people. Now all they are doing is moving here stirring up trouble and lowering the quality of education for our kids."

Hermon shudders as he imagines his board members reading such news articles over their morning coffee. "We have handled every single incident that has occurred in this district. We don't have racist teachers, we are working to be able to educate all students, and we certainly are not a racist district," Hermon says as he reviews the most recent Tribune *article with his cabinet.*

"No one is perfect, and we have had only a few isolated incidents of educators acting inappropriately. We handled them discreetly, involving as few people as we could, and once handled we don't speak of them again. Likewise, we are putting resources into schools so that we can be more successful with these kids from impoverished backgrounds. My goal is that when we look at the faces in a classroom, or out across the commons area at lunchtime, we don't see colors, we just see kids."

Later in the day at an emergency cabinet meeting, Winston Alexander, the assistant superintendent for business, clears his throat. "I'm not sure, Hermon, but do you think that we ought to hire a consultant? It might look good right now to bring in some outside experts so they can tell the press what a good job we are doing."

"That's a fabulous idea," exclaims Holly Kemp, the assistant superintendent for curriculum and instruction. "We just finished the Regional Association of Schools and Colleges (RASC) accreditation review, so the documents describing our programs and students are in order. We could hire consultants to provide a cultural accreditation of some sort. We are not bad people—surely they will know that."

His cabinet rarely lets him down, Hermon muses. That is why they have been honored as a nationally distinguished district three times in the past 10 years. Aloud he says, "A cultural audit. Good idea. Winston and Holly, can the two of you put together a request for proposal (RFP) this week? Ask our attorney friend, Barbara Latimer, to give you a hand. That should quiet her down for a while, and it will also let her know that we really mean to do well by her people."

"Winston, what kind of money can you find for this? We may need to dig deep to climb out of this hole."

CULTURAL PROFICIENCY: AN INSIDE-OUT APPROACH TO DIFFERENCE

In 1989 Terry Cross, executive director of the National Indian Child Welfare Association in Portland, Oregon, published a monograph that changed our lives. *Toward a Culturally Competent System of Care* provides several tools for addressing the responses to diversity that we have encountered in our work in schools and other organizations. Although Mr. Cross addressed the issues of difference in mental health care, his seminal work has been the basis of a major shift in how organizations across the country respond to difference. We adapted cultural proficiency to our work for several reasons:

- Cultural proficiency is proactive; it provides tools that can be used in any setting, rather than activities and techniques that are applicable in only one environment.
- The focus of cultural proficiency is values based and behavioral, not emotional.
- Cultural proficiency is to be applied to both organizational practices and individual behavior.

Cultural Proficiency

Cultural proficiency is a model for shifting the culture of the school or district; it is a model for individual transformation and organizational change. Cultural proficiency is a mind-set, a worldview, a way a person or an organization make assumptions for effectively describing, responding to, and planning for issues that arise in diverse environments. For some people, cultural proficiency is a paradigm shift *from* viewing cultural difference as problematic *to* learning how to interact effectively with other cultures.

Culturally Proficient Leadership

Culturally proficient leaders display personal values and behaviors that enable them and others to engage in effective interactions among students, educators, and the community they serve. At the organizational level, culturally proficient leaders foster policies and practices that provide the opportunity for effective interactions among students, educators, and community members. Culturally proficient leaders address issues that emerge when cultural differences are not valued in schools and other organizations.

This book is an approach for responding to the environment shaped by its diversity. It is not an off-the-shelf program that supplements a school's programs or a series of mechanistic steps that everyone must follow. As you will learn in this book, cultural proficiency is a powerful set of interrelated tools to guide personal and organizational change.

THE FOUR TOOLS

Cultural proficiency enables educators, schools, and districts to respond effectively to people who differ from one another. Cultural proficiency is a way of being, a worldview, and a perspective that are the basis for how one moves about in our diverse society. It is our experience that once people learn cultural proficiency, they embrace it as a natural, normal way to interact with and respond to people culturally different from them. We have also found that for some people embracing cultural proficiency entails a paradigmatic shift in thinking. People and organizations that view cultural difference as something to overcome are often surprised that it is they who have to change to be effective in cross-cultural situations.

Cultural competence is behavior that aligns with standards that move an organization or an individual toward culturally proficient interactions. There are four tools for developing cultural competence:

1. **The Barriers:** Caveats that assist in overcoming resistance to change

2. **The Guiding Principles:** Underlying values of the approach

3. **The Continuum:** Language for describing both healthy and non-productive policies, practices, and individual values and behaviors

4. **The Essential Elements:** Behavioral standards for measuring and planning for growth toward cultural proficiency

The Barriers

Creating conditions for effective personal and organizational change begins with an informed view of the landscape. There is no disputing the fact that our schools are not effective with all demographic groups of students. Since the end of World War II, public and private schools in Canada and the United States have served increasingly diverse groups of students. Students in today's P–12 schools are diverse in terms of race, ethnicity, gender, ableness, faith, and social class in ways that could not have been imagined in 1945. As the demographics of schools have changed, educators have been very successful in some locales but, for the most part, continue to struggle to serve all students equitably. Cross (1989) provided three caveats of which we must be mindful as we work with our colleagues to create personal and organizational change:

- The presumption of entitlement
- Systems of oppression
- Unawareness of the need to adapt

The **presumption of entitlement and privilege** means believing that all of the personal achievements and societal benefits that one has accrued are due solely to merit and the quality of one's character. It often makes people blind to the barriers experienced by those who are culturally different from them. **Systems of oppression and privilege** are the societal forces that affect individuals due to their membership in a distinct cultural group. Systems of oppression do not require intentional acts by perpetrators; they can be the function of systemic policies and practices. Resistance to change often is the result of an **unawareness of the need to adapt**. Many people do not recognize the need to make personal and organizational changes in response to the diversity of the people with whom they and their organizations interact. They believe, instead, that only the others need to change and adapt to them.

The Guiding Principles

The guiding principles are the core values, the foundation on which the approach is built. They are a response to the barriers, and they equip educators and their schools with a moral framework for doing their work.

- Culture is a predominant force; you cannot not have a culture.
- People are served in varying degrees by the dominant culture.
- The group identity of individuals is as important as their individual identities.
- Diversity within cultures is vast and significant.
- Each group has unique cultural needs.
- The family, as defined by each culture, is the primary system of support in the education of children.
- Marginalized populations have to be at least bicultural, and this status creates a distinct set of issues to which the system must be equipped to respond.
- Inherent in cross-cultural interactions are dynamics that must be acknowledged, adjusted to, and accepted.
- The school system must incorporate cultural knowledge into practice and policymaking.

The Continuum

Six points along the cultural proficiency continuum indicate unique ways of seeing and responding to difference. The first three points along the continuum are comprised of unhealthy values, behaviors, policies, and practices that emerge from the barriers to cultural proficiency:

1. *Cultural destructiveness*—Seeking to eliminate the cultures of others in all aspects of the school and in relationship to the community served

2. *Cultural incapacity*—Trivializing and stereotyping other cultures; seeking to make the cultures of others appear to be wrong or inferior to the dominant culture

3. *Cultural blindness*—Not noticing or acknowledging the culture of others and ignoring the discrepant experiences of cultures within the school; treating everyone in the system the same way without recognizing the needs that require differentiated interaction

The three points at the other end of the continuum are informed by the guiding principles of cultural proficiency and represent healthy individual values and behaviors, as well as healthy organizational policies and practices:

4. *Cultural precompetence*–Increasing awareness of what you and the school don't know about working in diverse settings. At this level of development, you and the school can move in a positive, constructive direction, or you can falter, stop, and possibly regress.

5. *Cultural competence*—Aligning your personal values and behaviors and the school's policies and practices in a manner that is inclusive of cultures that are new or different from yours and the school's and enables healthy and productive interactions

6. *Cultural proficiency*—Holding the vision that you and the school are instruments for creating a socially just democracy; interacting with your colleagues, your students, their families, and their communities as an advocate for lifelong learning to serve effectively the educational needs of all cultural groups

The Essential Elements

The essential elements of cultural proficiency provide the standards for individual values and behavior and organizational policies and practices:

- *Assess culture*—Identify the differences among the people in your environment.
- *Value diversity*—Embrace the differences as contributing to the value of the environment.
- *Manage the dynamics of difference*—Reframe the differences so that diversity is not perceived as a problem to be solved.
- *Adapt to diversity*—Teach and learn about differences and how to respond to them effectively.
- *Institutionalize cultural knowledge*—Change the systems to ensure healthy and effective responses to diversity.

A HISTORICAL CONTEXT

Our work with cultural proficiency has evolved from a number of efforts to address issues that emerge from cross-cultural contact. Some of the efforts are derived from legal processes and others from the need and desire to promote healthy interactions. Principle among those efforts have been desegregation, integration, race relations, human relations, antiracism, anti-oppression, tolerance training, cultural competence, and multicultural transformation. Each term represents changing responses to issues of diversity.

Societal response to diversity has changed a lot in the past 50 years. Each decade has spawned new social policies in response to the current issues of concern. Schools have responded to these changes as well. To understand fully the forces of policy evolution and the multiple factors that have led to policy shifts in U.S. society, particularly in schools, one must track the development of social policies related to the issues of diversity, the major movements in schools, and the concomitant resistance to these changes. Chapter 2 provides a more detailed historical context of cross-cultural contact. We invite you now to reflect on your knowledge of the major social movements, and the terms used to describe them, that affected schools and school policies over the past 50 years:

Prior to the 1950s: Segregation

1950s: Desegregation

1960s: Integration, equal access, equal rights

1970s: Equal benefits, multiculturalism

1980s: Diversity

1990s: Cultural competence

2000s: Cultural proficiency

Prior to the 1950s—Segregation

Before the 1950s, legal separation of cultural and racial groups in the United States was the norm. In the Southern United States, legal forms of segregation included slavery and Jim Crow laws, which defined racial groups, mandated the separation of those races in public settings (e.g., schools, buses, and restaurants), and dictated extremely different ways of treating individuals based on the physical characteristics that identified their ethnicity. The oppression of people of African descent through slavery and Jim Crow systems was based on legislative decisions by Southern states and upheld by state and federal court review. An understated reality in U.S. history is the widespread segregation that existed throughout the Northern states during this same period. Even without the force of law behind it, separation of the races was as evident in the North as it was in the South.

The remanding of people of America's First Nations, Native Americans, to reservations is another example of actions taken by federal and state legislatures, courts, and chief executives. As a further denigration of First Nations people, people of Northern European descent uprooted many and moved them to even less desirable locations when they discovered valuable mineral deposits or otherwise coveted property occupied by the First Nations. Beginning with the Mexican Cession of 1848 (though the encroachment had been underway for well over a century), native residents of what is now the Southwestern United States were often excluded from the political and economic mainstream and increasingly marginalized as European Americans immigrated into that area.

The Chinese Exclusion Acts of 1882 and 1902 were federal legislation supported by the executive and judicial branches of the U.S. government. These acts of Congress were specifically designed to control and minimize immigration once the Chinese were no longer needed in labor-intensive projects, such as building railroads throughout the Western United States. Another example of legally sanctioned segregation is Executive Order 9066, initiated by President Franklin D. Roosevelt and supported by Congress and the U.S. Supreme Court, which herded U.S. citizens of Japanese ancestry into relocation camps during World War II.

The 1950s—Desegregation

The 1954 *Brown v. Topeka Board of Education* decisions that ended segregation in public facilities had its genesis in countless legal initiatives. A few years before the Brown decisions, the state of California, in the 1947 *Mendez v. Westminster* decision, invalidated school attendance patterns that were drawn to exclude Mexican-American children from their local schools. In 1946, President Harry S. Truman issued an executive order to desegregate the military. However, it has taken the half century since Truman's order to desegregate the military. Even now, a compelling argument can be made that although the command structure has been desegregated, African Americans, Latinos, and other people of color and people of low socioeconomic status are overrepresented among the frontline combatants who receive the greatest casualties during conflict.

Throughout the history of the United States, disenfranchised groups have used the courts and the legislatures to seek redress of their grievances. The *Brown* decisions are widely acknowledged to have been the civilian apex of those efforts. Though the *Brown* decisions officially ended de jure (by law) segregation, de facto (actual) segregation did not end. To this day, de facto segregation—segregation practices that are not the result of legal mandates—continues. Nonetheless, the *Brown* decisions provided the legal and political leverage by which segregation policies and practices that permeated every region of this country could be legally dismantled.

The process of school desegregation has been fraught with problems from the very beginning. Despite many situations in which children have benefited from school desegregation (Hawley, 1983; Orfield & Frankenberg, 2007), public attention has chiefly focused on cases of resistance and failure. In Southern states, private academies quickly emerged to offer segregated alternatives to European American students. Throughout the country, families have fled to the suburbs to escape unwanted assignments to schools in urban areas. In some cases, these parents did not want to have their children attend a school outside their neighborhood, but in many cases, parents simply wanted to isolate their kids from children with cultural backgrounds different from their own. Often, they viewed different children as genetically or culturally inferior to themselves. In response, the children and parents who were the targets of these reactions were alienated from the dominant culture.

The 1960s—Integration
for Equal Access and Equal Rights

The shift from desegregation to integration was monumental. The 1960s was the decade of domestic revolutions. There were sit-ins, love-ins, bra burnings, freedom rides, and insurrection in urban centers. It was a period of activism for social justice, with the push for civil rights expanding from the Southern states and broadening to include women and other cultural groups. Although the focus was on the tension between black and white people, in the Western and Southwestern United States, Latino and First Nation children were included in desegregation programs.

In schools, the push to desegregate had two consequences. First, voluntary and mandatory school desegregation efforts were designed to provide children of color the same opportunities that white children were receiving. Second, the expansion of entitlement programs (e.g., Title I of the Elementary and Secondary Education Act and the Emergency School Assistance Act) led to many children of color being placed in programs for the culturally and economically disadvantaged. The unintended consequence of these programs is that certain labels became permanently associated with certain ethnicities, and students in desegregated schools continued to receive substandard educations. During this time, educators became aware of the effects of teacher expectations, gender bias, and second-language acquisition on the quality of instruction.

The 1970s—Equal Benefits and Multiculturalism

During this period, people of color in the United States were striving to extend the legal gains won during previous decades to broader societal contexts, such as the workplace. As educators engaged with more and more children of diverse cultures in their classrooms, they needed new approaches, strategies, and techniques for teaching them. Thus, the educational emphasis on multiculturalism was spawned. Multiculturalism represents a departure from the assimilationist, or melting pot, model, which had worked well for Eastern and Southern Europeans but did not work as well for people of color. Additionally, many educators questioned the appropriateness of assimilation as the goal for every cultural group. During this period, women's issues entered the multiculturalism discussion in many schools. In the broader society, Gay Men and Lesbians also began to claim their rights to equal opportunities and benefits in society.

The 1980s—Diversity

During this era, corporate America discovered that it was good business to address diversity-related issues. Many companies began offering diversity training for managers and other employees, and others began developing distinctive marketing strategies to target various sectors of society. As with most things, however, businesses did not uniformly embrace diversity throughout all companies or even throughout all industries. For example, the banking and the automobile sectors have recognized the money to be made in diverse markets, but the technology sector still appears to be lagging far behind. Similarly, while the leaders in some companies enthusiastically embraced diversity training, others bristled at the mere suggestion of it. During this period, the aspects of diversity included in this training were also expanded from ethnicity, language, and gender to include issues of sexual orientation, disability, and age.

The 1990s and the 21st Century—Cultural Proficiency

The essential elements of cultural competence provide basic behavior standards for interacting effectively with people who differ from one another. Cultural proficiency is a way of being that enables people to engage successfully in new environments. The work of Comer (1988), Levin (1988), Sizer (1985), and Slavin (1996) appears to be consistent with the basic tenets of cultural proficiency. These researchers believe that all children can learn, and they demonstrate that children from any neighborhood can learn well—if they are taught well. Although the national debate over school desegregation has not ended, it now focuses on the equitable distribution of human and capital resources. One of the many contemporary trends in education focuses on finding ways to appreciate the rich differences among students.

Many educators wonder how—or even whether—the previous decade's focus on multiculturalism really differs from the next decade's emphasis on diversity. This shift is not merely a superficial change in terminology but a much needed, profound change in perspective. Unlike multiculturalism, which focused narrowly on students' ethnic and racial differences, diversity responds to societal trends, urging us to take a broader approach to addressing equity issues and encompassing a wide range of differences, including race, culture, language, class, caste, ethnicity, gender, sexual orientation, and physical and sensory abilities among students.

"Culture" Is Inclusive

Culture involves far more than ethnic or racial differences. Culture is the set of practices and beliefs that is shared with members of a particular group and that distinguishes one group from others. Most people think of culture as relating to one's race or ethnicity. We define *culture* broadly to include all shared characteristics of human description, including age, gender, geography, ancestry, language, history, sexual orientation, faith, and physical ability, as well as occupation and affiliations. Defined as such, each person may belong to several cultural groups. An ethnic group is defined by shared history, ancestry, geography, language, and physical characteristics. Individuals may identify most strongly with their ethnic group, as well as several other groups that influence who they are.

Culturally proficient educators demonstrate an understanding of the cacophony of diverse cultures each person may experience in the school setting. Although they accept that they will not necessarily have intimate knowledge about each of the cultures represented in a classroom, school, or district, they recognize their need to continuously learn more. They develop a conscious awareness of the cultures of their districts or schools, and they understand that each has a powerful influence on the educators, students, parents, and communities associated with that district or school. By incrementally increasing their awareness and understanding, they begin to find the harmony within the diversity.

WHAT'S IN IT FOR US?

Cross, Bazron, Dennis, and Isaacs (1993) noted that a number of shifts in society gave rise to a cultural imperative: shifting population demographics, a shifting global economy, a shifting of the social integration and interaction paradigm, and a shifting of the goal from assimilation to biculturalism. Educators must respond to these and other issues of diversity, because effective responses to diversity target several mutually interactive goals about which educators care deeply. Following are effective responses to issues that emerge in a diverse environment:

- Enhance students' ability to learn and teachers' ability to teach.
- Prepare students to find their own places in the global community they will enter when they leave their school communities.
- Promote positive community relations.
- Prepare students for outstanding citizenship.
- Foster effective leadership.

LEARNING AND TEACHING EFFECTIVELY

Addressing the many complex issues associated with diversity is tough under any circumstances. Such issues become even more complex in school settings with large numbers of students whose experiences reflect diverse ethnicities, socioeconomic classes, languages, genders, and sexual orientations. Sometimes, the challenge may seem so daunting as to be impossible. Educators must rise to the challenge, however, if they are to teach their students effectively. For students to learn what their teachers have to offer, they must feel fully appreciated as individuals within the context of their own distinctive ethnic, linguistic, and socioeconomic backgrounds and with their own particular genders, sexual orientations, and sensory and physical abilities. Educators need to address the issues that arise in the midst of diversity and respond sensitively to the needs of students in ways that facilitate learning.[1] Additionally, educators need to address issues of diversity to provide mutual support to one another so that every educator feels understood and respected for who they are and the groups to which they belong.

LIVING IN A GLOBAL COMMUNITY

Over the last 10 to 15 years, it has become increasingly apparent that issues of diversity play a vital role in the economic and political life of the United States. During this time, our work has taken us to Canada, as well as the United Kingdom, France, and Korea. We find that the ability to understand and appreciate diverse peoples both within and across international borders profoundly affects one's ability to flourish in the global economy and the world political community. Educators must prepare learners to function well and to interact effectively with the richly diverse peoples of their worlds. To do so, educators can start by helping students to address issues of diversity in each of their school and home communities.

Educational leaders who are successful in creating culturally proficient learning communities will enable all students to play vital roles wherever they go in the global community. Technology has made the world much smaller. As the business community has learned, this nation's economic and political well-being depends on the ability of educators to foster an appreciation of diversity. If educators are to prepare future adults for this challenge, they must commit themselves to address effectively the issues that arise in diverse environments. These efforts will benefit students who are currently thriving in the public schools, as well as those who are being underserved.

PARTICIPATING IN THE COMMUNITY

Educators play a key role in enhancing the relationship between the school and the community, both as individuals and as participants in schoolwide and districtwide decisions. As you respond to issues of diversity, you can change policies and practices that may negatively affect

---

[1]Specific issues of instruction are addressed in our book *Culturally Proficient Instruction* (Nuri Robins, Lindsey, Lindsey, & Terrell, 2006).

community members whose ethnicity, gender, age, sexual orientation, language, or ability differs from that of school leaders. A holistic approach to issues that emerge in diverse environments provides tools for examining the school and the district to eliminate inappropriate policies, procedures, and practices that create negative outcomes for many students. If teachers and administrators have not been prepared to teach, lead, or work with people who differ from them, then the educational leader must take the initiative and create a learning community so that they can master these skills on the job.

PROVIDING LEADERSHIP

Through a successful approach to diversity, you can improve staff and student morale by improving the effectiveness of communication, reducing complaints, and creating a more comfortable and rewarding climate for all people in the school. As an educational leader, you can learn concepts and skills and translate these into new initiatives, curricula, programs, and activities that will enrich school life for all students and staff. As greater awareness and understanding develop in schools, so too will the awareness and understanding of the larger community be expanded. Very few educators intend to hurt their students or their colleagues. An effective approach to issues of diversity provides everyone with the information and skills that educators need to avoid unintentional slights or hurts (i.e., microaggressions) and to improve the quality of life for school and home communities.

THE CASE

We have worked with many school districts across the country and have spent our careers eavesdropping on conversations among educators. We present snippets of those conversations along with our observations of the people with whom we have worked. We hope that you are enlightened and encouraged by the stories we have woven into a case. In each chapter, we use vignettes from the case—at the beginning of the chapter and, sometimes, integrated into the chapter—to illustrate the points that we make.

To help you use the stories and to prevent them from becoming an impediment to your learning or slowing you down as you move through the text, we present here a description of the two school districts in our fictionalized county and the characters you will meet throughout the text (see Table 1.1). These are the people you will read about in the vignettes that introduce each chapter and who are used to illustrate the points we make in the text. The entire case is presented in the last chapter of the book.

Table 1.1   The School Districts

Rolling Meadows Unified School District	
District Administrators	
Hermon Watson	Superintendent
Winston Alexander	Assistant superintendent for business
Holly Kemp	Assistant superintendent for curriculum and instruction
School Administrators	
Dina Turner	First African American high school principal
Teachers	
Bobby	A consistently unhappy high school social studies teacher and counselor
Celeste	A seasoned high school teacher of mixed heritage
Parents	
Barbara Latimer	An attorney, one of the few black parents in the district. She is on the high school site council and is also on the board of the Citizens Human Relations Council, which deals with issues throughout the county. She is known in both school districts. Her daughter, Kim, attends school in Rolling Meadows.
Coolidge Unified School District	
District Administrators	
Bill Fayette	Superintendent
Leatha Harp	Director of credentialing and certification
James Harris	A diversity consultant who began his career as a social studies teacher
School Administrators	
Steve Petrossian	Elementary school principal
Richard Díaz	Middle school principal
Grace Ishmael	High school principal
Teachers	
Brittney	A naïve, second-year middle school teacher who is working with a provisional credential
Derek	A seasoned and effective middle school social studies teacher who is a friend of DeLois
DeLois	A middle school teacher with a big heart who will do anything to make certain that all of her students learn
Harvey	A jaded middle school teacher
Lane	A middle school teacher who is Harvey's friend

There are two school districts in the case. Rolling Meadows Unified School District is a suburban district serving a largely professional, European American student population. The Coolidge Unified School District is an urban district with an ethnically diverse population. Both districts are moving toward cultural proficiency, though at different paces and with mixed results.

Rolling Meadows Unified School District

Rolling Meadows is a bedroom community that has its own business and civic center. The majority of the population makes a long commute into the urban center for work. The district is growing; it currently has about 15,000 students in three high school clusters, a continuation high school, and an adult school. Ten years ago, 82 percent of the student population of the district was white with 4 percent Asian and Pacific Islander, 6 percent Latino, 2 percent African American, and 1 percent First Nation students. Five years ago, the percentage of white students had declined to 52 percent, while the Asian and Pacific Islander, Latino, African American, and First Nation student populations had increased proportionately. In contrast to the changing student demographics, the teaching force has been relatively stable for the past 10 years. Ten years ago, 90 percent of the teachers were white; today, the percentage has decreased by only 5 percent.

Hermon Watson, the superintendent of the Rolling Meadows District, decides to hire consultants to conduct a cultural inquiry study of the district. As you read the text, you will meet his cabinet and some of the teachers as they respond to the idea of a cultural study.

Coolidge Unified School District

On the other side of the county, Coolidge Unified School District serves the families that live in the urban center where many Rolling Meadows parents work. Coolidge High School continues to be among the schools in the county that earn top academic honors. The advanced placement classes have fewer than 10 percent African American and Latino students. In the last five years, the Title I population has increased from 5 to 35 percent. In that same period, the English as a Second Language (ESL) classes have grown from serving less than 2 percent of the student population to serving slightly more than 35 percent of the student population.

These trends have had two results. The first has been decreased sections of honors classes and a dramatic increase in remedial and heterogeneous classes. The heterogeneous classes in English and social studies were created to overcome criticism about the negative effect of tracking; however, placement in mathematics and science classes has served to stratify the English and social studies classes, despite their alleged heterogeneity. The second effect of the demographic changes has been that the school's standardized test scores have steadily declined, giving local media the impression that the quality of education at the school has deteriorated. Teachers still have an interest in a traditional academic approach to curriculum. They also place a high value on a tracked system in which the highest achievers are allowed to move at an accelerated rate.

The extracurricular programs of the school, except for football and basketball, tend to be associated with cultural groups. Though the sports program is nominally integrated, swimming is perceived to be a European American sport, wrestling a Latino sport, track an African American sport, and tennis a sport for Asians and Pacific Islanders. Student government reflects the demographic profile of the school, but one ethnic group dominates most of the clubs and other organizations. Of the major ethnic groups at the school, Latino students participate least in clubs and other organizations. In recent years, there has been tension among ethnic groups. Some fights and retaliatory attacks have received wide coverage in the newspaper.

Bill Fayette, the superintendent of the Coolidge District, recently hired a diversity consultant, James Harris, to provide training for faculty on cultural proficiency. As you read, you will be able to eavesdrop on conversations among these characters.

RESOURCES FOR DEVELOPING CULTURALLY PROFICIENT LEADERS

We use structured activities in this book to help schools and other organizations move toward cultural proficiency. The activities are not designed to be used as the sole vehicle for making change, nor are they designed to be used as the only intervention in a diversity program. Rather, they are intended for use as part of a comprehensive plan for approaching diversity issues in your school or district. Some of these activities will help you build trust among the members of the planning group. Others will help you introduce and reinforce the guiding principles and essential elements of cultural proficiency. The remainder of the activities will help you explore the concepts that we have presented in the book, or they will help you to facilitate the planning necessary to embrace cultural proficiency as an approach for a school or district.

While this book offers a number of activities that we believe are appropriate for reinforcing or exploring the concepts in the book, we encourage you to not limit yourself. Most of the activities have several variations and in different contexts will be useful for teaching more than one idea. Never conduct an activity simply as a space filler. Always relate the activity to something that the participants are learning and to concepts you want to reinforce. If you have new activities or variations on the activities we have provided, please contact us so that in future books, we can share your ideas with others who are on the road to cultural proficiency.

In most workshops, the papers that are distributed to participants are called *handouts*. In this book, we label any material that is intended for distribution a *response sheet*. The responses that these sheets elicit may be different for each sheet and each group in which you use them. Some have directions, others provide information, and some invite you to complete them with your own ideas and reflections. Most are tied to an activity. You have our permission to duplicate these pages as they are printed, with copyright notice intact, for work within your school or organization.

READ THE TEXT FIRST

With so many activities for getting people to think about issues of diversity and to reflect on their own developing cultural competence, you may be tempted to skip the text and to proceed to the activities. We do not recommend that approach; each activity is linked to the text and the portion of the case study found in each chapter. Reading the text and discussing the case study will provide a context for these activities.

Base your decisions to use a specific activity on its purpose, the skill of the facilitator, and the maturity of the group. Before conducting an activity, assess the readiness of the group and the expertise of the facilitator in working with groups on issues of diversity. We have rated each activity so that you can see the minimum level of experience and readiness we recommend for it to be successful.

Readiness is determined by the experience the group members have in doing the following:

- Effectively responding to conflict situations
- Openly discussing difficult issues
- Honestly articulating their feelings
- Comfortably interacting with people who strongly disagree with them
- Willingly examining their own values and behavior
- Candidly examining the school's policies, procedures, and practices for benign discrimination

The expertise of facilitators is determined by the following:

- The work they have done on their own issues related to diversity
- The amount of time and variety of experiences they have had facilitating groups as they address issues of diversity
- The experience they have had working with hostile or reticent groups
- Their sensitivity to the dynamics of group process
- The skills they have in focusing and supporting groups ready for change
- Their recognition that debriefing is the most important part of a structured activity
- The skills they have for eliciting and integrating insights and conclusions during debriefing sessions

THE MATRIX

No, not the movie—the one that follows Chapter 9! We are often asked to recommend our books for specific purposes. To assist you in deciding which book would be most appropriate as you continue your journey toward cultural proficiency, we provide you with a matrix that lists our other books and describes how you might use them. Once you are comfortable using the tools of cultural proficiency, you will find these books even more helpful as you approach your work from a culturally proficient perspective. Specifically, the books examine culturally proficient instruction, coaching, schools as systems, inquiry, leadership, learning communities, and approaches to poverty and counseling.

GOING DEEPER

At the end of each chapter, we include questions or activities that will take you farther along the path toward cultural proficiency. You may want to spend some time with these questions now.

1. When did you begin working in the field that is now called "diversity"?

2. What was it called when you started?

3. Have you heard the terms *cultural competence* or *cultural proficiency* before reading this book? In what context?

4. What are your personal goals for doing the work in this book?

REFLECTION

_____

_____

_____

_____

_____

_____

_____

_____

_____

_____

_____

_____

_____

_____

_____

_____

_____

_____

_____

_____

_____

_____

_____

_____

_____

_____

_____

The Culturally Proficient Professional

This is a description of the culturally proficient behavior of someone who works using the five essential elements of cultural proficiency. As you read it, think about how you would describe the specific culturally proficient behaviors of someone in your profession.

- **Assesses culture**. The culturally proficient professional is aware of her own culture and the effect it may have on the people in her work setting. She learns about the culture of the organization and the cultures of the clients, and she anticipates how they will interact with, conflict with, and enhance one another.

- **Values diversity**. The culturally proficient professional welcomes a diverse group of clients into the work setting and appreciates the challenges that diversity brings. He shares this appreciation with other clients, developing a learning community with them.

- **Manages the dynamics of difference**. The culturally proficient professional recognizes that conflict is a normal and natural part of life. She develops skills to manage conflict in a positive way. She also helps clients to understand that what appears to be clashes in personalities may in fact be conflicts in culture.

- **Adapts to diversity**. The culturally proficient professional commits to the continuous learning that is necessary to deal with the issues caused by differences. He enhances the substance and structure of his work so that all of it is informed by the guiding principles of cultural proficiency.

- **Institutionalizes cultural knowledge**. The culturally proficient professional works to influence the culture of her organization so that its policies and practices are informed by the guiding principles of cultural proficiency. She also takes advantage of teachable moments to share cultural knowledge about her colleagues, their managers, the clients, and the communities from which they come. She creates opportunities for these groups to learn about one another, to engage in ways that honor who they are, and to challenge them to be more.

2

A Cultural and Historical Context for Our Unfolding Democracy

I think we are still trying to educate the students who used to go to school here and haven't begun to address how to address the needs of our current students!

—Anonymous High School Teacher

As the demographics in Rolling Meadows changed, this very insular district, which had rarely hired administrators from outside the district, hired the district's first woman and first African American high school principal, Dina Turner. She had served as an assistant principal in another state, but this was her first principalship.

In the first two years, there was little evidence that anyone mentored her or showed her the "Rolling Meadows way of doing business." Another pressure on Dina was that last year, Rolling Meadows was given only provisional accreditation from the regional accrediting agency, a blow to the egos in the district and the community. Only after a consultant spent six days on campus interviewing teachers, students, aides, administrators, *and parents and issued a report of his findings did faculty confront the fact that the mission of the school had changed. It had been a school that "prepared students for college"; now it is a school that also has to prepare students to become citizens of this country.*

In our experience, the most effective and productive approach to addressing cultural diversity within schools is *cultural proficiency*. A culturally proficient environment acknowledges and responds to both individual and group differences. In a culturally proficient school, the educators and students know they are valued, and they involve community members in the school to facilitate their own cultural understanding. The culture of the school promotes inclusiveness and institutionalizes processes for learning about differences and responding appropriately to differences. Rather than lamenting, "Why can't *they* be like *us*?" teachers and students welcome and create opportunities to understand better who *they* are as individuals while learning how to interact positively with people who differ from themselves.

AN INSIDE-OUT APPROACH

Cultural proficiency is an inside-out approach that focuses first on those who are insiders to the school, encouraging them to reflect on their own individual understandings and values. It thereby relieves those identified as outsiders, the members of new or excluded groups, from the responsibility of doing all the adapting. The cultural proficiency approach to issues arising from diversity surprises many people when they find that it is learning about one's self, that it is not a diversity program involving learning about other people. The commitment to become culturally proficient results in a way of being that acknowledges and validates the current values and feelings of people, encouraging change without threatening people's feelings of worth.

The cultural proficiency approach prizes individuals but focuses chiefly on both the school's culture, which has a life force beyond that of the individuals within the school, as well as the values and the behavior of individuals. This focus removes the need to place blame on individuals and to induce feelings of guilt. The process involves all members of the school community in determining how to align policies, practices, and procedures to achieve cultural proficiency. Because all the participants are deeply involved in the developmental process, ownership is more broadly based, making it easier to commit to change. This approach attacks the problems caused by the diversification of students, faculty, and staff at a systemic level.

WHAT IT TAKES

Building cultural proficiency requires informed and dedicated faculty and staff, committed and involved leadership, and time. The transformation to cultural proficiency requires time to think, reflect, assess, decide, and change. To become culturally proficient, educators participate actively in work sessions, contributing their distinctive ideas, beliefs, feelings, and perceptions. Consequently, their contributions involve them deeply in the process and make it easier for them to commit to change. In contrast, educators cannot be sent to training for two days and be expected to return with solutions to all the equity issues in their school. Building cultural proficiency does *not* involve the use of simple checklists for identifying culturally significant characteristics of individuals, which may be politically appropriate but socially and educationally meaningless.

If you are truly committed to embracing diversity and effectively responding to the issues that emerge from a diverse environment, you can use the cultural proficiency tools to transform your classroom, school, or district at a systemic level. The culturally proficient school district closes the door on tokenism and stops the revolving door through which highly competent, motivated people enter briefly and exit quickly because they have not been adequately integrated into the school's culture. Culturally proficient educators can confidently deliver education knowing that their students genuinely want it and can readily receive it without having their cultural connections denied, offended, or threatened. Culturally proficient educators can also be sure that their community perceives them as a positive, contributing force that substantively enhances the community's image and the school's position in it.

Important to understanding how to use these tools is to recognize that cultural proficiency is not an off-the-shelf program that is implemented in all schools and districts in the same way. Rather, each classroom and each district that embraces cultural proficiency as a goal proceeds differently. The standards for a culturally proficient hospital or culturally proficient university will be different from those for a culturally proficient elementary or secondary school. A culturally proficient suburban school that is predominantly European American will have different standards than an urban school serving communities of color.

CULTURE IS . . .

Early anthropologists defined *culture* as that complex whole that includes knowledge, beliefs, art, law, morals, customs, and any other capabilities and habits acquired by a member of society. Every diversity trainer has definitions for *diversity* and *culture*. Some are quite complicated, whereas others are very simple. We define *culture* as everything you believe and everything you do that enables you to identify with people who are like you and that distinguishes you from people who differ from you. Culture is about "groupness." A culture is a group of people identified by their shared history, values, and patterns of behavior.

Culture provides parameters for daily living. The purpose of a culture is to assist people who are members of a group in knowing the rules for acceptable behavior and to provide consistency and predictability in everyday actions. These rules, a reflection of covert values, are called *cultural expectations.* The cultural expectations for a group assist in screening outsiders and controlling insiders, thus providing the basis for a group to sustain itself.

When people think of culture, they often think only in terms of *ethnic culture* and the behaviors associated with people who look different from them. Ethnic culture is related to ancestral heritage and geography, common history, language, and, to some degree, physical appearance. Ethnic cultural groups are commonly called *racial groups. Race,* a concept developed by social scientists, was misinterpreted and popularized by eugenicists and social Darwinists in the 19th century in an attempt to characterize people by their physical features and to use those differences in society to justify the subjugation of people of color and perpetuate the dominance of the white race. To become culturally proficient, you may need to expand your conceptual paradigm for culture to encompass everything that people believe and everything that they do that identifies them as members of a group and distinguishes that group from other groups.

Furthermore, organizational, occupational, and social cultures shape people's values and affect their communications. For example, *social cultures* are groups of people who share a common interest or activity (e.g., jogging, volunteer work, or arts and crafts). *Occupational cultures* are based on involvement in a common vocation (e.g., teachers, administrators, lawyers, and accountants—each group evokes an image). Dress, language, and beliefs are all aspects of occupational culture. People who work for the same school are members of an *organizational culture.* They share values of the larger district but differ from educators in other schools and offices in the district.

The culture of each organization—whether the organization is your family or your school—is what distinguishes it from other organizations. Each culture develops its own set of formal (overt) and informal (covert) processes to function. When you walk into a school building for the first time, you immediately get a sense of what type of school it is: whether it is a positive, healthy place for children; whether the administrator cares about what is going on; and whether someone will notice that you don't belong there. That feeling is your experience of the school's culture. You can go into several second-grade classrooms, and each one will feel different; those distinctions reflect the culture of each classroom. Harrison (1992) calls this cultural milieu the school's "climate."

The culturally proficient leader understands that the overlay of school climate, student cultures, and professional cultures provides a unique mix that affects each of the groups at the school in a different way. Your success as a culturally proficient leader is in part determined by your understanding of the cultures of your school or your district. The culturally proficient leader ensures that cultures within the school are identified, articulated, and taught to increase understanding.

Racial and ethnic cultures are tied to a common history, ancestry, language, and geographic origin. Additionally, people identify with the culture of their own gender and sexual orientation; these are influenced by the wider culture's expectations and roles for each gender and sexual orientation, as well as by the aspects of these cultures that are self-determined. In a society in which there are several ethnic cultures, one is usually dominant and consequently sets the norms for language and cultural expectations.

The dominant culture has disproportionately greater political and economic power in a society. Professional, school, and social cultures also affect the power relationships of people in a school environment. These types of cultures are important to recognize, because people usually identify with several cultural groups. Therefore, several types of cultures represent each person in the school. From this amalgam of culture types, the dominant cultural patterns emerge within the school. As the school culture's dominant pattern emerges, it either embraces or marginalizes educators, parents, and students of dominated cultural groups.

The broad spectrum of opinions among faculty and administration at Rolling Meadows High School reflects the range of views in the community. Many believe that the school can be organized into learning communities to provide a high-quality education for all students. A smaller and very vocal group, however, continually decries any changes that appear to lower standards and accuses the school and district administration of not supporting the school by getting tough with troublemakers. Members of this group believe that if the school returns to a well-defined tracking system that creates a vocational level for students who are not interested in learning, the needs of everyone will be served. They also believe that senior teachers should be given first choice for teaching courses. This vocal minority among the veteran faculty continues to protest loudly the many structural and curricular changes occurring at the high school.

Annoyed, Celeste, a teacher at Rolling Meadows High School, circled "sex" on the needs assessment form sent out from the district administrative offices. Beside it, she wrote, "Yes!" Then she wrote "gender" on the form, carefully drew a small box next to it, marked it, and wrote "female." Further down on the form, she was asked to indicate her race or ethnicity. "Ayy," she groaned and turned to her friend, Bobby, who was completing the same form. "I hate these forms. I am so tired of being forced into boxes that don't fit."

"Just fill out the form," Bobby chided. "It doesn't really matter. And besides, these are the categories that the U.S. Census uses."

"I don't care about the U.S. Census Bureau. They are wrong! Where is the box for me on this chart? I am not African American. My cultural identity is Brazilian. I am bicultural."

"Well, you are Black Hispanic, aren't you?"

"No. I am a U.S. citizen of African descent. I was born in Boston and moved with my parents to Brazil as a child. My first language is Portuguese. My father is Brazilian, and my mother is from Panama; they met when they were studying at Tufts University. I speak Spanish, but I am not Hispanic. I am black, and I relate most strongly to people from Central and South America."

WHAT HAPPENED TO RACE?

If you came of age in the 1960s, you may be most comfortable with the classification of people called race. *Race* is a false classification created in the 17th century by people seeking to describe and categorize the physical differences of humans to affirm the presumed superiority of Caucasians, or, more specifically, people of Northwestern European descent. Anthropologist George Armelagos said that "while biological traits give the impression that race is a biological unit of nature, it remains a cultural construct. The boundaries between races depend on the classifier's own cultural norms" (as quoted in Begley, 1995, p. 68). *Race* is a term that is used by the federal government, which in turn is used as a model for many other forms and applications. It is the most commonly used term but not necessarily the most accurate one.

In this book, we use the term *race* to denote the large groups of people distinguished from one another by their physical appearances. These groups are people of African descent, people of European descent, Asians, Pacific Islanders, First Nation, and Hispanics or Latinos/Latinas. Clearly, these groupings exclude a large number of ethnic groups and cultures. Such groupings do not speak to the widespread migration and miscegenation that has created what are sometimes called mixed-race, biracial, or multiracial groups. For instance, what should one call the people of African descent who live in Central and South America and who speak Spanish? Are they Hispanics of African descent? What about white South Africans? Are they Africans of European descent?

Racial terminology inadequately names the different racially defined ethnic groups. Rather than seeking to name the various groups of people, it might be more effective to develop ways of identifying, interacting with, and responding to anyone who differs from you in ways that demonstrate a value for human dignity. In this book, we use the term *ethnic group* or *ethnicity* to describe groups of people with shared history, ancestry, geographic and language origin, and physical type. Although *race* is a shorthand term that most people understand, in our efforts to move toward cultural proficiency, we choose to use terms that are more descriptive. When possible and appropriate, we use the name of a specific ethnic group. At the same time, we will continue to use the term *racism* when alluding to the social construct or describing the form of oppression that is based on the castes created by the physical appearance of people.

Importance of Cultural Naming

Does it really make much of a difference what names people call one another, whether they use racial, cultural, or other kinds of names? Yes. To grasp this importance, simply think about your own name and the names of your children or other family members. Each one has several names that are meaningful to them. A person may be Bob to his friends, Robert to his staff, Mr. Jones to his students, and Robbie with his family. Clearly, names mean a great deal to everyone. U.S. citizens are not alone in attaching deep meaning to names: across cultures, the naming process has great significance. In regard to personal names, many cultures have naming ceremonies for their children at which time it is believed the soul enters the body of the child. Almost every culture has traditions and rituals for the giving of names. Choosing, adopting, or changing one's name is sometimes part of a rite of passage. For example, most U.S. and European women, and increasing numbers of men, change their names upon marriage.

Because names connect people to their history, their families, and their culture, naming can be an act of dominance and a symbol of psychological and sometimes physical control of one person or group over another. (You may recall the scene in *Roots* when Kunta Kinte was forced to relinquish his African name to become "Toby.") Humans are objectified by assigning them names or labels for their particular behaviors or characteristics (e.g., *schizophrenic, blind, poor, girl*). By naming these ideas, we reify them and dehumanize the people to whom we attach the labels.

Dominant groups, the groups in power, do not name themselves; they name other people, specifically in relationship to the dominant group. When the first white explorers arrived in the territory called Alaska and asked the inhabitants what they called themselves, the people replied, "Eskimos," which means "people." Because the Eskimos were the only people around, they didn't need to name themselves in relationship to anyone else. The explorers, however, needed to distinguish the Eskimos as others, so they called them "Eskimos." In this book, we use names for the various racially defined ethnic groups in the United States that our clients have told us they preferred:

- African American
- Asian
- Pacific Islander
- European American

- Hispanic or Latino/Latina
- People of the First Nations

For other cultural groups, we use the terms for which our client populations have stated a preference, including the following:

- Differently abled
- GLBT: Gay Men, Lesbians, Bisexual, Transgendered people
- Older Americans
- Women
- Men

THE LEGACY OF SEGREGATION AND EXCLUSION

The terms *racism, ethnocentrism, sexism,* and *heterosexism* are often confusing and frequently misused. Racism has two components: (a) the belief that one racial group is superior to all others and (b) the power to create an environment where that belief is manifested in the subtle or direct subjugation of the subordinate ethnic groups through a society's institutions. Ethnocentrism differs from racism in that it suggests a belief in the superiority of one's own ethnic group, but it says nothing about the group's power to subjugate other groups via societal institutions. Like racism, sexism and heterosexism have two components: (a) a belief that men and heterosexuals, respectively, are superior to women and homosexuals, and (b) the power to institutionalize that belief, thereby marginalizing women and homosexuals both overtly and covertly.

Types of Minority Status

Economic classes that reflect overt national values stratify Canadian and U.S. societies. These classes are further stratified into caste groups by the ethnic groups within them. Some claim that the lines between social classes are flexible and that a person can move from one group to a higher one through hard work and determination. Others know that this movement is difficult, if not impossible, because of the caste status of certain groups. Ogbu and Matute-Bianchi (1990) describe two types of ethnic minority status: immigrant status and caste status. Table 2.1 shows how Ogbu and Matute-Bianchi distinguish between immigrant and caste minorities. In U.S. society, *immigrant status* is a flexible category through which people have moved voluntarily, first choosing to immigrate and then choosing to assimilate, leaving behind their distinctive cultural membership and identification. People with immigrant status reinforce the belief in flexible strata in our society, because they frequently cross class boundaries—if not within a generation then at least over several generations.

Table 2.1   Types of Minority Status

	Immigrant Minorities	Castelike Minorities
Definition	People who are assimilated into mainstream social and economic classes after one or two generations.	People who, as a group, are prevented from moving out of the lowest social and economic classes.
Reason for immigration	Moved voluntarily to the host society for economic, social, or political reasons.	Were brought to host society involuntarily through slavery, conquest, or colonization.
Characteristics	May be subordinated and exploited politically, economically, and socially.	Remain involuntary and permanent minorities.
	Are often successful in school.	Believed to be unalterably inferior as a group.
	May see themselves as "strangers" or "outsiders."	Perception of inferiority perpetuated by myths and stereotypes depicting the group as lazy, sexually primitive, violent, aggressive, and disease ridden.
	May consider their menial position in this country to be better than what they had back home.	Formal and informal barriers to assimilation (e.g., prohibitions of intermarriage, residential segregation) created by host culture.
	Do not internalize the negative effects of discrimination (as first-generation immigrants).	
	Negative effects of discrimination are not an ingrained part of their culture.	
	Affected by U.S. relations with country of origin in two possible ways: (a) worsening political ties between the country of origin and the host country lead to harsh treatment or (b) friendly political ties between the country of origin and the host country improve social and economic opportunities.	
	Biculturality and bilingualism are perceived as possible and acceptable.	
Effects	Attitudes toward schooling enhance strong desire for and pursuit of education.	Attitudes and behaviors internalize host culture's perception of them.
	Attitudes and behaviors help them overcome barriers to education and high-status careers.	Believe that schooling will not help them advance into the mainstream of society.

SOURCE: Ogbu, John U., & Matute-Bianchi, María Eugenia. (1990). Understanding sociocultural factors: Knowledge, identity, and school adjustment. In Bilingual Education Office, California State Department of Education, *Beyond language: Social and cultural factors in schooling language minority students* (pp. 73–142). Los Angeles: California State University. (ERIC Document Reproduction Service No. ED304241)

In contrast, *caste status* is an inflexible category in which a person's ethnic characteristics, such as physical appearance and language, differ so much from the dominant (white) caste that they prevent—or severely limit—that person's voluntary movement across class boundaries. For the rare individuals of lower castes who are able to cross class boundaries, caste continues to affect their status within their new social class. Thus, a person who has entered the middle class but belongs to a lower caste will be made to feel subordinate to other members of the middle class who are of a higher caste. The existence of a caste system violates the fundamental U.S. belief in the ability to cross class boundaries at will to improve one's position. Most people reject the notion of a caste system in the United States, because it contradicts one of the core overt values of the United States—freedom and justice for all.

A HISTORY OF CASTE IN THE UNITED STATES

The distinction between immigrant and caste minorities has been extremely important in the history of the United States, and much of U.S. society still functions in a caste system (Ogbu & Matute-Bianchi, 1990). Historically, as new generations of Europeans voluntarily migrated to what ultimately became the United States, they moved through immigrant status en route to assimilation. Initially, the caste minorities were chiefly enslaved African people and People of the First Nations.

For the most part, the second and subsequent generations of European immigrants were assimilated into the dominant culture of the United States. In contrast, Africans and First Nation people were prevented from entering the dominant culture by virtue of their caste. By denying their humanity, early European Americans readily justified stealing of the land of indigenous people and the importation and subjugation of African people. Religious zealots often justified this savagery through their ethnocentrism. They neither understood nor appreciated the beliefs and behavior of the Africans and the First Nation peoples, so they claimed it was their duty to civilize and Christianize these "primitives." They rationalized enslavement and brutalization as a means to converting these so-called heathens to the Christian faith. Over time, the colonists institutionalized slavery and the practice of exiling First Nations to small parcels of land, often thousands of miles from their homelands.

Following the war against the British, white men looked to British law and tradition to establish the U.S. government, society, and culture. These institutions formalized the political, social, and economic rights of landowning white men. This power, privilege, and entitlement was extended further through court cases, governmental policies, and a capitalist economic system. As new European immigrants arrived, if they were willing to work hard and to suffer many indignities, they—or at least their descendents—were granted entry into the dominant culture.

Meanwhile, racism became institutionalized in the new nation, and First Nations and African Americans were denied both the rights of citizenship and participation in the political and social life of the nation. Africans and African Americans were legally declared to be three-fifths of a white person. First Nations were slaughtered through direct aggression as well as by indirect means, such as exposing them to disease and preventing them from using their land to maintain their existence. First Nations were driven onto reservations and then moved again and again each time European Americans wanted their land or its mineral content. Africans were enslaved first as chattel and then in a politically acceptable fashion through Jim Crow laws, which carried the threat of mob violence against African Americans, including tacit legal sanction to lynch with or without cause.

By the time the United States was established as a new nation, slavery was firmly entrenched in the South, and racial prejudices pervaded the country on both sides of the Mason-Dixon line. Thus, the roots of oppression in racial prejudice against lower castes have a long-standing historical basis throughout the white community. In the early 19th century, Alexis de Tocqueville made a seemingly counterintuitive observation about prejudice and oppression in the United States. He said, "The prejudice of race appears to be stronger in the states that have abolished slavery than in those where it still exists; and nowhere is it so intolerant as in those states where servitude has never been known" (as quoted in Kovel, 1984, pp. 33–34). This statement becomes understandable only when we consider it in light of entitlement: Northern white abolitionists made Southern slaveholders painfully conscious of their racial prejudices and entitlement, but the Northerners failed to see their own. Folk wisdom among African Americans echoed Tocqueville 150 years later: *In the South, they love the people and hate the race; in the North, they love the race and hate the people.*

By the time de Tocqueville made his observation, the differentiation between immigrant and caste minorities had become deeply ingrained in our national psyche. If African Americans, First Nations, or women were to have any rights, those rights would not emerge organically as a natural outgrowth of social progress in a society that fully embraced these people as equal participants. Rather, vocal and often violent struggle was needed to extend the rights of citizenship to members of lower castes. Their strenuous efforts led to the passage of the Thirteenth (1865, abolition of slavery), Fourteenth (1868, equal rights for all people), and Fifteenth (1870, voting rights to all male citizens) Amendments to the U.S. Constitution.

Social Darwinism

By the beginning of the 20th century, racists were hard-pressed to use their old justifications for their oppressive beliefs and actions. Thus, in place of the rantings of the early Christianizers, the perpetrators of racism pointed to social Darwinism to rationalize their maintenance of racist institutions. Specifically, European American men perverted the work of Charles Darwin to suggest that they had all the power and all the privileges of society simply because they were the fittest to enjoy such power and privilege. The concept of Social Darwinism legitimized the power and privilege of a higher order of humans (i.e., themselves: white men).

Not everyone blithely accepted social Darwinism, however. Determined suffragists forced men to pass the Nineteenth Amendment (1920) to the U.S. Constitution, which granted women the right to vote nationwide for the first time. Similarly, outspoken blacks formed the National Association for the Advancement of Colored People (NAACP) and started pressing for social justice through the legal system. Their efforts led to such changes as the *Brown v. Topeka Board of Education* (1954, desegregation of public facilities) decision.

Sadly, it has taken urban violence to prompt many of the changes that ultimately benefited the lower castes. Throughout history and across the country, race riots have shown a consistent theme: people ultimately react violently to being denied human rights considered basic by the dominant classes. After a particularly turbulent summer in the 1960s, President Lyndon Johnson appointed a special panel headed by former Illinois Governor Otto Kerner to determine the causes of urban unrest. Among the many remarkable features of the study, two stand out: (a) that it was written at all and (b) that it was written by black and white moderates, not by radicals and fanatics (Terry, 1970). The *Report of the National Advisory Commission on Civil Disorders* (known as the Kerner Report; Riot Commission, 1968) identifies the causes of urban unrest as a white problem: "What white U.S. citizens never fully understand but what the Negro can never forget is that the white society is deeply implicated in the ghetto. White institutions created it, white institutions maintain it, and white society condones it" (p. 6).

The Kerner report was not the only outcome of angry and episodically violent reactions to oppression. Much legislation and many judicial decisions resulted that have extended civil rights to specific populations. This rich body of law that speaks to people's inalienable rights includes the Civil Rights Acts from 1866 to 1964, which have continually expanded the guarantees of citizenship to U.S. citizens who are not white, landowning men; the U.S. Supreme Court decision of 1954 (*Brown v. Topeka Board of Education*), which struck down 16 states' antimiscegenation laws; and the Voting Rights Act of 1965, which made it realistic for African Americans to exercise their right to vote throughout the country. These hard-won liberties are still not guaranteed without ongoing efforts to preserve them, however (witness the abdication of affirmative action both nationally and in many localities and the violation of voter rights in the 2000 presidential election).

Each of these historical and legal events had underlying moral issues. In each case, people identified a wrong and reacted angrily against it, often responding with legislative or judicial action. Perhaps surprisingly, the laws intended to right civil wrongs and inequities highlight the breadth and depth of entitlement: people have had to seek legal remedies to ensure the rights of all cultural groups except wealthy white men. (This is not to deny that most laws, drafted and passed chiefly by middle- and upper-class white men, primarily benefit this empowered group, however.)

By the 1970s and 1980s, the preponderance of U.S. immigrants arrived from Pacific Rim, Latin American, and Asian countries. Now there are large groups of people of color among which favorable and unfavorable distinctions are made. Compounding the problem is the fact that many Latin American immigrants also have African or First Nation backgrounds and they may speak Spanish, Portuguese, or French as their native language. This multiethnicity blurs the issues of immigrant versus caste status for some groups. For example, the caste and socioeconomic status of wealthy Hispanic (white) Cuban immigrants differs sharply from that of impoverished African (black) Cuban immigrants. Nonetheless, despite some blurring, the caste system is alive and well in contemporary America and perpetuated in large part by the labels ascribed to people.

LABELS FOR HISTORICALLY OPPRESSED PEOPLE

Labels ascribed to the emerging majority groups in our society that serve to perpetuate second-class status include the following:

- Genetically inferior
- Culturally inferior
- Deprived
- Disadvantaged
- Deficient
- Different
- Diverse

It is easy to see that these labels are pernicious, demeaning, and very much alive in our society and in our schools. You may be surprised to see *diverse* on this list of labels. Very often *different* and *diverse* are code words used to describe communities of color. It is not uncommon to hear educators indicate that their school has little or no diversity, meaning that there are few or no students of color. Of course, context is important, and when terms serve to label our students and members of our community as second-class members, we have constructed barriers to our own effectiveness.

Not Victims!

The labels in the list above reflect the power of dominant groups to define others in relation to the norms set by the group in power and to name them in such a way that their "otherness" is reinforced. However, let's be clear about one thing. Being a member of a historically oppressed group does not make one a victim!

Systemic oppression creates conditions such that students and educators who are targets of these labels, and the treatment that follows from those labels, must learn the overt educational messages from our schools and, simultaneously, be vigilant about covert messages of inferiority to be successful. Most often, in our experience, members of dominant groups are oblivious to and protected from such experiences. Historically oppressed people, (e.g., women, people of color, Gay Men and Lesbians, the aged, and the Differently abled) move through a progression of stages in reaction to both the social policies of the time and their current and historical position in society.

Note the progress from social Darwinist attributions of inferiority, deprivation, disadvantage, and deficiency to recognition of difference without the negative connotations. The social Darwinist attributions are classic labels that blame dominated people for their lot in life, even though these groups of people have been legally, educationally, and economically discriminated against. All disenfranchised and oppressed groups move through this system of being reclassified by the dominant society.

Across time, each cultural group has been assigned the same labels from the dominant society. In each case, the group labels were pernicious, and the societal response by each group was feelings of alienation from the dominant society. Prior to the 1950s, slavery and Jim Crow laws gave widespread sanction to the belief that African Americans were genetically and culturally inferior, despite numerous instances of free blacks making significant academic and economic accomplishments throughout U.S. history. During this period, the dominant society also commonly segregated black communities from white ones.

Similarly, most First Nations people were confined to reservations either by legal mandate or through economic disincentives for leaving the reservations. Though many Native Americans have built strong, independent lives separate from or within the dominant society, the vast majority have been treated by the dominant society as culturally and genetically inferior. As with African U.S. citizens, the labels of inferiority are often cloaked in seemingly beneficent terms describing (and treating) them as exotic. Although society is generally too sophisticated to use such terms as *noble savage* any more, it is not unusual for schools to invite First Nation people to wear their native "costumes," dance, and tell folk stories with little regard for learning the deeper societal and spiritual similarities and differences among cultural groups. A First Nation colleague of ours noted that "people wear costumes to be perceived as someone else; they wear clothes to be themselves. The appropriate term is not native costumes, but native *dress*."

For Latino groups in general and U.S. citizens of Mexican and Puerto Rican ancestry in particular, state laws that forbade children from speaking Spanish in schools heightened Latinos' alienation from the dominant society. Similarly, the various Asian groups that immigrated to this country were segregated from dominant society. By prohibiting the immigration of their compatriots, the dominant society continuously reminded Asians of their second-class status. Clearly, African American, First Nations, Mexican American, Puerto Rican, and Asian American feelings of alienation from the dominant society are not difficult to recognize and understand in this context of legally sanctioned segregation and exclusion.

Social Change and Labels

During the 1950s, 1960s, and 1970s—periods of great social change—the labels for historically oppressed groups subtly shifted from *inferiority* to *deficiency.* Inferior people were easy to provide for. They were perceived as simple and incapable of being like members of the dominant society. They were encoded as deviant, stupid, hostile, docile, childlike, or just plain backward. However as these groups moved closer to emerging as majorities in the social mainstream, different ways of experiencing them had to be developed.

Though referring to a person as *deficient* is hardly positive, it acknowledges a potential member of society. In fact, if it were not for a deficiency or two, these deficient persons could be just like members of the dominant society. Throughout this country, schools and other social agencies began to take the approach that because they were going to have to work with these groups, they had to figure out what was wrong with them and provide what they needed. It was widely held that the unidentified deficiencies could be cured through remediation via public education.

Unfortunately, this perspective led educators to self-fulfilling prophecies; they asked, "How could those people with such insurmountable deficiencies possibly be educated?" The educational tracking system became the vehicle by which inordinate numbers of African Americans, Latinos, and other people with low socioeconomic status were placed into lower-ability groups and continuously exposed only to basic curriculum. Throughout this period, few policymakers ever asked themselves: *Why do some children of color, girls, and low-income children throughout the United States succeed in schools, and what conditions contributed to their success?* The few policymakers who did ask often surmised, unfortunately, that success stories were meaningless anomalies.

Humanity, Policy, and Equity

Finally, during the 1980s and 1990s, educators began to use the terms *different* and *diverse,* which intended a common valuing of one another as fellow humans. Hopefully in the 21st century, educators will use terms such as the Mayan expression, *en la Kech,* which signifies that "you are in me and I am in you" and projects a high level of humanity into the discussion of policy and equity. To paraphrase a provocative question asked by Joel Barker (1996), a futurist: What seems impossible to do today, but, if we could do it, would radically change how we create equity across cultural groups? In 1950, the vast majority of people in this country probably could not have envisioned the changes that were to be made in human rights. Perhaps by the 2050s, people will accept as commonplace matters of equity beyond our imagination now.

Winston Alexander, Rolling Meadows's assistant superintendent for business, is reviewing the proposals he has received in response to the request for proposal (RFP) and is learning a lot. He gets some information from the specific responses to the questions the RFP team proposes, and the team gleans even more insight from the underlying values of the consultants. It is easy to discern what they believe from the way they present themselves and the extra materials they include. Right now, he muses over three ideas:

1. Our public schools work well for the students for whom they were designed.

2. No nation has ever sought to provide universal education for as broad a spectrum of social classes and ethnic or racial groups as does the United States.

3. We are more successful at education than any other nation in the world today, but our development of a de facto caste system has created great inequities. We are at a point in history where we must heed the warning to avoid creating "two societies, separate and unequal" (Riot Commission, 1968).

Having a palpable sense of history arms the culturally proficient leader with a context, grounding a vision of inclusiveness in knowledge of our different circumstances.

FROM SEGREGATION TO CULTURAL PROFICIENCY

Chapter 1 provided a brief overview of the historical progression of segregation to cultural proficiency within our country and the acknowledgment that vestiges of each succeeding historical phase linger. The task as an educator is to be aware of the effects of these dynamics as they impact students and their families. In this section, we provide a brief description of how people react and respond to various levels of discrimination. As you read, pause at the end of each subsection to see if you recognize any of the dynamics from within your own experience or those experiences of your students, their families, or your colleagues. Doing so places you on the road to cultural proficiency by being aware of your reactions and possessing an interest in the experiences of those around you.

Segregation and Assimilation

As social policies, motivations, and labels changed over the decades, the attitudes, feelings, and beliefs of historically oppressed people changed in response. Prior to the 1950s, while isolated and segregated from the dominant culture, they experienced intense feelings of alienation. During this time, everyone in society agreed that there was an *us* and a *them*, and everyone knew to which group he or she belonged.

As society began to invite some dominated people to assimilate into the dominant culture, they were expected to disassociate themselves from all vestiges of their primary or native culture, so they felt dissonance. Within the dominant culture, they faced tremendous obstacles and difficulties, yet they were obliged to resist reliance on their native cultural resources to help them overcome these problems. They knew that to be accepted into the dominant culture, they had to abandon all traces of their native culture. Similarly, they were expected to adopt the dominant culture's view, disparaging their native culture and denigrating the people in their respective native cultural groups. Thus, they felt dissonance not only with members of the dominant culture and in settings reflective of the dominant culture but also often with members of their native culture and in settings reflecting their native culture (Adams, 1996; Hudson, 1999; Kovel, 1984; Ladson-Billings, 2005; Locust, 1996; McCarthy, 1993; Milner IV, 2007; Ogbu, 1978).

Many U.S. citizens who had emigrated from Europe were able to overcome these obstacles as their distinctive native cultures melted into the dominant culture. Similarly, Gay Men and Lesbians were able to assimilate as long as they carefully avoided being open about their sexual orientation. Even some women were able to assimilate by accepting the dominant society's definitions of gender roles: if they wished to become chief executive officers (CEOs), they accepted that they must dress, speak, and act like CEOs—that is, like white men (Boyd, 1984; Gilligan, 1983; Miller, 2006; Tochluk, 2008; Weiss & Schiller, 1988).

The melting pot did not work for all people. Some people, no matter how thoroughly they abandoned their native culture, were still not welcomed into the dominant culture because their physical appearance continued to distinguish them as different, despite their best efforts at being indistinguishable. For instance, most women and people of color continue to look different from white men, even when they adopt the same values, attitudes, and behavior that white men show. Furthermore, much to the surprise of some members of the dominant society, many historically oppressed people rejected entirely the goal of assimilation into the great melting pot; they did not want to have their differences melted away.

Marginality

During the 1960s, many people outside the dominant culture experienced feelings of *marginality:* they knew two cultures but were not entirely accepted by members of either one, essentially because they could function in the other culture. Among those who experienced marginality were children bused to schools where very few members of their primary group were present; once they learned to cope with and thrive in the dominant culture, they often felt marginalized on returning to their home communities. They no longer felt at home while at home. Similarly, Latino children forced to speak only English in school, to the point of forgetting or becoming developmentally disabled in their native language, often feel marginalized in Latino culture. First Nation children educated in the long-running Bureau of Indian Affairs boarding schools too often fit neither in the white culture for which they were educated nor in their home cultures from which they had been separated. In all these cases, the insult added to the injury was that these children continued to be marginalized in the dominant culture while being marginalized in their native cultures (Cummins, 1990; Duchene, 1990).

Dualism

During the 1970s, many people were able to integrate successfully into a new culture while remaining comfortable in their native culture. Nonetheless, they felt unable to mesh the two worlds, so they experienced a sense of *dualism.* Unlike marginalized people, who live between two worlds, people who feel dualism live in the two worlds, moving back and forth yet never carrying one into the other. Many adults today experience a sense of dualism: they function successfully in corporate America yet continue to go home to a segregated community, where they socialize and worship with just the members of their native culture (Delpit, 1993; Fine, 1993; Miller, 2006; Sapon-Shevin, 1993). Closeted Gay Men and Lesbians experience dualism when they function in a straight business world in which most of the people with whom they work are straight and never imagine that their colleagues live in a world outside of work that is very different from theirs.

Negotiation for Acceptance

During the 1980s, many people attempted to bring aspects of their marginalized cultures into the world of the dominant culture. This process demanded that they negotiate for the acceptance of those in the dominant group. Members of the dominant culture assumed that they were inherently inferior and undeserving of the positions in society they occupied. So they also had to negotiate for a respect and acceptance in the workforce by proving that they did have the skills and credentials to do the job for which they were hired.

Bicultural Affirmation

Finally, starting in the 1990s, people have begun to feel bicultural affirmation, functioning effectively in two cultural worlds in which the people in each cultural world know they are a part of the other and respect their biculturality. The difference between dualism and *biculturality* is that although both involve knowledge of the norms and values of two cultural groups, with dualism, one group knows nothing about the other. With biculturality, both groups know about the other and celebrate that their group member is part of both. These situations both contrast with *marginality*, in which the person functions in two worlds and is accepted by neither. Perhaps in the 21st century, people will experience a multicultural transformation in which the norm for all people will be to know and function comfortably within several cultural groups and be changed for the better as a result (McCarthy, 1993; West, 1993; Willis, 1996).

Multicultural Transformation

In reviewing the changes across the past five decades, one can see historically oppressed people moving through a process of acceptance, internalization, and rejection of the labels given to them by others toward self-determination and self-identification. Although this discussion suggests that these general trends apply to all cultural groups, in fact, each cultural group moves at its own distinct pace. Furthermore, the individuals within each group vary widely in terms of how they view social policies, social impetuses and motivations, and labels, as well as in their responses to discrimination. For instance, even today, Gay Men and Lesbians may experience feelings ranging from alienation to multicultural transformation. New immigrants from Guatemala may still feel alienation, whereas their U.S.-born cousins may experience bicultural affirmation.

Implications for Culturally Proficient Leaders

What does this historical process mean? It means that the culturally proficient leader has to be adept at recognizing that a typical school faculty comprises teachers, aides, staff, counselors, and administrators who have had widely different life experiences. More important, the culturally proficient leader recognizes that the experiences of the school faculty and staff may be much different from the experiences of students and parents in the community served by the school. The culturally proficient leader recognizes that he or she must address issues of labeling in a way that helps people from the dominant culture to understand the pain caused by labeling and helps recipients of such labeling go beyond that pain to focus on self-determination and self-identification.

CULTURE AND HISTORY
PROVIDE PERSPECTIVE

As society moves from one social period to the next, it continues to include policies, attitudes, and practices from the previous periods. Many people may continue to be guided by outdated policies; hold attitudes acquired years ago; and implement long-standing practices in their work, home, and community interactions. Just as policies, attitudes, and practices are cumulative, so is the motivation to change any particular policy. The fact that we are at the beginning of the 21st century doesn't mean that previous social periods or the attitudes that characterized them are no longer with us.

The social impetus and motivation for a particular decade may appear isolated and past. However, closer inspection will reveal that the motivating forces from previous decades influence interactions today. Moreover, each social policy era spawns awareness in groups that did not initiate change before to press for social reforms affecting them, too. For example, the modern civil rights movement of the 1960s struggled to gain rights for African Americans and later for other cultural minority groups. These struggles then helped to spawn the modern reconvergence of both the feminist movement and the Gay Pride movement.

Over the past 50 years, each decade has been characterized by a particular impetus for social policy. The social impetus for the changes leading from segregation prior to the 1950s to desegregation and integration in the 1950s and 1960s focused on obtaining legal equity. During the 1960s, the social impetus continued to focus on legal equity, such as the provisions of the 1964 Civil Rights Act. In the push for integration, equal access, and equal rights, however, legal changes alone did not suffice. To broaden the application of legal measures, the social impetus shifted to activism for social justice. For instance, such activism included the development of programs to rectify inequitable distribution of resources, such as nutrition, prenatal care, child care, and early childhood education.

During the 1970s, the impetus for multiculturalism was almost exclusively motivated by the widely acknowledged need for equity in education. Educators sought to teach language arts and social studies in ways that recognized and included the increasingly multicultural populations found in U.S. schools (Banks, 1994, 1999). During the 1980s, the motivation for social policies of diversity was primarily economic issues. The business community recognized the changing demographics of consumers and workers. Once businesspeople recognized that diversity has an economic payoff, they started to make many changes addressing this issue—for example, changes in TV programming, images in commercials, and languages used in automatic teller machines.

During the 1990s, educators and other community leaders began to view cultural proficiency as a moral imperative. This book is an outgrowth of this social impetus, because we recommend social policies and school reforms that reflect cultural proficiency. For the 2000s and beyond, cultural proficiency is our vision of what this society will become.

GOING DEEPER

1. Before reading this chapter, how did you define culture? What do you think now? How does your definition affect the lens through which you observe and understand your school or district?

2. Find someone who lived through the Civil Rights Movement, attended a segregated school, rode with the Freedom Riders, or can tell you about some other significant time or event in this country's racial history. After talking with this person, write his or her oral history and your response to it.

3. Interview someone who has experienced overt discrimination because of his or her ethnicity, gender, sexual orientation, social class, primary language, ableness, or faith. Prepare a 10-minute presentation that you would deliver to your professional colleagues, including your response to the interviewee's lived experiences.

REFLECTION

_____

_____

_____

_____

_____

_____

_____

_____

_____

_____

_____

_____

_____

3

Leadership for Today's Schools

Principals working in a transactional world are expected to produce transformational changes.

—Lindsey, Daly, & Ibarra (2009, p. 7)

Superintendents Bill Fayette and Hermon Watson continue to have conversations about cultural proficiency. At one of their meetings, Bill shared this story with Hermon.

"My middle school and elementary school administrators had noticed for several years that large numbers of Mexican and Mexican American students regularly visit their families in Mexico around Christmas and Easter. What made this a problem was that the children were often gone for three or four weeks at a time. Consequently, they missed a lot of classroom work and lagged behind the other students.

"The teachers and the administrators at each school implored the parents to respect the school calendar and have their children back when school resumed, but most did not comply. The teachers even developed homework packets that the children could take with them, but those efforts had only mixed results.

"Finally it occurred to the leadership team that the school was organized around the living patterns of an agriculturally based community that had long ago become an urban center. The leadership team decided they needed to meet with parents and brainstorm ideas, share concerns, and see how best the school could respond to the educational needs of the children. From this meeting, the school people discovered that *rather than demanding that the parents respect an anachronistic practice, they could demonstrate respect for the families by organizing the school calendar around their lifestyles, in much the same way the school leaders' predecessors had done in generations earlier. So now, the schools are closed for four weeks in late December and early January and for two weeks during the observance of Passion Week and Easter. We make up the days in the summer.*

"You see," Bill concluded, "once people understood that the school calendar wasn't etched in stone, and parents were engaged as active partners, it was pretty easy to get our priorities in order and decide how we could best meet the needs of our students and their families."

OUR JOURNEY WITH CULTURALLY PROFICIENT LEADERS

As educators and consultants, we have been providing diversity or equity training since the early days of school desegregation. During our careers, many of the societal barriers to educational opportunities, particularly in the areas of race and gender equity, have been eliminated or reduced by state and national legislation. In Chapter 2 we provided a more detailed discussion of those barriers, the social movements that reduced or eliminated them, and the legislation and judicial decisions that promote equity in our society. In this chapter, we connect our expanding notion of equity to the role of formal and nonformal leaders.

By the latter part of the 20th century, accountability movements addressing the disparate achievement of social class, language acquisition, and special needs populations were well underway and helped prepare the political landscape for the reauthorization of Title I of the Elementary and Secondary Education Act, more commonly known as No Child Left Behind (2002). Most recently, issues of access to the full curricular offerings of schools due to faith and sexual orientation have emerged, demanding our attention. Schools are requested, and in some cases required, to provide space and time for religious groups to meet and to protect the rights of gay, lesbian, bisexual, and transgendered students and staff (Bochenek & Brown, 2001; Miller, 2006; Townley & Schmeider-Ramirez, 2007). Over the past 25 years, we have introduced cultural proficiency to schools throughout California and to organizations across the United States and Canada to address the many issues that arise out of our diversity. An increasing number of leaders are making strong commitments to culturally proficient leadership, instruction, and community engagement.

- Wichita, Kansas, School District 259 has established an Office of Cultural Proficiency and is engaging all district employees in related professional development.

- Howard County Public Schools in Maryland has established the position of Coordinator of Cultural Proficiency to guide professional development throughout county schools.
- The Medical Center at the University of California, San Diego, has trained all 3,500 managers, staff, and doctors in the approach. It has incorporated the essential elements into its core competencies used for performance appraisal and related the essential elements to the core values of the hospital, which are printed on the ID badges that staff wear every day.
- Elementary schools in the California communities of San Marcos, Sacramento, and Poway are using the tools of cultural proficiency to guide their instructional programs.
- The Commonwealth of Massachusetts Commissioner of Education has endorsed cultural proficiency as the approach he thinks will help close the achievement gap in Massachusetts's schools.
- The national offices of the Presbyterian Church (U.S.A.) have adopted a cultural proficiency initiative to help transform the cultural environment of the organization from "one of legalistic compliance with secular affirmative action and equal employment opportunity laws to one of genuine caring and valuing of all humanity where relationship building and God's agape love are modeled."[1]

Generally speaking, educators are always trying something new, yet processes in education change very slowly. Unfortunately, because of this pattern, the educators we encounter are either profoundly impressed with cultural proficiency or fundamentally weary at the prospect of having to add one more thing to their agenda—or they are both. The point we emphasize is that cultural proficiency is not an add-on program. It is an inside-out approach to addressing diversity in classrooms, schools, and districts. Cultural proficiency is an approach that is to be integrated into the culture of the school. Culturally proficient leaders forthrightly address issues that emerge when cultural differences are not valued in schools and other organizations.

In reading the case study, you perhaps noticed that both the Rolling Meadows and Coolidge districts started slowly and continued to enlarge and enhance the changes made as they worked toward becoming culturally proficient. Movement toward cultural proficiency usually begins with one or two people. We like to think of our sphere of influence as a pebble dropped in a pond. All of us get at least one pebble. We can choose to hold

---

[1]Advocacy Committee for Racial Ethnic Concerns (ACREC). (2004). *Task force to examine GA entities: Report on creating a climate for change within the Presbyterian Church (U.S.A.)*, Section VII: Summary. (Recommendation to the 216th General Assembly; retrieved February 4, 2009, from http://www.pcusa.org/acrec/pdf/climateforchange.pdf)

onto it and put it away in our pockets, or we can use it in some way. You can drop your pebble into a small puddle and make a big splash, you can toss it into a large lake and make almost no perceptible difference, or you can join with a few others and together toss your pebbles into the same place and create ripples that affects everything on the surface and, profoundly, those areas on which the pebbles fall.

Change takes place when people are open and ready for something new. Members are able to look around and see a future that is different and better. They are able to rally their colleagues around this vision and work together to make it a reality. Change occurs one step at a time, one classroom at a time, one school at a time, one pebble at a time. The first commitment is for members to trust the process. Culturally proficient leaders understand that personal and institutional change will take time and keep working at it until they begin to see changes in the attitudes and behaviors of colleagues and coworkers. There is a tendency to stop or alter programs when the agreed-on processes meet resistance. When this occurs, it is unfortunate, because resistance to change is a natural and expected step in the change process.

The process of cultural proficiency takes time to surface assumptions, reflect on values and behaviors, examine policies and practices, collect and examine data, and engage in conversations about the next near-term and long-range strategies. These processes need culturally proficient formal and nonformal leaders who have the vision, skill, and will to engage others in collegial discussions and dialogue for the purpose of continued improvement in serving all demographic groups of students. Culturally proficient leaders recognize that change is scary for some, that it will disturb the status quo, and that there will be barriers to surmount. They do not view barriers as impossible to overcome, only as factors that must be taken into account as professional plans for moving forward are formulated. Chapter 5 presents the first tool, the barriers to cultural proficiency, which is comprised of three caveats that describe and discuss personal and organizational barriers to change.

TRANSFORMATIONAL LEADERSHIP

The development of moral character and strength, an important cornerstone of public and private education, is the province of transformational leaders serving diverse communities. When an examination of privilege and power rests on a foundation of moral character, as described in Chapter 5, educators can construct a stronger foundation for the education of all. To serve the needs of all learners and their families, educators must clearly recognize that social privileges are given freely to some students and rationed meagerly to others. Recognizing these discrepancies is an important understanding for those who are most entitled in our society. In the same way that students from oppressed groups need role models, white and male students need role models to help them learn about unearned, unconscious privilege. Unearned, unconscious privilege transcends gender and racial/ethnic privilege and extends to those who experience few societal limitations due to our faith, sexual orientation, language, and ableness. Once we begin to acknowledge entitlement, we are better prepared to take a responsible role on the cultural proficiency continuum.

Rolling Meadows Superintendent Watson recognizes that during his tenure the demographics of the district have shifted from being almost totally white to increasingly multiethnic, and issues related to faith, ableness, and sexual orientation have emerged. He has gathered data on student achievement, noted the intercultural friction and fights at the high schools, and heard parents' complaints about the curriculum.

The request for proposal (RFP) that his staff prepares seeks consultants to conduct a year-long cultural inquiry study and needs assessment that tap into the views and beliefs of all sectors of the district—the educators, the staff, the students, and members of the community. Although he has not yet been introduced to the concept of cultural proficiency, Superintendent Watson knows intuitively to move in this comprehensive direction and to involve all district administrators in ways that support their understanding and share his vision for all students in the district. He uses his formal position to lead the district into this process.

Too often, transactional leadership and transformational leadership are presented as dichotomous, but, in fact, both approaches to leadership are needed in today's schools (Bass, 1997; Ibarra, 2008). The major skill sets used by transactional leaders involve extrinsic systems, such as setting clear goals and expectations, arranging for resources, and providing incentives for needed work. In the complex school systems where most educators work and which most students attend, these are needed skill sets. In complementary fashion, the transformational leader appeals to intrinsic motivation and, in visionary fashion, appeals to the greater good (Lindsey, Daly, & Ibarra, 2009).

Ibarra (2008) noted that transformational leaders influence followers to look beyond self-interest. In terms of cultural proficiency, this begins with wanting to know how best to serve the educational needs of your students, irrespective of the demographic characteristics of your school. We have adapted Bass's four components of transformational leadership (Ibarra)—idealized influence, inspirational motivation, intellectual stimulation, and individualized consideration—to the work of culturally proficient educators. School leaders, such as Superintendent Watson, embody the four components of transformational leadership in these ways:

- **Idealized influence**—They are leaders who have strong convictions, take stands on difficult issues, focus on vision and purpose, and are ethically committed to their work. Such leaders use assessment data to pose questions like, *Given the low reading scores of this demographic group of fourth-grade students, what might we do differently to reach these students better? What barriers within us or the school restrict our ability to meet the needs of our students?*

- **Inspirational motivation**—They are leaders who provide context and meaning for the work to be done, a vision for what can be accomplished, and standards for educators to employ. Transformational leaders ask questions of themselves and their fellow educators, such as, *In what ways do the essential elements of cultural competence enable us to serve better all demographic groups of students?*

- **Intellectual stimulation**—They are leaders who seek to replace old assumptions, traditions, and beliefs with values, behavior, policies, and practices that serve the needs of local populations. Leaders such as Superintendent Watson are likely to pose questions such as, *Have we made the commitment to teaching the students in our school, or are we still trying to educate the children that used to go to school here or who we wish were here?*

- **Individualized consideration**—They are leaders who mentor, instruct, and coach fellow educators and members of the community. In response to fellow leaders who highlight the shortcomings of fellow educators, they ask, *What are some things you are "doing" to improve the learning environment of our students?*

Culturally proficient leaders are mindful of their transactional roles in providing for the structures and resources necessary for the effective functioning of schools. Similarly culturally proficient leaders engage their educator colleagues, students, and community members to share their vision and context for schooling that is inclusive of all demographic groups of students.

FORMAL AND NONFORMAL LEADERS

When asked about school leadership, most people in the school community focus on specific behaviors they observe in formal leaders, then judge how those behaviors measure up against what they believe to be appropriate behaviors. Some people prefer leaders who leave them alone, whereas others prefer leaders who are deeply involved with them in their classrooms. Everyone has a different list of specific characteristics. We prefer to broaden our vision to look at the overall qualities of leadership, particularly qualities that facilitate movement toward cultural proficiency. In this section, we provide a context for understanding the leadership at your school, a necessary step for developing culturally proficient leadership skills in yourself and in those with whom you work.

Leaders can motivate others to excel and to move in desirable directions or diffuse or otherwise block plans for change. In either case, contemporary researchers have found that effective leaders consistently show several key characteristics, whether they are in private businesses, corporate enterprises, or local school districts (Argyris, 1990; Banks, 1999; Collins, 2001; Heifetz & Linsky, 2002; Marzano, 2003; Senge, Roberts, Ross, Smith, & Kleiner, 1994; Senge et al., 2000; Wheatley, 1994, 2002). These characteristics include the following:

- Taking responsibility for one's own learning
- Having a vision for what the school can be
- Effectively sharing the vision with others
- Assessing one's own assumptions and beliefs
- Understanding the structural and organic nature of schools

We have observed that culturally proficient leaders show these characteristics, whether they do so intuitively or as a result of carefully studying how to lead effectively. Furthermore, culturally proficient leaders learn and use what they learn about themselves, those with whom they work, and within the schools they work.

Whereas management, or school administration, is the process of getting work done through others, *leadership* is the process of inspiring others to work together to achieve a specific goal. Almost any book on school leadership emphasizes the importance of leaders having and communicating a vision, guiding the creation of a shared mission, and building strong school cultures (Argyris, 1990; Blankstein, 2004; Fullan, 2003; Gilligan, 1983; Oakes & Lipton, 1990; Ogbu, 1978; Owens, 1991; Reeves, 2008: Sizer, 1985; Wheatley, 1994, 2000).

Coolidge Middle School Principal Richard Díaz is also ready to conduct a needs assessment. This urban school's student demographics have changed from virtually all African American to about one-fourth Latino in fewer than five years. Among the many changes he has initiated at the middle school is to provide instruction in Spanish to all students. This not only provides those whose primary language is Spanish the opportunity to develop bilingual skills in both their native tongue and English, but it also offers native English speakers the chance to learn Spanish, which will prepare them to function in multilingual settings as teenagers and adults. His vision helps African American students learn about the lifestyles of the Spanish-speaking students, and it mitigates tensions that could result from having two language-based cultural groups in the school.

It is our experience that when people speak of leaders, they are usually referring to formal leaders, those who have titles and official positions according them a certain degree of authority and coercive power. Although nonformal leaders have no official role assigning them the authority to direct a group, they have personal attributes, such as charisma, vision, and eloquence, often in combination with the leadership skills of communication, facilitation, and collaboration that cause people to listen and to take action. A nonformal leader can be more powerful than a formal leader, because the attributes of leadership are internally driven rather than externally conferred. Culturally proficient school leaders use effective collaborative and communication skills to engage nonformal leaders in ways that makes use of their knowledge and skills.

COLLABORATIVE LEADERSHIP

Successful superintendents and principals are adept at amplifying their efforts by working with teachers, staff members, students, parents, and other community members who are respected by their constituents. In this section, we focus mainly on formal leaders, secondarily addressing the key role of nonformal leaders in school. We do so because although we can attest to the tremendous influence of nonformal leaders, we believe that formal leaders should bear the primary responsibility for creating the changes described in this book. The formal leaders of schools—namely, the superintendents, district office administrators, site-level administrators, and teachers—are employed to educate all children. How well formal leaders use the skills of the nonformal leaders, including students, parents, community members, and key staff members, is a measure of their success. Following is an example of a formal leader, Ms. Harp, using data to identify and engage nonformal school leaders.

> Leatha Harp, director of credentialing and certification in the Coolidge Unified School District, has gathered a small team of teachers and administrators who have agreed to serve on employment interview panels this school year to hire administrators for the district. They are reviewing anonymous comments written by other teachers and administrators when asked to discuss the type of leaders desired at Coolidge schools. The team has pulled out the comment sheets that reflect patterns or themes in the responses. About the formal leaders in the district, they read the following:
>
> - That school needs a strict disciplinarian so the kids will know who is in charge.
> - The Latino kids need a Latino administrator so they can have a positive role model.
> - Principals come and go, but I will always be here.
> - This school is entirely too tough for a woman administrator!
> - I may not agree with her, but I know where she stands.

- One thing I will have to give the principal, he sure does relate well to the parents.
- She may be an expert in instruction and supervision, but how can she evaluate my physics lesson?

"I had no idea the comments would be so personal," exclaims Brittney. She is one of the middle school teachers, with a provisional teaching credential. "Some of them sound so jaded."

"Oh, they are not all bad," says Leatha. "They tell us a lot about what people want in their leaders. Look at this pile of comments. They tell us a lot about where the nonformal leadership is in this district."

"What do you mean by 'nonformal'?" asks Brittney.

"Nonformal leaders are not officially appointed or chosen but rather emerge from the group, based on the needs and aspirations of those who work in the environment," explains Leatha.

"Nonformal leaders are usually people like teachers, aides, students, or parents. People whose positions don't give them a lot of power but who have a lot of influence nonetheless. Barbara Latimer, who is on the board of the Citizens Human Relations Council, is a nonformal leader. She doesn't have a formal position of leadership, with a title, but everyone respects her and listens when she speaks. She is always at the district office and the board meetings, even though her daughter attends school in Rolling Meadows.

"Look at these comments; they acknowledge the nonformal leadership we have in this district."

- That secretary has trained seven principals!
- If you want to reach out to the parents, just tell Mrs. Latimer—Kim's mother—that woman is well respected in this community.
- To include more bilingual parents in school governance, you may want to use the services of the aide in Room 7; she knows all of the parents, and they respect her highly.
- The union representative is a very important member of the leadership council, but DeLois Winters is the teacher to whom the others look for guidance.

"You can see from these comments that our job is very important. What is expected in a school administrator varies widely, which is why we have assembled this team to assist us in this search for new administrators. We fully realize that a prospective administrator has to be a technician and a visionary, one who knows the skills and artistry of formal and nonformal leadership. We are looking for leaders who display personal values and behaviors that enable them and others to engage in effective interactions among students, educators, and the communities they serve."

Leaders come from all sectors of the school and the community it serves, and student leadership is vital to culturally proficient schools. Schools exist for students to gain knowledge and skills for adult life. In the 21st century, these skills and knowledge must include the ability to work in multicultural environments. Although students should not have to lead change efforts, effective leaders will find ways for them to contribute to change. Effective leaders acknowledge and support student leaders while assuming their own primary responsibility for making the school work for all students. Ideally, they do so proactively with foresight and vision, rather than reactively by responding to student or community pressures. Lindsey, Jungwirth, Pahl, and Lindsey (in press) hold that culturally proficient learning communities are places where the skills of formal and nonformal leadership merge in ways that benefit educators, staff, and, most important, our students and their parents/guardians. Lindsey et al. reviewed the prominent literature about learning communities and communities of practice (DuFour & Eaker, 1998; Hord, Rutherford, Huling-Austin, & Hall, 1987; Kruse & Seashore Louis, 1995; Oxley, 2004; Senge, 1990; Senge et al., 2000; Wenger, 1998) and identified common themes of professional communities focused on learning:

- A common vision
- Learning and collaborating with others
- Setting goals
- Using disaggregated student achievement data
- Focusing on standards, instructional practices, and student learning

We believe that the sustainability of learning communities requires reflection on a personal and organizational level, using a systems thinking approach as found in Hord and Sommers's (2008) five tenets for a professional learning community. To Hord's work, Lindsey et al. (in press) added the lens of cultural proficiency whereby participants in the collaborative learning community also engage in

- examining their own personal beliefs and values,
- examining the policies and practices of the school/district, and
- examining the culture of the community.

CULTURALLY PROFICIENT LEADERSHIP

When analyzing current school practices, leaders must be able to identify issues of class, caste, culture, and gender. Ogbu's (1978) notion of a caste system in the United States yields a crucial observation about poverty and racism: it is no accident that low-achieving students in the United

States are disproportionately African American, Latino, and First Nations students from families of lower socioeconomic status. In the United States, the apparent permanence of these socioeconomic groups gives rise to the reality of caste systems not unlike those many people assume exist only in other countries.

Similarly, Freire's (1970, 1997) view of the inadequate teaching offered to the lowest economic groups of the United States provides a stark perspective on the role of schools. His work with people around the world, most notably in Central and South America, has illustrated time and again that students and their families are capable of high levels of achievement if they are taught how to learn, provided with the resources to learn, and given a reason to believe that they can control their own destinies. Gilligan's (1983) work on gender issues illustrates how the male-centered perspective in this country has too often denied women the educational and other advantages afforded to half of the population.

The teachings of Ogbu (1978), Ogbu and Matute-Bianchi (1990), Freire (1970, 1997), and Gilligan (1983) align with culturally proficient practices. Culturally proficient leaders first develop a vision and then a mission that serves the needs of all students. In addition, they recognize and use both the formal and nonformal systems in the school. They know about the cultural issues that affect learning, and they have access to the resources necessary for an appropriate learning environment within the school. Culturally proficient school leaders know and appreciate how different school systems have evolved. Leaders are equipped to work with people and to guide others in challenging assumptions and translating perspectives, perceptions, values, and goals into agendas for school change. Having this knowledge of systems enables leaders to access the formal and nonformal leadership structures of their schools. Culturally proficient leaders are able to support and lead school personnel in formulating plans for school change.

Leadership in Action

A school cannot become culturally proficient without effective leadership focused on meeting the academic and social needs of all demographic groups of students enrolled at the school. Someone or some group has to have a vision of a culturally proficient school or district. Someone has to communicate a clear, culturally proficient vision to the administrators, teachers, and community members. These leaders inspire and expect transformative actions by all members of the educational community.

Although Rolling Meadows Superintendent Watson, the formal leader, has not been formally introduced to cultural proficiency, his values and many of his current practices are precompetent with an eye forward to what is possible. He has vision for maintaining the school district's excellence during a time of changing student population. Instead of accepting declining test scores, initiating repressive disciplinary measures at the high schools, or turning a deaf ear to parents, he gathers data so that the district can examine its practices and make necessary changes based on the data and consistent with the district's values. In this case, Superintendent Watson identified the following leverage points for change strategies within the school system:

- Student achievement data
- Teachers' perceptions of a need for higher expectations
- Interracial clashes among students
- Parental complaints about curriculum

Rather than blaming the teachers, the students, the students' families, or their cultural experiences for these areas of weakness, Watson gathers information to improve the school's processes. As he examines student achievement data, he realizes standardized test data is only one measure of student progress. Sharing the data and the vision, Superintendent Watson engages the leadership team to explore and seek alternative ways to teach and test students.

Typically, leaders either reinforce existing structures or promote change through dialogue and collaboration. Effective leaders evaluate the needs of the group. As those needs change, culturally proficient leaders provide appropriate support for making adjustments to those changes:

- Culturally proficient leaders help the school's faculty and staff assess its culture and determine how the school affects the students and its community.
- Culturally proficient leaders develop strategies for resolving conflict effectively and for addressing the dynamics of difference within the school.
- Culturally proficient leaders shape the school's formal and nonformal curricula to include information about the heritages, lifestyles, and values of all people in society.

Teachers, administrators, and educational consultants have seen that culturally proficient leadership can be exercised well independent of the leader's gender, ethnicity, social class, sexual orientation, or physical or sensory ability. Leaders who are effective are most often formal leaders who know how to collaborate with and support the talents of nonformal leaders. Culturally proficient leaders hold and share a vision of what education at the school can be for all students. They actively engage others in this shared vision, and they have the knowledge and skills to work with others to assess the school's needs and devise ways of providing for student needs so as to achieve their shared vision.

SO WHERE DO YOU START?

First and foremost, *commit to your own learning* by reading and studying Chapters 4 through 8. As a leader, it is important to do your own work first and to know how to use the tools of cultural proficiency. Once you have embraced the tools of cultural proficiency as part of your own personal and professional development, then we recommend you consider these activities:

- Use the Cultural Proficiency Continuum (Resource F, Activity F2) to assess situations that have taken place in your school.
- Use the Human Relations Needs Assessment (Resource C, Activity C10) to get the pulse of your school/district.
- Use the Cultural Competence Self-Assessment (Resource G, Activity G3) to begin conversations about what you and your colleagues need to learn and do personally.
- Connect the Guiding Principles of Cultural Proficiency (Resource E, Activity E1) to the core values or a mission statement for the district.
- Conduct the Examining Your Organizational Values activity (Resource E, Activity E5) at a staff development meeting to get a collective commitment to addressing the issues of diversity.

Once you have gathered these data, you may want to examine the school or district through different lenses:

- The data you gather using the Continuum (Resource F, Activity F2) provides you with a perspective on how you and others view the school. You may find widely different points of view on where school or district activities place on the continuum. Some may think an activity is culturally competent, whereas others may see it as culturally blind. Sharing your views and earnestly listening to the views of others is an important step in developing consensus about where you are and in what direction you need to go.
- Data from the Needs Assessment (Resource C, Activity C10) provide even more detailed information on how different groups experience the school or district. When analyzed along with the assessments of where the school activities lie on the Cultural Proficiency Continuum, powerful images begin to emerge. You will come to understand why some groups are pleased with the school's approach to diversity and why other groups are discontented.
- When you analyze your school or district's Examining Our Organizational Values Response Sheet (Resource E, Activity E5), you will begin to see how perceptions about the school and its needs are aligned—or not—with the core values, the mission statement, and the essential elements. By the time your group is ready to identify the shared values of your school or district, you and your colleagues will

be ready to commit to becoming an open, inclusive learning environment by embracing cultural proficiency as the approach that will support all students' access to learning.

With these activities, the culturally proficient leader creates agreement to examine schools through a different lens. The new lens frames assumptions about access, oppression, and entitlement. This new lens will guide you beyond the angst of guilt and anger to taking responsibility for effectively educating all students. Culturally proficient school leaders redirect conversation *from* explaining why groups of students fail *to* engaging colleagues in collaborative dialogue about creating powerful teaching-learning environments that ensure student success. Culturally proficient educators recognize and respond to both individual and group differences. Culturally proficient leaders organize the human and material resources of the school in a manner that considers the education of all students the fundamental responsibility of the school.

GOING DEEPER

1. What kinds of changes are needed at your school?

2. What type of leader is needed at this time?

3. What strategies might you use to identify nonformal leaders at your school?

4. In what ways might you support and engage nonformal leaders in culturally proficient practices?

5. In what environments are you a formal leader? In what environments do you rely on your nonformal leadership?

REFLECTION

_____

_____

_____

_____

_____

_____

_____

4

Framing Your Work With the Cultural Proficiency Tools

A sociocultural conception of oppression and privilege . . . enables us to see both the oppressed and the privileged as full and equal participants in a common history and an ongoing dialogue that, although it may not be easy (and may in fact at times seem impossible), is our only hope for both personal and social transformation.

—Cornel West (1993, p. 18)

The key to understanding cultural proficiency begins with recognizing the existence of different worldviews. Differing cultural worldviews become problematic when one's worldview causes one to judge a culture as "inferior" or "less than" rather than "different." Cultural worldviews range from seeking to eliminate other cultures to seeking to interact with other cultures in a way that builds on the best of both worlds. This range of worldviews is reflected in the points along the cultural proficiency continuum.

Those who commit to cultural proficiency have worldviews at the transformative side of the continuum—precompetence, competence, and proficiency. People who begin at the reactive end of the continuum—destructiveness, incapacity, and blindness—and end up at the transformative end of the continuum experience a paradigmatic shift from viewing diverse groups as problematic to working with people different from themselves in a manner that ensures healthy practices, mutually beneficial practices, and transformative relationships. Table 4.1 displays the points along the continuum.

Table 4.1   The Cultural Proficiency Continuum

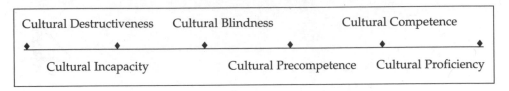

INSIDE-OUT CHANGE

Movement toward the transformative side of the continuum represents the shift to a commitment of educational equity for all learners in our schools. Educational theorists and researchers are unrelenting in calling our attention to the moral imperative inherent in transforming our country's schools (Baca & Almanza, 1991; Banks, 1999; Fullan, 2003; Gay, 2000; Hooks, 1990; Kozol, 2007; Senge et al., 2000; Singleton & Linton, 2006; Sleeter & Grant, 2007). These voices are aligned with current state and national reform efforts acknowledging that our schools continue to serve well those for whom our schools have been historically effective, while they need to be transformed to meet the needs of students who are English learners or are from low-income, African American, Latino, First Nations, and special needs populations.

Like every long journey, cultural proficiency begins with a first step. The first step includes understanding that the personal and organizational change that must take place is an inside-out process that begins with these commitments:

- A commitment to examining your own values, assumptions, and behaviors
- A commitment to working with your colleagues to examine your school's and district's policies and practices
- A commitment to being an integral part of the community you serve by learning with and from the community

These commitments involve using the processes of introspection, reflection, examination, analysis, and planning. The journey toward cultural proficiency will involve you in

- introspection as a means to understand your own thoughts, feelings, and motives;
- reflection as a means to examine your actions;
- examination as a means to study the current policies and practices of your school and district;
- analysis as a means to understand the relationship of all parts of the schooling processes; and
- planning as a means to be intentional in providing for the social and academic needs of all demographic groups of students.

Cultural proficiency is a worldview that reflects a commitment to serving students in unprecedented ways. The "tools" of cultural proficiency are processes that can be used by both historically dominated and dominant group members to replace old myths and stereotypes with the images, information, and skills that equip them to have substantive dialogue that results in equitable actions within schools (Cross, 1989, Tappan, 2006). We have organized the tools into a conceptual framework that graphically depicts the interrelationship of the tools.

CULTURAL PROFICIENCY CONCEPTUAL FRAMEWORK

Senge et al. (2000) used the term *mental model* in much the way we use the term *conceptual framework*. Simply put, a conceptual framework is a pictorial representation of one's thoughts, values, actions, policies, and practices. In this case, the conceptual framework is akin to a road map in that it allows sojourners for social justice to determine where they are on the journey to cultural proficiency and to develop plans for getting to where they want to be.

You will recall that the tools of cultural proficiency are as follows:

- **The Barriers:** Social constructs that, when understood, assist in overcoming resistance to change
- **The Guiding Principles:** Underlying values of the approach
- **The Continuum:** Language that describes both healthy and nonproductive policies, practices, and individual values and behaviors
- **The Essential Elements:** Behavioral standards for measuring, and planning for, growth toward cultural proficiency

Table 4.2 on the next page represents the tools and the manner in which they interact with and inform one another. The manner in which they interact and inform one another raises the tools from being separate and discrete to being a conceptual framework for how we improve our practice as educators. Take a few minutes for a close look at the information in the table.

Guidance in Reading Table 4.2

First, read the table from bottom to top. It may be useful to use these prompts:

- At the bottom of the table, notice the manner in which the arrow flowing from the "Barriers to Cultural Proficiency" informs the left side of the Continuum, fostering practices that are culturally destructive, incapacitating, and blind.
- Notice how the arrow flowing from the "Guiding Principles of Cultural Proficiency" informs the right side of the Continuum, leading to practices that are culturally precompetent, competent, and proficient. In effect, adherence to the guiding principles as core values enables people and organizations to overcome barriers to cultural proficiency.
- For those on the right side of the Continuum, the Five Essential Elements serve as standards for educator and school practices, enabling cross-cultural effectiveness.

Table 4.2   The Conceptual Framework for Culturally Proficient Practices

The Five Essential Elements of Cultural Competence

Serve as standards for personal, professional values and behaviors, as well as organizational policies and practices:

- Assessing cultural knowledge
- Valuing diversity
- Managing the dynamics of difference
- Adapting to diversity
- Institutionalizing cultural knowledge

Informs

The Cultural Proficiency Continuum portrays people and organizations who possess the knowledge, skills, and moral bearing to distinguish among healthy and unhealthy practices as represented by different worldviews:

Unhealthy Practices:

Differing
Worldviews

Healthy Practices:

- Cultural destructiveness
- Cultural incapacity
- Cultural blindness

- Cultural precompetence
- Cultural competence
- Cultural proficiency

Informs

Informs

Resolving the tension to do what is socially just within our diverse society leads people and organizations to view selves in terms Unhealthy and Healthy.

Barriers to Cultural Proficiency	E t h i c a l T e n s i o n	**Guiding Principles of Cultural Proficiency**
Serve as personal, professional, and institutional impediments to moral and just service to a diverse society by		*Provide a moral framework for conducting one's self and organization in an ethical fashion by believing the following:*

Barriers to Cultural Proficiency:

Serve as personal, professional, and institutional impediments to moral and just service to a diverse society by

- being resistant to change,
- being unaware of the need to adapt,
- not acknowledging systemic oppression, and
- benefiting from a sense of privilege and entitlement.

Ethical Tension

Guiding Principles of Cultural Proficiency:

Provide a moral framework for conducting one's self and organization in an ethical fashion by believing the following:

- Culture is a predominant force in society.
- People are served in varying degrees by the dominant culture.
- People have individual and group identities.
- Diversity within cultures is vast and significant.
- Each cultural group has unique cultural needs.
- The best of both worlds enhances the capacity of all.
- The family, as defined by each culture, is the primary system of support in the education of children.
- School systems must recognize that marginalized populations have to be at least bicultural and that this status creates a distinct set of issues to which the system must be equipped to respond.
- Inherent in cross-cultural interactions are dynamics that must be acknowledged, adjusted to, and accepted.

The tools of cultural proficiency equip individual educators and their schools with the means to make meaningful, intentional change that benefits all students. A brief orientation to each of the tools is provided in the section that follows. Then Chapters 5 through 8 provide detailed descriptions of each of the tools. To deepen further your understanding of each of the tools, the Resources section at the back of this book provides activities and instruments to guide your use of the tools of cultural proficiency. As you read this chapter and each of the subsequent chapters, turn frequently to the Resources and review the activities and instruments there.

THE FOUR TOOLS OF CULTURAL PROFICIENCY

Cultural proficiency is an interrelated set of four tools, *not* strategies or techniques. Being culturally competent or proficient is exemplified by how educators develop and implement school board policy, allocate resources, use assessment data, deliver curriculum and instruction, interact with parents and community members, and plan and use professional development. The tools assist in executing these tasks. In combination, the tools of cultural proficiency—overcoming the barriers, the guiding principles, the continuum, and the essential elements—provide a conceptual framework for analyzing your values and behaviors, as well as your school's policies and practices. Table 4.2 shows how the tools relate to one another.

Two of the tools provide a framework to guide personal values and organizational policies in schools:

- **The Barriers to Cultural Proficiency** provide persons and their organizations with the understandings that enable them to overcome resistance to change.
- **The Guiding Principles of Cultural Proficiency** are *values* related to issues that emerge in diverse environments and when engaging with people who are not members of the dominant culture.

The other two tools provide ethical choices relating to behaviors and standards that will guide your work:

- **The Cultural Proficiency Continuum** provides language to describe unhealthy and healthy *values and behaviors* of persons and *policies and practices* of organizations. In addition, the Continuum can help to assess the limitations of current practices and to plan for learning and using effective practices. Movement along the Continuum represents a shift in thinking *from*, at best, tolerating diversity *to* transformation for equity. It is not a subtle shift in worldview. It is paradigmatic.
- **The Essential Elements of Cultural Competence** serve as standards by which one develops healthy individual values/behaviors and organizational policies/practices.

Barriers to Cultural Proficiency

In the manner that the guiding principles provide a moral compass for culturally proficient actions, barriers to achieving culturally proficient actions exist to resist constructive actions. The barriers to cultural proficiency are the following:

- Resistance to change and unawareness of the need to adapt
- Systems of oppression and privilege
- A sense of entitlement and unearned privilege

These barriers are often manifested in statements such as, *It is not me who needs to change. I have been a successful educator for years. These kids/parents just need to get a clue!* Similarly, it is rare to find the person who doesn't acknowledge that racism, ethnocentrism, and sexism exist in society. However, one often fails to see that when one group of people loses rights and privileges due to systemic oppression, those rights and privileges accrue to others in unacknowledged or unrecognized ways. When one recognizes one's entitlement, one has the ability to make constructive choices that benefit the education of children and youth.

A conversation gap exists among educational policymakers and educators when focusing on the achievement issues of nondominant students. The gap in conversation, often unrecognized or unacknowledged, is in educators not having the perspective to see roadblocks encountered by members of nondominant groups. This selective invisibility leads to a sense of privilege and entitlement for members of the dominant group. Whereas systems of oppression impose barriers for members of nondominant groups, concomitant systems of privilege and entitlement impose barriers for members of the dominant group. Not being able to see, or refusing to see, the barriers erected by a sense of privilege and entitlement involves a skewed sense of reality, which can impede one's ability to pursue ethical and moral avenues in meeting the academic and social needs of nondominant groups.

The position of privilege often fosters educators voicing biased or ill-informed assumptions about parents from nondominant groups. The following are typical comments:

> *Their parents won't come to parent conferences because they don't care about the education of their children.*

> *Why try to help them? They will just end up as gangbangers, just like their dad!*

> *Why should I learn anything about their culture? This is our country—let them learn about us!*

Educators who make these comments are in need of different lenses, tools, and structures to understand their students and the barriers that impede their students' access to education. Cultural proficiency is an approach for surfacing assumptions and values that undermine the success of some student groups and a lens for examining how we can include and honor the cultures and learning needs of all students. Educators feel enriched and successful when they engage in intentional conversations about how parents and students who are different from them behave and learn. Chapter 5 provides a detailed discussion of the barriers to cultural proficiency and, in combination with activities and instruments in Resources, opportunities for improving your professional practices as well as those of your school or district.

The Guiding Principles of Cultural Proficiency

To counter the pernicious effect of the barriers, the guiding principles provide a framework for the examination of core values of schools. Use of the guiding principles provides educators opportunity to match their expressed values with what they actually do (Argyris, 1990; Schein, 1985). The guiding principles provide a framework for how the diversity of students informs professional practice in responding to student learning needs. Does your school or district have a mission, vision, or beliefs statement? If so, these are good places to see if the stated values in your school align with predominant behaviors in the school. Most likely you will encounter phrases such as *all students, valuing diversity, 21st-century education,* or *high-tech skills.* Do leadership behaviors align with those expressed values?

The guiding principles of cultural proficiency are as follows:

- Culture is a predominant force in society.
- People are served in varying degrees by the dominant culture.
- People have individual and group identities.
- Diversity within cultures is vast and significant.
- Each cultural group has unique cultural needs.
- The best of both worlds enhances the capacity of all.
- The family, as defined by each culture, is the primary system of support in the education of children.
- School systems must recognize that marginalized populations have to be at least bicultural and that this status creates a distinct set of issues to which the system must be equipped to respond.
- Inherent in cross-cultural interactions are dynamics that must be acknowledged, adjusted to, and accepted.

In *The Culturally Proficient School* (Lindsey, Roberts, & CampbellJones, 2005), we noted that

understanding and acknowledging the principles and choosing to manifest them in your behavior are demonstrations of culturally proficient leadership. The choice you make to align your leadership actions with the principles of cultural proficiency communicates a strong message throughout your school's community that you value diversity and fully expect that every individual will do the same. Indeed, the guiding principles are attitudinal benchmarks that enable you and others to assess progress toward acknowledging and valuing cultural differences, and while this assessment yields crucial information, it is insufficient by itself in provoking the development of culturally proficient behaviors. (p. 52)

Chapter 6 is designed for you and your colleagues to learn the guiding principles and apply them to your practices. In combination with the associated activities and instruments in Resources, you have the opportunity to make an expressed commitment to being the educator you want to be in the school community you want your community to become.

The Continuum of Cultural Proficiency

The first three points on the continuum may find educators referring to students as *underperforming*, while the next three points would find them referring to the ways in which they are *underserving* students and their communities. The first three points of the continuum (cultural destructiveness, cultural incapacity, cultural blindness) align with the barriers and focus on *them* as being problematic; the next three points of the continuum (cultural precompetence, cultural competence, cultural proficiency) align with the guiding principles and focus on our *practice*. Such change is a paradigmatic shift in thinking. We refer to this shift as an "inside-out" approach to change. Following are the points on the Continuum:

- *Cultural destructiveness*—Seeking to eliminate vestiges of the cultures of others
- *Cultural incapacity*—Seeking to make the cultures of others appear to be wrong
- *Cultural blindness*—Refusing to acknowledge the culture of others
- *Cultural precompetence*—Being aware of what one doesn't know about working in diverse settings. From this initial level of awareness, a person/organization can either move in a positive, constructive direction or falter, stop, and possibly regress.
- *Cultural competence*—Viewing one's personal and organizational work as an interactive arrangement in which the educator enters into diverse settings in a manner that is additive to cultures that are different from that of the educator
- *Cultural proficiency*—Making the commitment to lifelong learning for the purpose of being increasingly effective in serving the educational needs of cultural groups; holding the vision of what can be and committing to assessments that serve as benchmarks on the road to student success

Chapter 7 describes each point of the continuum in ways that allow you to examine your own values and behaviors and the policies and practices of your school. Use of the information in Chapter 7 and the related activities and instruments in Resources will provide you with the perspective to identify inequitable and equitable values, behaviors, policies, and practices.

The Essential Elements of Cultural Competence

The essential elements are the standards for culturally competent values, behaviors, policies, and practices. The essential elements are the embodiment of the guiding principles and frame what we do as educators:

- *Assessing cultural knowledge*—Being aware of what you know about your own and others' cultures, about how you react to others' cultures, and what you need to do to be effective in cross-cultural situations
- *Valuing diversity*—Making the effort to be inclusive of people whose viewpoints and experiences are different from yours and will enrich conversations, decision making, and problem solving
- *Managing the dynamics of difference*—Viewing conflict as a natural and normal process, which has cultural contexts that can be understood and can be supportive in creative problem solving
- *Adapting to diversity*—Having the will to learn about others and having the ability to use others' cultural experiences and backgrounds in educational settings
- *Institutionalizing cultural knowledge*—Making learning about cultural groups and their experiences and perspectives an integral part of your ongoing learning

Chapter 8 provides detailed descriptions of each of the essential elements. Used in combination with the associated materials in Resources, Chapter 8 gives you the opportunity to be intentional in how you approach your role as a nonformal or formal leader in your school or district.

GOING DEEPER

1. How comfortable are you with your knowledge of cultural proficiency?

2. What questions do you have?

3. What more do you want to learn about the tools of cultural proficiency?

4. How do you see the tools of cultural proficiency helping you and members of your school community narrow and close educational gaps?

REFLECTION

_____

_____

_____

_____

_____

_____

_____

_____

_____

_____

_____

_____

_____

_____

_____

_____

_____

_____

_____

_____

_____

_____

_____

_____

_____

PART II

Using the Tools of Cultural Proficiency

5

The First Tool

Overcoming Barriers

If we tell ourselves that the only problem is hate, we avoid facing the reality that it is mostly nice, non-hating people who perpetuate racial inequality.

—Ellis Cose (1998, p. 20)

The Rolling Meadows consultants are making a presentation to Superintendent Watson's cabinet, and Holly, the assistant superintendent of curriculum and instruction, is not so sure they really understand the situation at Rolling Meadows because she hasn't seen any of these problems. The consultants say, "Throughout U.S. educational history, students have been taught close to nothing about the caste system in this country and very little about U.S. citizens of lower castes. In recent decades, however, most textbooks and school curricula have inserted some materials and lessons mentioning women and people of color, although these insertions have generally been few and segregated from the sweep of U.S. history.

"Acknowledgment of African Americans is too often limited to brief lessons on slavery, the celebration of Dr. King's birthday, and observances of Black History Month in February. Lessons about People of the First Nations often range from highlighting their nobility to underscoring their savagery; usually, their only significant role is to

> attend the first Thanksgiving. Lessons about Latinos are frequently relegated to music, dance, and a lesson about Cesar Chavez or Che Guevara, if they are mentioned at all outside of New York and the Southwestern United States. Students learn about Asians as the celebrants of Chinese New Year, the sneaky attackers at Pearl Harbor, and the reluctant recipients of our 'help' during the Korean and Vietnam Wars. Lessons about women often resort to the 'great woman' approach, focusing on a few heroic individuals rather than the historic and continuing role of women in the United States. These discrete lessons lead to the objectification and invisibility of females and people of color."

In professional development sessions similar to that at Rolling Meadows, we have posed this question: "As reasonable people, can we agree that systems of oppression like racism, ethnocentrism, sexism, and heterosexism have existed historically in this country and people have lost rights, benefits, and their lives?" Uniformly, people either nod in assent or verbally agree with the statement. Then we continue by asking, "As reasonable people, then, can we agree that vestiges of these systems persist and that people are still penalized by these systems?" Again, people nod in agreement or express verbal agreement. Then we ask the important question, "If people have lost, and continue to lose, rights and benefits due to systems of oppression, what happened to those rights and benefits?" One can sense the discomfort as participants begin to have an emerging awareness of the powerful dynamic of entitlement.

Failure to recognize, acknowledge, and commit to overcoming the barriers is the result of a deficit model worldview. A deficit worldview legitimates the misuse of power; embraces privilege as inalienable; and holds that those who are not in the economic, social, and political mainstream are solely responsible for their lot in life.

BARRIERS TO CULTURAL PROFICIENCY

The first tool of cultural proficiency is a set of caveats—systemic oppression, the presumption of entitlement, and unawareness of the need to adapt—all of which result in resistance to change. They warn of the individual and systemic barriers to becoming culturally proficient. To confront and overcome the barriers to cultural proficiency requires will, knowledge, and skills. These barriers are present throughout society, as well as in schools, and are instrumental in perpetuating the deficit model worldview. Table 5.1 presents the barriers to cultural proficiency.

Table 5.1   Barriers to Cultural Proficiency

- **Systems of oppression**—That racism, sexism, heterosexism, ableism, and classism exist is without refute, historically and currently. Data are on the side of documenting and describing the ill effects of such systems. Being able to understand oppression as a systemic issue apart from personal behavior is important.
- **A sense of privilege and entitlement**—Systems of oppression have two effects—on those who are harmed and on those who benefit. Those harmed from systemic oppression respond from an emotional connection, as well as from being well informed of practices that impact them negatively. On the other hand, many of those who benefit from historical and current practices are oblivious to the negative effects of systemic oppression, because they can choose not to see.
- **Unawareness of the need to adapt**—Many educators and schools often struggle with change that involves issues of culture. For those who are resistant, change often is experienced as an outside force that judges current practices as deficient or defective. Whether accurate or not, an adversarial relationship exists between those forcing the change and other members of the school community.

- Power in the form of *systemic oppression* is represented by the inequities that persist due to past and prevalent policies and practices. Most often, organizational and societal policies and practices that are discriminatory get acted out in individual values and behaviors. As you will see later in this chapter, even when we don't discriminate intentionally, inequities persist in the system. The persistent achievement gap is an example of unresolved historical inequities.
- People with a *presumption of entitlement* believe that they have acquired all the personal achievements and societal benefits they have solely on the basis of their own merit and character; therefore, they don't feel a need to release or reorder any societal or organizational perquisites they may have. Having schools where some students get a world-class education and other schools where failure is expected is an example of systemic privilege. When this disparity is allowed to continue, this is another example of systemic privilege.
- *Unawareness of the need to adapt* means failing to recognize the need to make personal and school changes in response to the diversity of the people with whom one interacts, perhaps because it never occurs to anyone in the dominant group that there is a problem. People who are unaware of the need to adapt often believe that if the others—the newcomers—change or adapt to the environment, there will be no problems. They do not yet understand that once the commitment to cultural proficiency is made, everyone changes to create a new school culture.

Edward Ball (1998), a descendant of slave owners, links historical practices to current realities:

No one among the Balls talked about how slavery helped us, but whether we acknowledged it or not, the powers of our ancestors were still in hand. Although our social franchise had shrunk, it had nevertheless survived. If we did not inherit money, or land, we received a great fund of cultural capital, including prestige, a chance at education, self-esteem, a sense of place, mobility, even (in some cases) a flair for giving orders. And it was not only "us," the families of former slave owners, who carried the baggage of the plantations. By skewing things so violently in the past, we had made sure that our cultural riches would benefit all white Americans. . . .

At the same time, the slave business was a crime that had not fully been acknowledged. It would be a mistake to say that I felt guilt for the past. A person cannot be culpable for the acts of others, long dead, that he or she could not have influenced. Rather than responsible, I felt accountable for what had happened, called on to try to explain it. I also felt shame about the broken society that had washed up when the tide of slavery receded. (pp. 13–14)

For decades, educators and other leaders have recognized that an important step in creating change in schools is to identify barriers to the acceptance of new ideas, as well as the implementation of programs, procedures, or techniques that challenge long-held and unexamined beliefs (Freire, 1970; Fullan, 1991; Giroux, 1992a; Owens, 1995). The barriers to cultural proficiency are manifest in the dominant society's view that the issues concerning marginalized or targeted groups (e.g. people of color; women; Differently abled people; Gay, Lesbian, Bisexual, and Transgendered people) are the problems of those groups and have little relevance to the issues of apparently straight, white males.

THIS CHAPTER IS FOR EVERYONE

In this chapter, we introduce the terms *dominant group* and *historically oppressed groups*. We recognize and acknowledge that reading or discussing these concepts makes some people uncomfortable. If you are discomfited, please read on, because your discomfort is a sign that you may be on the verge of deeper learning about your own values and behaviors. Our intent is not to cause distress; our intention is to raise awareness and encourage self-reflection. You cannot be an agent of personal or organizational change or make improvements in the system if you have not first examined your role and function within it. If you are experiencing any level of discomfort, you may be in the first phase of awareness.

CAVEAT: SYSTEMIC OPPRESSION

Systems such as racism, sexism, ethnocentrism, heterosexism, and ableism serve to create unlevel playing fields by ensuring access to society for some members and impeding access for others. Throughout history, the disenfranchised have had to seek legislative and judicial remedies to gain power in this country, but wealthy, white, landowning men have held and retained power from the very beginnings of U.S. history. Jacksonian democracy broadened the participation of U.S. citizens in the political and economic spheres of this country, but it denied such participation to anyone other than white men. U.S. white men have enjoyed power, as manifested in the form of privilege or entitlement, as an integral part of their history, tradition, and economic status.

The power that accrues to the entitled in society is so widespread that those who have it do not see its pervasiveness. If you don't notice your culture or the privilege you have within it, you are probably a member of the dominant culture. Delpit (1988) notes two distinct responses to entitlement: (a) those with greater power are frequently least aware of, or least willing to acknowledge, its existence; and (b) those with less power are often most aware of power discrepancies. In much the same way that people do not appreciate their liberties until they are threatened, most entitled white men do not appreciate the power of their entitlement because they have never experienced the systemic absence of power. Moreover, the milieu of entitlement insulates them from the cries of those who live in fear of sexual assaults, battering, racist acts, and other forms of discrimination.

The same system of privilege keeps dominant group members from hearing those who protest against the systematic denial of their access to societal power and insulates them from day-to-day microaggressions. Smaller systems also reflect inequities in the distribution of power and privilege. Think about your school or worksite. People with tenure, degrees, and formal leadership roles have many more resources than those who do not. In the classroom, children who are attractive, bright, and compliant receive disproportionately more of the teacher's time than those who are simply average. School districts with wealthy student populations have higher achievement scores than districts that are populated by poor, immigrant, or nonwhite students.

"What is at stake for white America today is not what [oppressed] people want and do but what white people stand for and do" (Terry, 1970, p. 15). We would say the same for men in relation to gender, to heterosexuals in relation to sexual orientation, and to mentally and physically fit people in relation to ableness. Once all U.S. citizens understand and accept that some people receive entitlements based on gender and race, that other people have impediments placed before them for the same reason, and that all U.S. citizens have a responsibility to recognize that everyone is an integral part of both the problem and the solution, then true progress toward cultural proficiency begins.

Recognizing Power in Education

Since the late 1970s, we have involved thousands of educators, parents, and students in the simulation *StarPower* (Shirts, 1969). In an hour of facilitated interaction, participants in *StarPower* notice the effects of entitlement and inequity. Participants create a three-tiered society in which power and access are disproportionately distributed. Participants experience interactions within and among the three groups, then debrief by discussing the feelings and perceptions that surfaced during the simulation. The participants reflect on the roles they played in this simulated society and then transfer their learnings to new interpretations of their experiences in the real, inequitable world.

Delpit's (1988) observation of educators debating issues related to educating children of color supports this notion of unawareness:

> For many who consider themselves members of liberal or radical camps, acknowledging personal power and admitting participation in the culture of power is extremely uncomfortable. On the other hand, those who are less powerful in any situation are most likely to recognize the power variable most acutely. My guess is that white colleagues . . . did not perceive themselves to have power over the non-white(s). . . . However, either by virtue of their position, their numbers, or their access to that particular code of power of calling upon research, the white educators had the authority to establish what was to be considered truth regardless of the opinions of people of color, and the latter were well aware of that fact. (pp. 283–284)

Given that most educational policymakers and decision makers are white, this absence of information and insight becomes especially crucial to the culturally proficient leader. Many entitled members of society believe that all people in this country have the opportunity to succeed but choose instead to pick the scabs on old wounds so that they do not have to put forth effort in new endeavors. Entitlement creates either unawareness or denial of the reality that not all U.S. citizens have a common base of inalienable rights. These beliefs and denials are supported by curricula that are silent about the pluralistic nature of our country's history and development.

The authors of history textbooks have routinely excluded some cultural groups from their writing; more insidiously, they have also excluded major events. When authors exclude this information from students' textbooks, they romanticize history, thereby failing to help young people understand many social conflicts. Both the teaching of history and the outcomes of the simulation illustrate how entitlement is reinforced by experience.

An illustration of how white men often lack awareness of entitlement and deny its existence comes from the many sessions on cultural proficiency that we have conducted in recent years.

During an inservice session on cultural proficiency at the Coolidge district, James Harris, the consultant, overhears this conversation between European American Principal Steve Petrossian and Puerto Rican Principal Richard Díaz:

Steve says, "You know, this activity in determining how prejudice differs from racism or sexism gives me some new ideas to work with. I had never considered the concept of power; it just never occurred to me. Let me ask you this: One of my African American teachers said that his student is 'a good athlete for a white boy.' Now isn't that racism?"

"Steve," Richard replies, "let me get this straight: You have been on this planet for decades, and you have never thought about the power that European American people have in this country?"

Steve is defensive. "Hey, why attack me? I'm being honest with you. Power is something I've just never considered. Just because I'm white doesn't mean that I have power. Besides, you haven't answered my question. Isn't my story an example of racism?"

James responds to Steve, "No, it isn't. Although your story illustrates an ethnocentric use of a stereotype and is definitely cultural incapacity, the teacher in your example lacks the power to institutionalize his beliefs. The term racism implies the power to act on one's bigotry. Or reflects the systems within our institutions that discriminate against people of color without the consent or the conscious participation of dominant group people in the system."

James continues, addressing the whole group, "Steve's story also shows his lack of awareness of—as well as his wish to deny—his own entitlement. The teacher in Steve's story was not reinforcing or perpetuating institutional racism, which affects every single person and has grave social consequences, no matter whether it is recognized or acknowledged. More often than not, people who are not directly affected by oppression fail to understand when cultural groups speak out about their experiences. Members of the dominant group, whatever that group tends to be, usually fail to notice their power or entitlement."

Richard interrupts: "Yeah, they say, 'If I didn't experience the oppression, or witness it, then you must be overreacting.' Or they want to start talking about their own pain, like this was the oppression Olympics."

James goes on, "If we are to create an effectively functioning society—and, by extension, a school system that is culturally proficient—we must find ways to address issues of entitlement. By doing so, we can minimize gaps in the education of our educators that perpetuate their lack of awareness and their denial of their own empowerment."

CAVEAT: PRIVILEGE AND ENTITLEMENT

While our society is generally knowledgeable about the historical inequities caused by systemic racism and sexism, too few people ever acknowledge how the deficit model worldview benefits privileged populations. To become a culturally proficient educator or develop a culturally proficient school, you must understand entitlement as a facet of the deficit model worldview.

Entitlement is the converse of the institutionalized forms of oppression—racism, sexism, ethnocentrism, and heterosexism—phenomena that penalize people for their membership in dominated cultural groups. *Entitlement* is the accrual of benefits solely because of membership in a dominant group. Just as dominated people are penalized because of their culture, other people benefit because of their membership in a privileged group within the dominant culture. If examined on a continuum, entitlement is the end at which some people—chiefly, heterosexual white men—predominate and have great power and control because of their membership in the dominant cultural group; *institutionalized oppression* is the other end, at which people—chiefly, people of color, women, persons who are differently abled, and homosexuals—are more sparsely represented and, therefore, have relatively little institutionalized power or control.

An illustration of this "disconnect"—of being aware of the downside but not the upside of systemic oppression—is the recently emerged awareness of the achievement gap. One of the disquieting outcomes of the current standards-based accountability movement has been the "discovery" that achievement gaps correlate with membership in demographic groups, such as race, gender, language, social class, and ableness. The educational community has been aware of the achievement gap for over 30 years, but gave it little attention until accountability measures for schools were called for (Perie, Moran, & Lutkus, 2005). This system of oppression existed because those who benefited from existing practices felt no need to address the disparities. The differences in achievement reinforced their deficit worldview. When one's environment is in alignment with one's perception of reality, there is no need to question or change the status quo.

The hierarchy of power poses issues that must be addressed within at least two contexts, local and societal. For example, only a few years ago, elementary schools had predominantly female faculties and male principals. The recent trend is to have a school that is predominantly female in its administrators, faculty, and staff, which means that the dominant culture often becomes a female-influenced culture. For a man to thrive in such a school, he must adapt to it. In that environment, a group that has been historically underrepresented becomes the dominant group. However, in most environments outside of the school, or in interactions with particular women within the school, the man retains systemic privilege. Once he leaves campus, he moves back into a social, economic, and political system that benefits his gender. The point here is that even though he is a minority in this particular environment, the man has power and privileges that contribute to his sense of entitlement that come from the larger, dominant culture.

Understanding One's Role in Ending Oppression

Your role in shifting the balance of power must begin with understanding your own distinctive role in ending oppressive actions. Which role you play may depend on whether the cultural group to which you belong is the dominant one. For people in dominant groups, your role requires a moral choice to assume personal responsibility and to take personal initiative to change it. For people in dominated groups, your role is to recognize, name, and challenge the oppressive systems and to commit yourself to self-determination, continue to confront dysfunctional systems, and network with others to take control of your personal and professional lives.

As a culturally proficient leader, you will guide colleagues to recognize how some people are disenfranchised and, at the same time, others benefit from current practices. The newest skill for you is to coach members of dominant groups to examine and reflect upon their roles in our many systems—educational, political, and economic. It is important for our colleagues to recognize that the disparities that exist in each of these systems are not happenstance; they are the result of historical inequities, and as such, they can be remediated and overcome.

Most dominant group members in U.S. culture do not view themselves as more powerful or privileged than others in society, so they do not see themselves as stakeholders in these issues of power. Therefore, more often than not, dominant group members view issues of oppression and entitlement as issues solely for oppressed people. In fact, the traditional manner of studying issues of equity and diversity is to study the powerlessness of people of color, women, and other historically underserved groups.

Why don't discussions of diversity include white people and men? The answer is "entitlement." White people, and more particularly white men, choose—consciously or unconsciously—whether to participate actively in issues of equity and cultural proficiency. They may become angry, guilty, or indifferent to these topics. They may decry their forefathers' actions, they may protest that they never owned slaves, they may become depressed learning of some of the history that was never taught when they were students, or they may shrug it off and quietly declare that it is not their problem. The reality is that once entitled people react, they still can choose whether or not they will address issues of power and oppose acts that perpetuate oppression. The first step in addressing these issues and opposing these actions is simply to acknowledge that the dynamics of entitlement do not accord people of color, women, LGBT people, or Differently abled people the same opportunity to choose whether to deal with issues of entitlement and oppression. These issues are part of their daily existence, just as power is an unacknowledged reality for straight white men.

To understand entitlement, we must understand how the empowered members of society are often oblivious to the ways in which they have benefited from their entitlement. Even as awareness emerges, they may still be reluctant to acknowledge the dynamics of race, gender and sexual orientation, ableness, and socioeconomic class in the expression of power. For example, socioeconomics is clearly a major factor in determining who wields power in this country. The effects of poverty have blinded poor white people to the oppression experienced by other people based on their ethnicity. As a result, impoverished white people often feel a disregard for—and even an antagonism toward—people of color. This dynamic results in dysfunctional conversations where the participants attempt to prove whose pain is greater. We refer to this as "oppression Olympics" and find that it results in circular arguments that spiral downward and are not productive.

Entitlement and the Teaching of History

Prior to World War II, white males were the primary recipients of public and private education, and the version of history taught in schools reflected the views, beliefs, and interests of white males. To this day, most U.S. history textbooks fail to address either the country's historical caste system or the distinction between caste and immigrant status, as described in Chapter 2, and its legacy in persistent educational and social disparities. Oppressed U.S. citizens appear as single chapters, cursory comments, or footnotes, if they appear at all. The effect of this legacy of omission is an assumption of entitlement by members of dominant U.S. society, particularly white men.

This dominant cultural perspective has thus been institutionalized in U.S. public schools. The effect on women has been to ensure their role as subordinate to men. The effect on people of color has been to ensure their second-class citizenship and to deprive members of most cultural groups, including white people of lower socioeconomic status, of the education and access that would facilitate their success in the U.S. mainstream.

The unfortunate reality of most history textbooks is that they glorify the accomplishments of politicians, barons of industry, and warriors but spend comparatively little time on the social issues of each historical period. The accomplishments of white men are the major foci, because government, business, and the military have been, and remain, the province of white men. When women and people of color have been recognized for their contributions to the development of our country, history textbooks have recorded their contributions as exceptions. This sends an insidious message to students about who is valued in this country.

The struggle for the rights of oppressed people predates the U.S. Revolutionary War, yet history textbooks have consistently failed to present the role of women and people of color in the development of the United States. For example, though urban violence has historical roots going back to the 18th century, the race riots of the 18th and 19th centuries are rarely recorded in modern U.S. history textbooks (Franklin & Moss, 1988). Hence, most U.S. citizens see urban race riots as an artifact of the modern civil rights movement. The view that urban violence is a recent phenomenon is further enhanced by modern media, which compete to provide the most sensational accounts of contemporary upheavals.

> The consultants at Rolling Meadows direct the cabinet's attention to a chart with these quotations from the focus groups they conducted during the cultural audit:
> "If we are celebrating diversity, why don't we have celebrations like European American History Month?"
> "The teacher wrote on my child's paper that she didn't understand the black inner-city experience and, therefore, couldn't grade her essay fairly. This child has never lived in the inner city! Her father is a chemist, and I am vice president of the Red Cross. Her teacher knows we are a middle-class family."
> "These immigrant students don't even have magazines and books in their homes. They are at a tremendous disadvantage when compared to the other students."
> "I don't believe we have to point out people who choose their sexual preference or orientation or whatever the politically correct term is! Does that mean we, then, need to identify George Washington as a heterosexual?"
> After giving the cabinet a chance to reflect on the effect of these statements, the consultant remarks, "Each of these comments assumes that entitled students, the European American students and families of the dominant culture, are the standard of measure for other students. In the first comment, it is not recognized that most traditional school curricula celebrate the dominant culture daily. The second illustration shows the unawareness of the relationship of economic class to ethnic culture. The second to the last quote reflects the assumption that the speaker knows what is in students' homes and that students with books and magazines read them. The final quote assumes that sexual orientation is chosen."

These segregated lessons fail to teach students about how women, people of color, and LGBT people have played vital roles throughout all aspects and periods of U.S. history. Lessons about a few isolated events and people cannot help students understand how such people and events relate to all of U.S. history. Furthermore, because the history of racism and other forms of oppression is absent from these lessons, most students fail to understand how current societal tensions have emerged from historical events and trends.

Although all students are kept ignorant of the history of women, people of color, and LGBT people in U.S. life, straight white male students suffer the least from this omission: they are still able to feel a connection to their past. Their forebears appear on every page and in every lecture. They are clearly a part of the U.S. pageant. In contrast, students of color, LGBT students, and female students often feel disconnected from U.S. history: none of their forebears appears to have been involved in any significant way, and LGBT persons, people of color, and women are largely absent from the history being taught. As a result, students of color, female students, and LGBT students gain a sense of invisibility in history and literature due to the omissions, distortions, and fallacious assumptions being taught in school.

White boys, never having this experience, have no idea how it feels to be absent from history. Howard (1993) summarizes their experiences well: "The possibility of remaining ignorant of other cultures is a luxury uniquely available to members of any dominant group" (p. 38). This luxury extends to ignorance of the oppression experienced by people of other cultures. This situation places a heavy burden on the culturally proficient educator.

Without an accurate historical perspective, both entitled and oppressed people will continue to be intensely defensive and protective when assessing contemporary and historical social issues. People of color confront racism daily and are often exasperated by white people, whose responses to their frustrations range from hostility to indifference based on profound ignorance. For their part, white U.S. citizens who do not feel personally responsible for racism, men who do not understand their role in perpetuating institutionalized sexism, and heterosexual people are often frustrated by apparently unsympathetic people of color, women, and LGBT people. Consequently, discussions of oppression and entitlement often lead to miscommunication and resentment. One side speaks from painful personal experience, whereas the other side perceives only apparently inexplicable anger and personal attack. As a culturally proficient leader, you can guide teachers to learn, understand, and teach all of American history and the implications of history for the alpha and beta groups in this country. In addition to being more cognizant of the entitlement of some groups, culturally proficient educators are more proactive in ending oppression.

The deficit model worldview reflects the entitlement of people in dominant groups. The skewed teaching of history and misinterpretation of its lessons are ways that educators manifest a deficit model worldview and their sense of entitlement. Entitlement is also demonstrated through the language used for describing oppressed people, the ways in which oppressed people are objectified, and the differing access to power available to entitled people versus oppressed people.

The Language of Entitlement

To understand the empowered end of the entitlement continuum, it is important to recognize how language dehumanizes people by objectifying them (making them objects). Historically, the dominant white male society has used demeaning terminology to focus social attention on groups with less power, implying that they are the cause of their own marginalization.

Thus, language reflects the realities of power in this society. Educators are no strangers to language that blames the victims for their oppression. Since the mid-1950s, educators have bombarded students, educational literature, and their colleagues with terms attempting to explain the disparities between oppressed and entitled groups. Table 5.2 presents some of the more common terms.

Table 5.2   Words Used to Describe Oppressed and Entitled Groups

Oppressed	Entitled
Inferior	Superior
Culturally deprived	Privileged
Culturally disadvantaged	Advantaged
Deficient	Normal
Different	Regular
Diverse	Uniform
Third World	First World
Minority	Majority
Underclass	Upper class
Poor	Middle class
Unskilled workers	Leaders

Each of the terms in the left column in Table 5.2 describes groups that occupy the oppressed end of the entitlement continuum. The ideas represented by these terms are used to explain why students from these groups fail to perform at criterion levels. These terms serve two purposes: (a) they frame the students, and their student cultures, as the source of any educational problem they may have; and (b) they discount the institutionalized oppression to which beta students are subjected.

Terms of oppression focus on what is wrong with the oppressed, thereby implying that they must be studied (to detect their specific flaws) and then fixed. The unquestioned use of these terms suggests that people of color, who are disproportionately represented on the oppressed end of the continuum, suffer from a pathological condition. At best, they are viewed as *others* (not us) and at worst, as deviants. This polarity of language and perceptions is reflected in the daily workings of schools. Notice that some labels have no comparable terms for the entitled groups—unless, of course, we wish to use *normal* or some other term signifying that white men are the standard against which other people are measured.

The terms in the right column in Table 5.2 describe the students representing the dominant culture of our country. Pause for a moment to consider this question: How often do you use these terms in your interactions with students and with fellow educators? Most of the people we ask answer *not much* or *never*. Most people rarely utter these words because entitled people do not objectify or name themselves. Entitled people name only others, people they perceive to differ from themselves. Thus, when the terms *deficient* and *deprived* are used in their many permutations, the speaker implies that entitled people are the norm to which other people are compared. That norm is based on white middle-class U.S. values and behaviors and, more specifically, on the values and behaviors of white middle-class people.

Labeling traps dominated people in two ways. First, it reinforces their marginalization from the dominant culture and ensures that they will be denied access to the privileges of the dominant culture. Second, it pronounces them deficient for failing to meet the cultural expectations of the dominant culture, reinforcing their unworthiness to have the privileges associated with the dominant class. The holds true for socioeconomic status as well: oppressed people are denied access to the middle class, and then they are rebuked for failing to show middle-class values, attitudes, and behavior. In addition, they are denigrated not only as individuals who receive personalized oppressive labels but also as members of cultural groups that are castigated because of their likelihood to be given such labels. They are marginalized into a socio-cultural-economic caste and then rebuked for it.

Few entitled people, however, can see the irony of these cultural and economic traps. Culturally proficient educators have to work hard to resist these labeling traps so that they can avoid referring to students and their families with multiple oppressive, deficiency-based terms. You can use the Cultural Proficiency Continuum to guide your colleagues in choosing terminology that affirms the value of each student rather than focusing on how students deviate from the dominant culture.

The Language of Entitlement: Objectifying Nondominant Groups

Objectifying others creates and maintains distance between the dominant U.S. society and others. Kovel (1984) used the term *thingification* to describe how members of the dominant society use language to objectify others. Whether one uses the term *objectify* or *thingification*, the result is the same—language is used to maintain privilege and entitlement.

Entitlement gives the dominant group the power to establish, define, and differentiate outsiders as others. When people use such terms as *them* and *you people*, they objectify others. They manipulate people's self-perceptions and perceptions of others while reinforcing a sense of otherness. Similarly, when they continue to use *man* and *he* as inclusive terms for women and men, they *thingify* women, placing women in the category of other (i.e., not men, the acknowledged norm).

Thingification is an extension of the institutionalized oppression never experienced by members of the dominant culture. It is part of a "matrix of culturally derived meanings" (Kovel, 1984, pp. 6–7), which allows the larger and empowered segment of society to communicate that members of oppressed groups are never quite as good as the dominant group members of society. Is it surprising that oppressed people often react in a hostile manner to the use of these expressions of privilege and entitlement?

> *Derek is in his first year as a teacher-coach in the Coolidge district. He has been working to help his colleagues understand how much is communicated to children by the language and tone that is used by the teachers.*
>
> *"Well, they are not going to do as well as the regular students," Harvey said of his Vietnamese students, "so I think it is a disservice to ask them to do as much as the others."*
>
> *"No, no," said DeLois. "If they need more help, we give more help. That's our job! We don't lower our expectations for them."*
>
> *Breathing deeply to calm himself, Derek opened the door of the next classroom in time to hear the teacher, Lane, say to his Latino students, "Your parents are poor and uneducated, so I know they won't be able to help you with your homework. I am going to have an afterschool homework session with all the needy kids like you. I really want to help you so you don't grow up to be like your parents."*

Entitlement breeds thingification by rendering the humanity of thingified people invisible. A person becomes invisible as an individual in many ways: by being viewed as unable to learn, by representing an entire group of people during an interview, or by having value only as a cog in the economic system. When whites perpetuate thingification and invisibility, incessantly view nonwhite groups negatively, and then refuse to acknowledge those realities, nonwhites often feel enraged (Ellison, 1952; Gilligan, 1983; Giroux, 1992a; Kovel, 1984; Wright, 1940). The vast majority of white people, particularly white men, are astonished at this furor, however, because they have never experienced thingification. When confronted with this information, white men often respond by denying their individual participation in the process. They say, *I identify myself as a person, not as a white man.* Only the members of the dominant group are entitled to make such an assertion.

Granted that straight white men have many pressures to perform, succeed, and survive, these pressures occur in a context absent of the additional and insupportable pressures of institutionalized oppression. Educators must understand these pressures, particularly if they belong to the dominant group in U.S. society. Such understanding is the foundation for creating a school system that addresses the needs of children as members of groups capable of learning, as opposed to being members of groups with deficiencies that limit their full participation in school or society.

CAVEAT: UNAWARENESS OF THE NEED TO ADAPT

Unawareness of the need to adapt means failing to recognize the need to make personal and school changes in response to the diversity of the people with whom one interacts, perhaps because it never occurs to anyone in the dominant group that there is a problem. People who are unaware of the need to adapt often believe that if the others—the newcomers—change or adapt to the environment, there will be no problems. They do not yet understand that once the commitment to cultural proficiency is made, everyone changes to create a new school culture.

> At their staff development meeting with the diversity consultant, Richard Díaz, Coolidge Middle School principal, writes on the board, "That [women and] men do not learn very much from the lessons of history is the most important of all the lessons that history has to teach. Aldous Huxley, 1959."
>
> "There he goes again," Harvey whispers to Lane. Richard has developed a mantra of change and a rallying cry for the new order of things he is trying to establish at Coolidge Middle School. He knows that one speech, one memo, or one staff meeting will not do it. Every time the faculty and staff see him, Richard talks about change and what it will mean for whomever he is addressing, as well as how it will affect the students and the school's community. He communicates regularly with the district's consultant, James Harris, so that each reinforces the work of the other when making presentations.
>
> "These diversity staff development meetings are a waste of time," Harvey continues. "No one's going to change. I've been here for 17 years, and I've seen it all. I have tenure, so I'll just sit tight. These administrators are only here until they get a promotion. Each one brings his or her own program, and each program leaves with the administrator. If I wait long enough, I won't have to do a thing."
>
> Across the room, DeLois and Derek are eagerly taking notes. "I wish I had taken more history courses when I was in college," DeLois sighs. "I'm sure that I could be more effective if I had a stronger historical foundation for what we are doing."
>
> "We're not here to teach history, we're here to teach kids," Derek retorts. "I wish he would just tell us more about this cultural proficiency model so I can figure out what I need to change in my classroom."
>
> "You're right," DeLois sighs. "Richard just needs to mandate what he wants done. Understanding history is not going to change some of the bigots in this room."

Change can be difficult for some people and like a fresh breath of air for others. However the change is experienced, there are certain hallmarks to change that involve one's worldview—paradigms are challenged, myths are dispelled, and change is an uneven process.

CHANGING EDUCATIONAL PRACTICES

The deficit model worldview is prevalent among educators. Unfortunately, the education system not only fails to enlighten students and educators about oppression and entitlement, but it further institutionalizes the oppression of dominated cultural groups by its very structure and practice and resistance to change. Two particularly egregious systems are the process of tracking and the communication of educator expectations.

Systems of Tracking

Tracking emerged during the late 19th and early 20th centuries, when educators were seeking ways to incorporate myriad European immigrants into the U.S. mainstream. The biases of entitlement built into the tracking system and its negative effects on students, as well as on society at large, are well documented (Burris & Garrity, 2008; Oakes, 1985; Oakes & Lipton, 1990; Wheelock, 1992). Today, educators know that the latent—and perhaps often unintended—function of tracking has been to harm students at the oppressed end of the entitlement continuum. Throughout the country, as schools move toward culturally proficient practices, they are beginning to dismantle tracking systems and to focus on grouping systems that provide all students with equal access to information, skills, and values that foster success.

Even without a formal tracking system, however, U.S. students are tracked because of their color and the caste status that color imbues. The power of caste and entitlement is reflected in this playground rhyme:

> If you're white, you're alright,
> If you're black, get back,
> If you're brown, stick around,
> If you're yellow, you're mellow,
> If you're red, you're already dead.

Educator Expectations

Extensive research has shown that educators have differing expectations of students depending on the students' race, ethnicity, and gender. These studies have provided consistent data demonstrating stark disparities of class, caste, and entitlement in educators' interactions with students. Interactions based on poor expectations clearly lead to devastating consequences for students in terms of both academic performance and self-image (Burris & Garrity, 2008; Oakes, 1985; Oakes & Lipton, 1990; Rosenthal & Jacobson, 1966; Wheelock, 1992).

CULTURALLY PROFICIENT EDUCATORS

Educators who are committed to educating all students to high levels have three characteristics:

- Culturally proficient educators have an emerging awareness of their strengths, their limitations, and what they need and want to learn.
- Culturally proficient educators are not afraid to change their world-view or paradigms about their students' cultures.
- Culturally proficient educators are eager to begin the change process, both individually and institutionally.

Culturally proficient educators can strive to overcome obstacles to learning through programs that provide models that teach verbal and nonverbal behaviors that project the cultural expectation that all students can learn, thus providing them with equal opportunity in the classroom. In this book, the activities selected for the Resources section introduce concepts basic to understanding the cultural bases for expectations.

At Coolidge Middle School, consultant James Harris overhears this conversation in the parking lot:

Teacher DeLois says, "I am really enjoying these sessions on cultural proficiency. I can see where I can use a lot of this information to prepare the girls and Latinos in my classes to assume a responsible role in society."

Harvey, cynical as always, lashes back, "Are you for real? I would like you and this 'cultural expert' to spend a day in the vice principal's office. All day long, he deals with the scum of this school. If those kids were in your classroom, you would know why those people are so behind in school."

DeLois can't believe what she is hearing. "Let me tell you something," she hisses at him. "First, if you think the girls and the Mexicans are the ones who need help, you are in worse shape than you know. The true scum in this school are the educators who don't see students when they come to their office. All they see is the color of their skin . . . and you judge the kids and their families in the same way."

To deny either the overt or the covert presence of the attitudes reflected in this conversation is to be blind to the kinds of oppression to which unentitled children, particularly children of color, are subjected daily. Cultural proficiency is not color blindness. Rather, culturally proficient educators see what color, gender, sexual orientation, and ableness mean in the context of entitlement and oppression. Once educators see how they make judgments based on entitlement and oppression, they recognize how such judgments influence their expectations and evaluations of students, the tracking of students, and the creation of instructional programs. Consider a discussion that takes place among some teachers at Coolidge High School.

Harvey doesn't limit his discontent to his middle school colleagues. Consider a discussion that takes place among some teachers after a union meeting at Coolidge High School.

"I have been in this district for 17 years, and have I seen some changes!" says Harvey.

"Like what?" his friend Lane asks.

"Well, first of all," Harvey responds, "when I first came here, this was a nice, stable, working-class community where the parents wanted their children to have more than they did. Sure we had problems, but nothing like today. Then, 14 years ago, the school became all minority in no time at all!"

"And?" Lane challenges.

"What do you mean, 'And?'" Harvey was getting annoyed. "You know exactly 'and what.' That was when our test scores dropped, drug problems began, and the schools became one more ghetto nightmare. And I'm not a racist; these are just facts!"

Belief: We Can Learn

In Chapter 3, we posed a question for your consideration, "So Where Do You Start?" We recommended data collection activities from the Resources section of this book that would guide your own reflection and provide valuable information about the culture of your organization, how your organization perceives the diverse cultural groups you serve, and the extent to which your vision of inclusivity is shared among your colleagues.

The important next step toward cultural proficiency is embracing the guiding principles of cultural proficiency in Chapter 6 as a means to overcome the deficit model worldview, which misuses power; embraces privilege as inalienable; and holds that those who are not in the economic, social, and political mainstream are solely responsible for their lot in life. Although white men are particularly needful of gaining awareness, all successful public school educators have been indoctrinated in a system that perpetuates racism, sexism, and other forms of oppression. All educators pass through this system as they prepare to transmit the values and the culture of the dominant society to public school children. This preparation is couched in such terms as *responsible citizenship* and *civics*. In reality, through this system, educators learn to prepare students to sustain the status quo and to maintain and support U.S. democratic society as it exists today. Educators might risk being accused of treason or labeled as anarchists if they were to teach students to challenge societal norms overtly, to accept lifestyles and values considered deviant by Middle America, or to advocate for societal change. Public schools were not designed to stimulate controversy, and public school educators are not expected to teach students to question, let alone defy, authority.

Culturally proficient leaders understand this process and are aware of the subtle ways in which entitlement and oppression are fostered. They understand that educators have furthered the programs and practices that have served to enhance opportunities for some people while denying access to those opportunities for others, whether intentionally or unwittingly. They encourage their colleagues to recognize that a student's native culture and values are important for the student's survival in his or her family and community. They encourage teachers to complement their own native values with an understanding of the values of dominant U.S. society. At the same time, culturally proficient leaders work with colleagues to challenge some of the assumptions of dominant U.S. values and to raise the dynamics of entitlement to a conscious level.

Culturally proficient educators must interpret their discomfort with these issues as a sign of where they need to become more aware of their own entitlement. Often, when one discusses, debates, and argues about the manifestations of oppression, deep and intense emotions erupt. On the one hand, people who are targets of oppression often feel angry and frustrated with their day-to-day experiences. On the other hand, people who have never experienced these forms of oppression often feel guilty or defensively angry at being held responsible for things they never intentionally created. That anger, in turn, feeds the frustration of those who are victimized, for they cannot believe the naïveté of the dominant groups. And the spiral of ire winds ever higher.

Various educational practices have been developed and studied; when used by educators who understand the oppression-entitlement continuum, they result in positive educational experiences for students regardless of their social status. Many researchers (e.g., Comer, 1988; Levin, 1988; Sadker & Sadker, 1994; Sizer, 1985; Valadez, 2008) have demonstrated that all children are capable of excelling in all areas of schooling. Culturally proficient leaders must value the diversity present in the school setting and then take steps to evaluate the culture of the school and its educators by clarifying values, assumptions, and cultural expectations. They must learn about the cultures of the students and their families and assess the dynamic nature of the differences in values and expectations.

Culturally proficient leaders work with their colleagues to adapt the school program so that it addresses the needs of all students, not just the entitled ones.

Belief: Paradigms Can Change

Culturally proficient educators use the Cultural Proficiency Continuum presented in Chapter 7 to learn of paradigms they might hold that cause them to be resistant or blind to learning ways to meet the needs of people who are culturally different from them. As examples of paradigms we hold, do you remember when a cell phone was considered a luxury too expensive for children to have? If you made lists called "working mother's" or "father's jobs" in 1965, how would they differ from the same lists written in 2009? These are examples of paradigms that have changed. A *paradigm* is the set of rules or criteria you use to judge whether something is correct or appropriate. A paradigm is a filter of perception; it is a frame you put around a concept to understand it and make it fit with your understanding of the world. The cultural expectations of your school or district are paradigms.

Everyone uses paradigms to order his or her world. When you do a double take because you have observed or experienced something odd, or when you argue intensely against a new idea, it is because your paradigms have been challenged. Joel Barker (1989, 1996) is a futurist who has taken the concept of paradigm, used initially solely by scientists, and reframed it for the world at large. He uses the concept of paradigm to help explain the process of change.

Most people resist change because they feel threatened. They fear that they may lose something that they value. The new idea or process does not fit within the boundaries of their current paradigms, so they resist or actively seek to prove that the new idea is wrong, inappropriate, or unnecessary. *Paradigm shifters* are perceived as misfits or outcasts who move along the margins of the group. They may be older and venerated and, therefore, have no fear of losing their power or prestige, or they may be new and unseasoned, seeking to prove themselves to veterans in the field. *Paradigm resisters* are people who are vested in a system or who are among the system's elite. They have the most to lose and are among those who denounce a proposed change most vociferously. They suffer from "hardening of the categories." The culturally proficient leader is a paradigm shifter who prepares for various types of resistance to change while building a team of paradigm shifters who, as formal and nonformal leaders, help take the school or district through the transition.

Belief: Change Is Beneficial

Culturally proficient educators use the essential elements of cultural competence in Chapter 8 as standards to guide how to make personal and organizational change. William Bridges's book, *Transitions* (1980), focuses on personal change and how it affects your relationships and your work. The key to understanding change, said Bridges, is to recognize the stages: endings, transition, and beginnings.

Most people fail to acknowledge that starting something new begins by ending something else. Even the most joyous occasions—birth, marriage, promotion, and retirement—involve huge losses. During the ending times, you may mourn your losses or just need time to say goodbye to old friends, familiar places, comfortable ways of doing things, and a changing sense of yourself. If you end well, your beginnings will be easier to manage. Between your endings and beginnings, however, are periods of transition that also must be managed.

Imagine the process that children go through to learn new things. Like walking, for example. They don't just stand up and walk. They practice a lot. They go through a period of practicing, having small successes, making adjustments in their approach, practicing some more, and experiencing greater success. They also fall down a lot. You can use this image when you are learning or adjusting to new things, because this process is not just what children do. It is how all people learn. Transition periods mark the times that you are changing from one way of doing things to another. You have accepted that the old way is no longer available to you or acceptable in your new environment, yet you have not quite mastered the new way of doing things.

The change process is both simple and difficult. Similarly, cultural proficiency is very easy to describe but difficult for some people to achieve, because it challenges their existing worldview. Culturally proficient leaders implement the steps in the appropriate order: ending by releasing the old paradigms, transitioning between the old and the new, and beginning to use new behaviors and processes in a consistent way. Most leaders add to people's resistance to change because they don't acknowledge the true order in which change takes place. Table 5.3 outlines the process.

Table 5.3   Phases of the Change Process

Phase of the Change Process	Characterized by These Emotions	Individual Challenges	Organizational Challenges
Release the old **Endings**	• Denial, shock • Anger, hostility • Elation, relief • Disbelief • Confusion • Disappointment • Grief	• Accept the reality of change. • Release attachment to people and to the old ways of doing things. • Acknowledge losses.	• Create the need for change. • Connect to the history. • Allow people to get used to the idea. • Include people in the planning process.
Change **Transition** *Change*	• Resistance • Sabotage • Depression • Support • Facilitation • Resignation • Humor • Denial • Excitement • Frustration	• Review what has been learned in the past. • Overcome resistance. • Commit to the future. • Connect with the transition.	• Communicate a vision of the future. • Dismantle old systems. • Mobilize commitment to the new vision. • Stabilize transition management. • Create effective balance of the old and the new. • Establish appropriate timelines or phases. • Establish and use feedback systems.
Beginnings *Embrace the new*	• Fear • Exploration • Resolution • Commitment • Excitement • Resistance • Anger • Disillusionment • Anxiety	• Master new routines. • Learn new cultural norms. • Embrace the new organizational climate.	• Institutionalize the change. • Reward and reinforce the new systems. • Introduce new cultural norms. • Affirm old values. • Identify and respond to unintended consequences. • Realign structure and staffing to accommodate the change.

SOURCE: Adapted from William Bridges. (1980). *Transitions: Making sense of life's changes.* Reading, MA: Addison Wesley.

Endings

Culturally proficient leaders understand that change begins by ending something. You end the way you have been doing things, for example, your focus on similarities in the diversity program or your goal of cultural blindness. Even if your faculty has intellectually accepted cultural proficiency as the model for addressing issues of diversity, they will be more willing to move forward toward new goals if you acknowledge their losses and their need to grieve those losses.

During the endings phase, culturally proficient leaders facilitate the process by spending time with members of the school community to acknowledge their feelings of perceived loss and by guiding them through the stages of denial and shock, anger and hostility, and elation and grief. In this phase, the leader is challenging the school to create the need for change and the staff members to accept the reality of change. The culturally proficient leader develops a mantra of change and a rallying cry for the new order of things.

Transition

The transition period is marked by activities in which people are no longer doing what they used to do but still aren't doing what they want to do. At this time, the leader introduces the new concepts and strategies and works to create a collective vision for how the school will be different as a result of this change. The leader then has the school community dismantle the old systems and initiate most of the changes. Some people will be ready to participate immediately; others will be convinced that it won't work; and most will just sit back, waiting to see what happens. During this time, many people will try out new ideas yet revert back to old and comfortable ways of doing things.

It is important during the transition period to remember the seven dynamics of change. When changes are made in a relationship or in an organization,

1. people are at different levels of readiness for change.

2. people will think first about what they are going to lose.

3. people will feel awkward, uncomfortable, and ill at ease.

4. people tend to be concerned that they will not have enough resources.

5. people will feel alone, even though others are going through the same thing.

6. people can only handle so much at a time.

7. when the pressure is off, people will revert back to old behavior.

The culturally proficient leader continues to challenge, encourage, and shepherd staff members forward while managing the transition. Many staff members complain and sing their songs of lament, foreboding, and ire. They resist, they sabotage, and they fall into depression. The culturally proficient leader remembers at this time that human beings do not change overnight. Children don't learn to read after one lesson, and adults don't learn new behaviors after one structured activity. Just as proficient teachers coach, support, and praise children for incremental improvements, culturally proficient leaders coach, support, and praise staff members as they try out new attitudes and new behaviors.

Beginnings

The beginnings of change follow the transition period, which comes some time after the endings have been acknowledged. It is during the beginnings phase that changes become institutionalized. It is also during this phase that resisters look for evidence that change is not working. Culturally proficient leaders are ready for the naysayers by explaining the process of making changes and setting realistic expectations for everyone. They are also prepared to point out where progress has been made. They find ways to reward the participants for their commitment to change and to reinforce changes in the school. This is not, however, the time to stop and rest on one's laurels. Once one set of changes has been put in place and systems within the school are supporting it, leaders look to see what else can be changed and how.

OVERCOMING RESISTANCE

With diversity programs, the first barrier of resistance is the unawareness of the need to change. Expect that people will attempt to assign blame and abdicate responsibility. Be prepared to hear the following:

> *"We didn't do anything to those people. Why do we have to change?"*
>
> *"This is America. They should be adapting to us."*
>
> *"This is reverse discrimination."*
>
> *"Why are we trying to fix something that's not broken?"*
>
> *"I don't want to have to apologize for being white."*
>
> *"It seems like white men are the ones being oppressed now."*

Culturally proficient leaders respond to resistance in two ways:

1. They acknowledge the feelings of the complainers: change is seldom easy and is often unwanted, especially when a commitment to cultural proficiency means having to do more work.

2. They explain that the changes are being made to serve the students and their families better. The plan is not to fix something that is broken; it is to grow as a school community for the students' benefit.

This is also the time to refer back to the appropriate principle or element so that people can see how the cultural proficiency tools can be applied to each problematic situation.

Your team of paradigm pioneers can then support one another and provide the appropriate kind of support to the paradigm settlers. *Paradigm settlers* are the ones who wait until the new paradigm is almost in place, then shout to the pioneers, "Is it safe out there yet?" (Barker, 1989).

Rolling Meadows High School Principal Dina Turner is conducting a meeting with her site council. "We are at the midpoint of our year, and our plan specifies that we are to assess our progress by examining our benchmarks. As you recall, our goals for this year were for schoolwide academic improvement in reading and for learning more about our interaction patterns with students."

Bobby, one of her consistently unhappy teachers, replies, "You know, I am all for academic improvement, but I still don't see how it is related to having a teacher observing me in my classroom."

Another teacher, Celeste, speaks up in Dina's defense. "I am not sure I agree with you. Since we have started the schoolwide focus on reading, it's easier for me to talk with my students about reading for fun."

Barbara Latimer, a very active parent in the district, adds, "That is a good point! Just this weekend my daughter asked if I didn't think that we watched way too much television. I hated to admit it, but she is right. I was just wondering how parents who are not members of the site council are reacting."

Dina says, "Obviously, I am very supportive of our reading initiative. I am also deeply committed to our continued study of student-teacher interactions. Has anyone tried any of the teacher expectations behaviors in their classrooms?"

"I have," said Celeste. "You know, Bobby, even though I know I am a good teacher, those activities are helping me see some of my blind spots. I am beginning to see how my unintentional behaviors can keep kids from learning!"

"What occurs to me," adds Dina, "is that if these unintentional behaviors occur between teachers and students, they must occur among adults, too. It scares me to think about the damage we do to one another without even realizing it."

Barbara has an idea. "You know, we may want to consider some of that training for parents. From what you are saying, it may be very enlightening, possibly a little uncomfortable, but very worthwhile."

"Most teachers are comfortable with the process," Dina replies. "I believe if everyone sees oneself as a student and is willing to commit the energy it takes to walk this path to improvement, we will all grow, and our kids will really benefit. And, I agree, it would be good for this group too. It would be an excellent topic for training all our parents."

Across town, neophyte teacher Brittney is looking at a framed list hanging on the wall near the desk of her mentor teacher, DeLois. "What is this?" Brittney asked.

"Oh," DeLois said, "I am a quilter, and once, as I made a quilt of ribbon and lace, sewing one small strip after another, I thought about the life lessons that I was learning

through quilt making. I try to remember these things whenever we are trying to implement some change in the district." This is what was on DeLois's list:

- There is no rehearsal. It all counts.
- Sometimes you need the big picture before you can start.
- Don't skimp.
- Be patient with yourself.
- Do one square at a time.
- Try it out.
- Take it apart, start over.
- Nonconformity, although beautiful, is sometimes very disruptive.
- Stop when you are tired. It's better to have only three things to do when you are fresh than to have three things to do over when you are frustrated.
- Sometimes you won't know the best process to use until after you have finished.
- Good work is not always transferable. What works well in one setting may be totally wrong in another.
- Perfection is perception.

Perhaps you can put DeLois' list near your desk as well.

VERY GOOD NEWS

At this point, you should understand how the deficit model worldview is supported through the perpetuation of systems of oppression, the prevalence of systemic privilege, and the unawareness of the need to adapt to diverse communities. The very good news is, you can change your worldview. Chapter 6 presents the guiding principles of cultural proficiency, which serve as core values for a culturally proficient worldview.

Because change affects people in such personal ways, we have provided a larger number of reflection questions in the "Going Deeper" section of this chapter. They are separated into three categories: entitlement, personal change, and organizational change.

GOING DEEPER

Entitlement

1. What is your initial response to the notion of entitlement?

2. Do you believe that ending racism is the responsibility of white people? That it is the responsibility of men to end sexism?

3. People who are members of the dominant group tend not to see their privilege and not recognize their sense of entitlement. In every

group, however homogeneous it may appear to outsiders, there is some type of stratification or hierarchy. Think of your school or some other group to which you belong. What are the cultural groups within it? Which group has the most privilege and power? How is that manifested?

Personal Change

1. Think of a personal change in your life or the life of your family. Describe the change process in terms of endings, transitions, and beginnings.

2. How many things in your life are in transition today? Do you need to say goodbye or mourn the loss of anything or anyone? Refer to Table 5.3. How well does it reflect the transition periods you have experienced? How would you personalize the chart?

3. If you find yourself stuck at the beginning of an ending process, ask yourself, "What am I holding on to?" Remember some of your aborted transitions. List them. Perhaps some of these unfinished transitions could still be completed, allowing you to bring more energy and less anxiety to your present situation. What might you do to complete an aborted transition? Completion may involve no more than a belated farewell, a letter, or a call to someone. It may involve an inner relinquishment of someone whom outwardly you left behind years ago, of some old image of yourself, or of some outlived dream or outworn belief that you have kept long past its usefulness.

4. Talk with a few people about their personal rituals for managing the transitions in their lives. Create a personal ritual to mark your transition process.

Organizational Change

1. After reading about the dynamics of change, go back to the list and select one that invites you to reflect a little more deeply. How has this dynamic of change affected you? What does it relate to in your life? Is there something you need to ask of your colleagues to help you to adjust to some changes in your district? Is there something you need to say to your staff to help adjust to the changes they are experiencing?

2. What are the changes that have been implemented at your school or in your district in the past three years? How many of the changes were permanent? Do you recall how people responded? How did you respond?

3. Make a list of barriers in your school or district. When do people fail to see the need for change? To what do people feel entitled?

REFLECTION

6

The Second Tool

The Guiding Principles of Cultural Proficiency

Accepting diversity enables us to see that each of us is needed. It also enables us to abandon ourselves to the strengths of others, acknowledging that we cannot know or do everything on our own.

—Max De Pree, U.S. writer on leadership,
as quoted in Zadra (2008, p. 37)

Bill Fayette, the superintendent of the Coolidge district, has hired a diversity consultant, James Harris, to provide training for faculty on cultural proficiency. At the first staff development session, James explains the underlying principles that inform his approach to dealing with the issues that emerge in a diverse environment. He also explains that the response to these issues usually falls within one of four categories:[1]

- *Right the wrongs:* Some people are angry or have a strong sense of justice. If something is wrong, they think that it should be fixed immediately and, if necessary, the wrongdoers should be punished.
- *The golden rule:* These people want everyone to get along. "If we all just treated everyone equally, with courtesy and kindness, there wouldn't be a problem," they say.

---

[1]Thanks to our colleague Stephanie Graham for sharing this model with us.

- *My pain equals yours:* Then there are those who say, "Everyone has been discriminated against about something. I got over it; so should they. We need to forget the past and move forward."
- *Oppression Olympics:* These people recognize that every group has suffered some form of discrimination. They are, however, certain that the group they are in has suffered the most and should not be minimized by discussing anyone else's alleged experiences of oppression.

"Each of these perspectives has some serious drawbacks," says James, "and each one also is useful." He presents the group with a list of comments he has collected from teachers and administrators in a number of districts:

Doesn't focusing on differences just make it harder for us to get along?

I don't have a culture. I'm just a generic person. Heinz 57 American.

He sure didn't sound black on the phone when we talked.

I didn't know there were Chinese people over six feet tall.

You are different, but we're comfortable with you.

We would have more of your kind around if they were just like you.

Why do they have to have a special program?

I think everyone should be given the same attention and information. That's fair.

It's the culture of that school that needs to be changed! After all, what can you expect from a school in that community?

James uses these comments to illustrate the need for the guiding principles of cultural proficiency.

THE GUIDING PRINCIPLES OF CULTURAL PROFICIENCY

James had studied culture and diversity in the context of P–12 education and embraced the guiding principles of cultural proficiency for his personal work and for his work with educational institutions. The principles that James shared with his Coolidge colleagues, from Cross's (1989) seminal work, are as follows:

- Culture is a predominant force.
- People are served in varying degrees by the dominant culture.
- People have individual and group identities.
- Diversity within cultures is vast and significant.
- Each cultural group has unique cultural needs.
- The best of both worlds enhances the capacity of all.

- The family, as defined by each culture, is the primary system of support in the education of children.
- School systems must recognize that marginalized populations have to be at least bicultural and that this status creates a distinct set of issues to which the system must be equipped to respond.
- Inherent in cross-cultural interactions are dynamics that must be acknowledged, adjusted to, and accepted.

Prominently placed in most of the schools we have worked in, usually in a beautiful frame, is the organization's mission and values. In some school districts, employees wear identification badges; often laminated on the back of the ID is a list of the district's mission statement and/or core values. In every public place and in the staff lounge are statements that say what the district believes in and how it intends to treat people. We usually find a noticeable difference in the espoused values of the school or district and the practices of the educators in that district, and another gap between the practices and how they are experienced by the students and their families. Our interest is not only how people are treated as members of cultural groups but in how the district's and the schools' cultures are communicated to groups that are not part of the dominant culture.

We spend the initial hours of our time with clients assessing the culture of their organizations. As part of a cultural proficiency inquiry, we examine personnel policies, look at memos sent to employees, and listen to people as they tell us what it is like to work at that particular school or in that particular district office. Invariably, a disconnection exists between what the district says it is and how the employees, the parents/guardians, the students, or the community members experience the district. In simple things like the personnel policy, we see major conflicts. The values statements speak of trust, honesty, harmony, and cocreation. The personnel policies are written in legalistic terms from the underlying assumption that employees cannot be trusted and must fear punishment so they won't do anything wrong.

Clients—in this case, students and their families—tell us how they are treated as unwelcome interlopers in the school community. Office staffs complain that if it weren't for the students, they would be able to get their work done. Students tell of teachers who are rude, insulting, and vindictive while demanding unquestioning obedience and extreme deference from the same students whom they oppress through their abuse of power and position. Now you may be thinking something like this:

- *This doesn't happen where I work;* or
- *You must be citing extreme cases;* or
- *There is a reason that these things happen. After all, we can't . . .*

In many cases, you have significant and valid points to make. The point that we seek to make here with you is that if you say that you represent an open, inclusive, learning community that values all people and their contributions, then everything that you do and say must reflect that. There cannot be a disconnection between what you say you are or want to be and how you behave on a daily basis. Your character is who you are under stress, not how you are when everything is peaceful and going smoothly. Moreover, if only one teacher or one person in the front office is the cause of complaints from your clients, and (a) no one knows about it or (b) there are no checks in the system to stop it, then your school or office is culturally blind or worse.

It is easy to articulate good values as an expression of the culture of your school. It is much harder to incorporate those values into all of the systems and structures of your school and district. It is even harder as a leader to hold the people in the organization accountable for policies, practices, and procedures that are consistent with the mission and the values of the organization. If you can do this, then you not only have learned the importance of a strong core culture, but you also have learned how to create an environment where all members of the community understand their role in maintaining it. What we look for is not what you say but what you do. A tool that will help you close this gap is the Guiding Principles of Cultural Proficiency.

CULTURAL PROFICIENCY AS AN EXPRESSION OF VALUES

Your worldview is an expression of the world in which you want to live. It is an expression of your belief about the world as it should be. It is an expression of your core values. Whether your core values are derived from a religious creed, spiritual beliefs, or secular understanding, you have a mind-set that shapes and informs how you assess your behavior as well as the behavior of others. When you come together with other educators in the place called school, your shared values represent your organizational worldview.

In this chapter, we describe a worldview that is in sharp contrast to the deficit model worldview described in Chapter 5. Cultural proficiency as a worldview is a model for a system of people and organizations committed to healthy and effective cross-cultural interaction. In our work, we have witnessed educators and schools undergo major shifts in thinking (i.e., paradigm shifting) as they moved from viewing differences in culture as problematic to examining and applying ways in which they could be successful with people culturally different from themselves or the dominant group.

When educators and schools make this transformative shift in thinking and behaving, the principles of cultural proficiency guide their professional practice. They become more mindful of their own values and behaviors and the policies and practices of their school or district, from the classroom to the grade levels or departments to the organization in its entirety.

PRINCIPLE: CULTURE IS EVER PRESENT

You cannot *not* have a culture. Nor can there be an environment that is culture-free or without cultural bias. Culture is like the air; it is everywhere, and you don't notice it until it changes. People in dominant groups often say that they don't notice culture. And that is the main point. If you are in the dominant group, you don't have to pay attention to cultural norms and cultural expectations. You just know what they are. Just as you know the rules for riding in a public elevator or the rules for entering a concert that is in progress, if you are part of the group that makes the rules, you know them intuitively. That is part of your privilege, and it is a source of your power. You know what to do. Culturally proficient educators recognize that what they experience as normal or regular is part of their culture. This may create a sense of entitlement, but by recognizing these feelings, they can then acknowledge and appreciate the subtle cultural differences among members of the dominant culture.

Your culture is a defining aspect of your humanity. It is the predominant force in shaping values and behaviors. Occasionally, you may be inclined to take offense at behaviors that differ from yours, but as a culturally proficient leader, remind yourself that offensive behavior may not be personal; it may be cultural. Recognize that members of emerging majority populations have to be at least bicultural, and this creates its own set of issues, problems, and possible conflicts.

All people who are not a part of the dominant group have already gained competence in one culture before they began to learn standard forms of English or dominant cultural norms. Therefore, when members of dominated cultures resist or hesitate in using the language or cultural norms of the dominant culture, they are not necessarily ignorant or incompetent; rather, they simply may be using language or cultural behaviors with which they are more familiar or more comfortable. The culturally proficient leader remembers that culture—the culture of the individuals and the culture of the organization—is always a factor.

PRINCIPLE: PEOPLE ARE SERVED IN VARYING DEGREES BY THE DOMINANT CULTURE

Common knowledge is not common, and things are only self-evident to those who share your worldview and culture perspective. Just because a person is working in the school district or a child has made it to the fifth grade doesn't mean that they have learned all of the rules—the cultural expectations—that the dominant group uses as criteria for success. Think about the last time someone new joined your staff. Although most people made gestures of welcome and courtesy, there was also a bit of standing back to watch and wait. You wanted to see who this person was and whether he or she would fit in. After three or four days, you could hear people saying, *Boy, she is really great,* or, *Well, he's not going to last long around here.* These comments reflect the unconscious evaluation of the person by using the cultural expectations of the group as the criteria for determining the person's *fit,* or success.

Imagine what it would be like to welcome someone into the school by saying, *Here's the personnel policy manual, and here are the employee procedures, and here are our cultural expectations—our practices. Read these practices first, and when they contradict something in the other two documents, go with the cultural expectations. That is how we really do things around here.* It's hard to imagine, but that is what would happen in a culturally proficient organization. Moreover, before inviting new people into the community, there would be a conscious effort to align the policies and procedures with the practices. Additionally, as the group became diverse, the policies, procedures, and practices would be examined to eliminate unintentionally discriminating policies and practices.

Culturally proficient educators adjust their behaviors and values to accommodate the full range of diversity represented by their school populations. They recognize that some individuals from minority cultures find success in varying degrees in schools where only the dominant culture is acknowledged and valued. Although educators and students in the dominant culture may profit from such a setting, and members of some dominated groups may do well despite such a setting, many other students and educators will find such an atmosphere stifling and limiting. Such an imbalance of power puts the total burden for change on one person or group. Culturally proficient leaders see the need to ensure that members of dominant groups, dominated groups, and emerging groups share the responsibility for change.

PRINCIPLE: PEOPLE HAVE GROUP IDENTITIES AND PERSONAL IDENTITIES

A common experience among people of historically oppressed groups is the *model minority syndrome.* This occurs when one member of the dominated group learns the cultural norms of the dominant group. Because model minorities are bicultural, they can assimilate into the dominant culture without causing discomfort to those in the power group and without calling attention to their differentness. The guest, not the host, does all of the accommodation. The only acknowledgment of this syndrome is when one of the members of the dominant group says something like this:

- *You know, you aren't like the other _____. You're different.* or
- *You seem to fit right in.* or
- *Your English is so good, I can understand everything you say.* or
- *You read speech so well that I totally forget that you are deaf.*

Although these comments are meant to be compliments, they are not. They are insulting, because they deny that the person has any connection or identification with the group being denigrated. In essence, these statements say, *Thanks for selling out. I can tolerate you because you act just like me.*

It is important to treat all people as individuals, as well as to acknowledge each group's identity. It demeans and insults individuals and their cultures to single out particular assimilated members of ethnic groups and to tell them that they differ from members of their own group, implying that their differentness somehow makes them better than others of their group—or more acceptable to the dominant group. Culturally proficient leaders know that to guarantee the dignity of each person, they must also preserve the dignity of each person's culture.

Often, so-called personality problems are actually problems of cultural differences. Culturally proficient leaders address these problems. They recognize that cultural differences in thought patterns (e.g., those of non-Western, non-European people versus those of Westerners) reflect differing but equally valid ways of viewing and solving problems. No cultural group appears exclusively to use just one particular approach for processing information and solving problems. Although some cultures are traditionally associated with one approach more than others, there is no evidence that one approach is superior to others across all situations. Culturally proficient leaders recognize these and other cultural differences, and they use this knowledge to promote effective communication among diverse people.

PRINCIPLE: DIVERSITY WITHIN CULTURES IS IMPORTANT

A prospective client who was responsible for "minority recruitment" to an exclusive postsecondary school said to us that she was not going to be successful because the bus lines didn't run past the school. She assumed that all people of color were poor and would be riding the bus if they attended the school. She did not realize that within any group are vast differences in wealth, income, education, and lifestyle. Because diversity within cultures is as important as diversity between cultures, it is important to learn about ethnic groups not as monoliths (e.g., Asians, Latinos, or whites) but as the complex and diverse groups that they are. Within each major ethnic group are many distinctive subgroups. Although a significant portion of a historically oppressed group may occupy the lower rungs of the socioeconomic ladder, within each group is great diversity. Often, because of the class differences in the United States, there is greater commonality across ethnic lines, between groups that share the same socioeconomic status (SES), than there is within an ethnic group between the upper and lower SES of that group.

For example, upper-middle-class U.S. citizens of European, African, and Japanese descent are more likely to share values and similar worldviews than members of any one ethnic group who come from socioeconomic backgrounds varying from working class to upper class. For the client to be successful in her recruitment, she would need to know this and know how to access people of color who fit the socioeconomic profile of those who attend the school. Culturally proficient leaders recognize these intracultural differences and provide their faculty, staff, students, and parents with access to information about people who are not like themselves in various ways. Culturally proficient schools create an environment that fosters trust, safety, and the inclusion of all people who work and learn there.

PRINCIPLE: EACH GROUP HAS UNIQUE CULTURAL NEEDS THAT MUST BE RESPECTED

There was a time in the history of educational practices when all children were expected to dress, talk, and respond to their teachers in the same way. Adults who are creative, intuitive, extremely bright, or dyslexic often talk about the horrible experiences they had in school because they didn't conform to the one-size-fits-all mode of education that was offered to them. They grew up thinking they were defective in some way because they could not learn the way they were being taught. In the past 50 years, educators have learned to acknowledge in their curricula and in their teaching different learning styles, different cognitive styles, and the different ways people process information. Still, some schools refuse to change their policies to adapt to differences in grooming needs, dietary restrictions, or physical accommodations.

European Americans can assume that a public school in Canada or the United States will have information about the history and culture of their people, as well as about their countries of origin. Other citizens and immigrants cannot make such assumptions. The desire to learn about oneself and one's people is unique only in that each group wants different information. Additionally, schools may be invited to accommodate students in large and small ways—all of which are significant to the people who are not in the dominant group. These changes in how things are done are also teachable moments for members of the dominant groups to learn about others. The culturally proficient educator teaches and encourages colleagues who are members of the dominant culture to make the necessary adaptations in how they provide educational services so that all people have access to the same benefits and privileges as members of the dominant group in society.

PRINCIPLE: THE FAMILY, AS DEFINED BY EACH CULTURE, IS THE PRIMARY SYSTEM OF SUPPORT IN THE EDUCATION OF CHILDREN

The traditional relationship between home and school is to place most of the responsibilities for involvement directly with parents. While that holds true for most cultural groups, cultural proficiency provides a different frame of reference by which teachers, parents, and education leaders assume greater responsibility for finding authentic ways to engage in culturally proficient practices to support student achievement. Traditional approaches to parent involvement have parents coming to the school to demonstrate their care and concern for their children within the school setting. Culturally proficient practice assumes the school setting includes the community and parents.

We find that too often educators and parents have different perceptions of the often-used term *parent participation*. When the educators and the parents are from different socioeconomic, racial, or ethnic cultural groups, often they have different perceptions of this term. Lawson (2003) used the terms *communitycentric* and schoolcentric to describe these contrasting perceptions:

- *Communitycentric*—"Parents involved in activities that meet the basic needs of their children such as going to school well fed, rested, and clean."
- *Schoolcentric*—"Parents involved in activities that are structured and defined for parents by schools" (p. 79).

Effective and meaningful partnerships between parents and schools require sensitive, respectful, and caring school leaders who are willing to learn the positive nature and culture of the community, as well as identify barriers that have impeded progress in school-community relations. The elementary school in Sacramento, California, located in a low income neighborhood (mentioned in Chapter 5) is an example of a school that, once educators identified their core values about parent/guardian involvement to include culturally proficient practices, has been successful in engaging parents in productive ways through home and other off-site meetings.

Furthermore, there are multiple definitions of *family*. In the traditional, often stereotypic, image of European American homes, the family has been identified as one mother, one father, and the children. However, there are many other family configurations—single-parent, multiple-generation extended family, same gender parents, foster care, and residential care homes. Whatever the configuration for the children in our schools, their family is their family.

PRINCIPLE: PEOPLE WHO ARE NOT A PART OF THE DOMINANT CULTURE HAVE TO BE AT LEAST BICULTURAL

Parents have to be fluent in the communication patterns of the school as well as the communication patterns that exist in their communities. They also have to know the cultural norms and expectations of schools, which may conflict or be different from those in their communities, their countries of origin, or their cultural groups. In ideal conditions, their children are developing bicultural skills, learning to code switch appropriately as the cultural expectations of their environments change, yet parents may not have these skills. They are then penalized because they do not respond as expected to the norms set by educators, nor do they negotiate well the educational systems of the public schools.

PRINCIPLE: INHERENT IN CROSS-CULTURAL INTERACTIONS ARE SOCIAL AND COMMUNICATION DYNAMICS THAT MUST BE ACKNOWLEDGED, ADJUSTED TO, AND ACCEPTED

People who belong to groups that have histories of systemic oppression have heightened sensitivities to the societal privileges they do not receive and to the many unacknowledged slights and put-downs that they receive daily. These microaggressions are usually unnoticed by dominant group members and, when brought to their attention, are often dismissed as inconsequential. Cumulatively, microaggressions create the same hurt and oppressive environment as an activity or policy that is obviously at the culturally destructive end of the continuum. The historical mistrust that emanates from a national history of racism, ethnocentrism, sexism, heterosexism, classism, ableism, and discrimination based on religion and spiritual beliefs is usually more obvious to the members of targeted groups than members of agent groups. Awareness of issues of systemic oppression by all educators is fundamental to effective cross-cultural communication.

Historically marginalized populations face many issues. For example, children from marginalized populations are vastly overrepresented in special education programs and woefully underrepresented in advanced placement or gifted and talented programs. In too many cases, educators try to explain to parents that placing children in special education or "opportunity" programs is in the best interest of the child. Likewise, underrepresentation in gifted programs is associated with failure to score adequately on standardized tests, which tend to favor European American populations. The issue facing parents in either of these scenarios is that the burden of proof is implicitly assigned to them to prove that their child does not belong in special education or does qualify for gifted programs. Educators aware of such dynamics employ strategies and tactics that engage parents as partners in beneficial placements for their children.

PRINCIPLE: THE SCHOOL SYSTEM MUST INCORPORATE CULTURAL KNOWLEDGE INTO PRACTICE AND POLICYMAKING

Culturally proficient educators are self-consciously aware of their own cultures and the culture of their schools. This is crucial knowledge, because in addition to the cognitive curriculum, the cultural norms and expectations of the school must be taught as well. Each time a student or parent fails to respond appropriately to a cultural norm, they are judged and penalized. Judgmental comments are usually prefaced with "It is common sense . . . ," "Everyone knows that . . . ," "It's the parents' responsibility to teach their kids . . . ," "Well, they should have known. . . ." All of these comments reflect assumptions made by members of a dominant (alpha) group as they witness marginalized outsiders experiencing conflicts with the dominant culture.

First, culturally proficient educators must assess and raise consciousness about their own individual and organizational cultures. Then, as they teach the cultural expectations of the school and classroom to all students and their families, educators must learn about the cultures of their students. When educators begin the process of learning what they need to know about the cultural groups they serve, we often hear, *How can we possibly learn about all of the cultural groups in our district? We have to teach, too!* Cultural learning can be daunting, but it is important and it is possible to learn enough to make a difference. One way is to engage the community, identifying people who know both cultures and can serve as a bridge for the educators. Another is to identify other experts who can provide needed information. And finally, and most easily, if educators use their own expertise, sharing information and institutionalizing it, individual knowledge will ultimately become institutional knowledge.

An example is an elementary school in Roseville, California, that had experienced a sustained immigration of families from the Ukraine and Russia. In addition to learning about Ukrainian and Russian cultural practices in their professional development sessions, educators devoted a full-day professional development day to visiting three sites within the community and talking with local business and church leaders. Not only did they learn a bit more about these new immigrants, but more important, they demonstrated to their clients' communities a willingness to go to the communities to learn.

In Anaheim, California, teachers are regularly making home visits to teach parents what they need to know about the schools, at the same time learning more about the students' communities and cultures. They share what they have learned and taught informally and formally in professional development sessions. Of course, professional development sessions at school and in the field, though valuable, are only a first step. The follow-up steps have to include the involvement of members of the community in purposeful decision-making activities in the school for their voices to be heard and to facilitate meaningful contact with other parents/guardians.

MAKE IT COUNT

The tools of cultural proficiency assist you in shifting the culture of the organization. This is not something that can take place after a few staff development sessions; it requires commitment at the top, accountability systems at the bottom, and an ongoing intention of everyone to pay attention to the things that count. According to a popular legend, Albert Einstein had a sign in his office that said, "People spend too much time counting things that don't count, and not counting the things that do." Nicely framed values statements don't count. Educators who consistently model courtesy and respect to one another and to all of their students do count. A beautifully articulated mission statement doesn't count if there is no relationship between the mission and the programs that operate on a daily basis or if the front office staff does not see its work as one of the ways in which the mission is fulfilled.

By deliberately and systematically implementing the behavior outlined in the essential elements of cultural proficiency, your school or district can become culturally proficient. To carry out this ambitious task, you need strong core organizational values (Collins & Porras, 1997; Senge et al., 2000). In addition to the values you currently hold, you can use the values of cultural proficiency—the guiding principles—as the foundation on which you re-create your classroom, your school, or your district.

GOING DEEPER

1. Take the statements made by the educators in the case study and decide which of the guiding principles apply to each.

2. As you reflect on how your school or district responds to the issues of diversity, can you cite examples of counting what doesn't count? Can you identify some things that should be counted?

REFLECTION

_____

_____

_____

_____

_____

_____

_____

_____

_____

_____

_____

_____

_____

_____

_____

_____

_____

_____

_____

_____

_____

_____

_____

_____

_____

_____

7

The Third Tool

The Cultural Proficiency Continuum

You really can change the world if you care enough.

—Maya Angelou, African American poet,
as quoted in Zadra (2008, p. 52)

The faculty at Rolling Meadows Middle School has heard that the district is going to hire consultants to evaluate their ability to teach and assess students in an effective cross-cultural manner. They are neither impressed nor pleased. Sitting in the staff lunchroom, they speak wistfully about when their own children attended the district, failing to acknowledge that the demographics have change dramatically. Their comments about the children and the impending work with the consultants range from culturally destructive to culturally proficient.

In one corner of the room we hear the following:

"This is America, everyone should speak English—they should be adapting to us. This is reverse discrimination. We didn't do anything to those people, so why do we have to change?"

"Our goal for examining our school policy on student grouping must be to enhance student achievement. If we get some quality consultants in here, they can *help us to disaggregate these test data. Then we can really understand student needs."*

"Why are we trying to fix something that's not broken? When I walk into a classroom, I do not see color or ability or gender—I only see children."

"I believe that conflict is natural and normal; I'm glad we will be learning how to do things differently when conflict occurs."

Across the room, some teachers are discussing their students:

"I didn't know his father was gay. He doesn't look gay to me."

"She catches well for a girl."

"I can't believe my Asian boys only scored in the 80th percentile!"

Over by the copier, some of the teachers are trying to be proactive:

"We need a Korean vice principal to help us with the Korean students."

"We celebrate Cinco de Mayo and Martin Luther King's birthday. What holiday can we use for American Indians?"

"Let's look at the school calendar to make sure we don't schedule our potlucks during Ramadan, Ridvan, or Yom Kippur."[1]

Cultural proficiency is a way of being that enables one to respond effectively in a variety of cultural settings to the issues that emerge in diverse environments. A culturally proficient school or school district interacts effectively with its employees, its parents/guardians, its students, and its community. Culturally proficient people may not know all there is to know about others who are different from them, but they know how to take advantage of teachable moments, how to ask questions without offending, and how to create an environment that is welcoming to diversity and to personal and organizational change. Culturally proficient individuals use the four tools for developing the cultural competence of their organizations or in themselves.

In this chapter, we describe the Cultural Proficiency Continuum. It provides language for describing both unhealthy and healthy policies, practices, values, and behaviors. Six points along the Cultural Proficiency Continuum indicate distinct ways of seeing and responding to difference. Table 7.1 displays the points along the Continuum with brief descriptions of each. Later in the chapter, we provide expanded descriptions of each point of the Continuum.

---

[1]These are the holidays of the Muslim, Baha'i, and Jewish faiths, respectively, that require the faithful to fast during the day. Ramadan and Ridvan last for several weeks, so your Muslim and Baha'i colleagues and students may be at school while fasting.

Table 7.1   The Cultural Proficiency Continuum

REACTIVE > > > > > > > > TOLERANCE			PROACTIVE > > > TRANSFORMATION		
CULTURAL DESTRUCTIVENESS	CULTURAL INCAPACITY	CULTURAL BLINDNESS	CULTURAL PRECOMPETENCE	CULTURAL COMPETENCE	CULTURAL PROFICIENCY

- **Cultural destructiveness**—Educating in a manner that seeks to eliminate the cultures of others in all aspects of the school and in relationship to the community served
- **Cultural incapacity**—Educating in a way that trivializes other cultures and seeks to make the cultures of others appear to be wrong
- **Cultural blindness**—Educating so that you don't see or acknowledge the culture of others, choosing to ignore the discrepant experiences of cultures within the school
- **Cultural precompetence**—Educating with an increasing awareness of what you and the school don't know about working in diverse settings. At this level of development, you and the school can move in a positive, constructive direction, or you can falter, stop, and possibly regress.
- **Cultural competence**—Educating with your personal values and behaviors and the school's policies and practices being aligned in a manner that is inclusive of cultures that are new or different from yours and those of the school
- **Cultural proficiency**—Educating as an advocate for lifelong learning for the purpose of being increasingly effective in serving the educational needs of cultural groups in your school and community; holding the vision that you and the school are instruments for creating a socially just democracy

The left side of the Continuum—cultural destructiveness, cultural incapacity, cultural blindness—are reactive and focus on tolerance and *the other* as being problematic. The three points on the right side of the Continuum—cultural precompetence, cultural competence, cultural proficiency—are proactive and focus on transforming *one's practice*. Language on the left side of the Continuum would refer to students as *underperforming*, while language on the right side would refer to the ways in which educators *underserve* students and their communities.

The points on the Continuum represent the vast range of intercultural and intracultural interactions found in an educational setting—within one school or one person. Neither individuals nor organizations occupy one point on a continuum. If you assessed your assertiveness on a continuum, for instance, you might determine that you are very assertive as a consumer, moderately assertive when talking with your boss, and a total wimp when trying to confront your mother. Assigning a particular point on an assertiveness continuum for each interaction is both more descriptive and more instructive than giving you a fixed point for assertive behavior. The Cultural Proficiency Continuum works in the same way. A school might have a mission statement that embodies the guiding principles and have policies that reflect each of the essential elements, but the practices of the people in the school office might be culturally blind or even culturally destructive. On the other hand, you might have a teacher with an exemplary culturally competent classroom who is functioning in a school that is rife with practices that can only be described as cultural incapacity.

MACRO- AND MICROAGGRESSIONS

Understanding and performing culturally proficient behaviors and institutional practices begins with recognizing and comprehending the experiences of people who are targets of unwanted behavior. Table 7.2 aligns macro- and microaggressions with the first four points of the Cultural Proficiency Continuum—destructiveness, incapacity, blindness, and precompetence.

- Macroaggressions are obviously wrong and offensive behaviors or policies.
- Microaggressions are often treated as isolated incidents. Violators may not even know they did something wrong. Because they are often missed and usually repeated over time, microaggressions become egregious.

Table 7.2   Macro- and Microaggressions on the Continuum

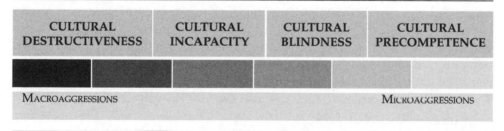

CULTURAL DESTRUCTIVENESS	CULTURAL INCAPACITY	CULTURAL BLINDNESS	CULTURAL PRECOMPETENCE
MACROAGGRESSIONS			MICROAGGRESSIONS

In any setting, you may witness practices or behaviors that, by themselves, may be slightly questionable or even unnoticed but are experienced as microaggressions. They are wrong, but often, when the targeted person complains, his or her protests are dismissed as inconsequential, or the person is judged as overly sensitive. Comments that imply that a minority person only got a job because of affirmative action, that a woman is overemotional, or that someone who has an observable difference looks stupid are microaggressions.

What makes culturally proficient behavior difficult is that it is not precise; it is ambiguous and contextualized. What is appropriate in one environment may be highly inappropriate in another. To be culturally proficient, you have to assess the environment and determine the cultural expectations for that particular setting. To be part of a diverse and inclusive organization means that you share cultural expectations with newcomers, instead of waiting for them to figure them out, or you teach people, instead of punishing them because they don't know the rules of the environment.

The Cultural Proficiency Continuum is particularly useful when discussing a particular situation or a specific policy or in articulating why someone's behavior is inappropriate. Culturally proficient leaders are able to identify macro- and microaggressive behaviors and practices, and they use the Continuum to provide perspective for examining policies, practices, and procedures in a school by giving reference points and a common language for describing historical or current situations. It is easy to assign a point on the Cultural Proficiency Continuum to events that have resulted in people being murdered, maimed, or exploited by dominant and destructive groups. Identifying how students' opportunities have been preempted, denied, limited, or enhanced, however, may be more difficult to categorize. So use the activities in the Resources section of this book to practice with your colleagues by describing situations, events, and policies as they arise.

THE CONTINUUM

The six points of the Cultural Proficiency Continuum represent distinctly different ways in which individuals and organizations respond to those who are culturally different from them. In this section, we provide a description of each point of the Continuum, which includes examples from history, current organizational practices, and representative observations from current educators. The observations from current educators were gathered in professional development sessions conducted with P–12, higher education, and agency educators across the United States and Canada. We used the Cultural Proficiency Continuum activity (Resource F, Activity F2). The activity is an effective way to teach the Continuum and to collect data about the climate of the school. In conducting the activity, the presenter delivers six mini lectures to define, describe, and provide examples of each point of the Continuum.

Participants are instructed to think of their current context and to write on sticky notes comments, behaviors, policies, and practices they have known to occur in the past two years at their school or office. Participants are requested to confine their examples to those involving people who are employed by the school, district, or agency and to avoid using comments from students, parents/guardians, or community members not so employed. The presenter makes six such presentations and pauses for a minute or two after each mini presentation for participants to record their examples. At the conclusion of the six mini presentations, participants are invited to post their examples on six easel-size sheets taped on nearby walls, each of which is titled with the points of the Continuum—destructiveness, incapacity, blindness, precompetence, competence, and proficiency.

Cultural Destructiveness—
See the difference; stomp it out.

The extreme form of macroaggression is cultural destructiveness. Cultural destructiveness is any policy, practice, or behavior that effectively eliminates another people's culture; it may be manifested through an organization's policies and practices or through an individual's values and behaviors. The easiest form of cultural aggression to detect, it is at the most negative end of the Continuum. It is represented by attitudes, policies, and practices destructive to cultures and, consequently, to the individuals within a culture. Extreme examples include cultural genocide, such as the U.S. system of enslaving African peoples and the westward expansion of American territory that resulted in the near-extinction of First Nations. Other examples of cultural destructiveness are the Bureau of Indian Affairs educational programs that took young people from their families and nations and placed them in boarding schools, where the goal was to eradicate their language and culture.

Additional examples include the ethnic cleansings and holocausts in Europe and Africa. The Nazi extermination targeted Jews, Gypsies, Gay Men, and Lesbians, as well as others viewed as less than desirable by occupying forces. Other destructive acts have included the pogroms of Russia; the Turkish extermination of Armenians, Cypriots, and Greeks; the killing fields of Southeast Asia; the genocide in Darfur; the wars of Hutu and Tutsi in Central Africa; and the wars in the former Yugoslav Republic.

Elementary and high schools historically have been places where students were socialized for active participation as U.S. citizens and taught basic skills for functioning in the workplace. In the 19th and early 20th century, this process of acculturation involved socializing people from all parts of Europe into an emerging dominant European American culture. This melting pot approach to public school education was relatively effective within two to three generations for European immigrants. Over the past 50 years, compulsory attendance requirements have brought into schools increasing numbers of Latinos, African Americans, First Nation people, immigrants from Southeast Asia, and European Americans from low socioeconomic groups.

Although some members of these groups have been successful in school, their acquisition of English proficiency and dominant society mores has not necessarily ensured their access either to higher education or to the dominant culture in the United States. The cultural destructiveness that these groups have experienced in schools is manifested in markedly lower achievement, higher dropout rates, and lower social mobility. Specific examples of cultural destructiveness in schools include English-only policies that prohibit students from using their native language at school; Bureau of Indian Affairs schools; dress policies that single out specific ethnic groups; and tracking programs that systematically allocate specific ethnic groups to low-achieving courses, which limit students' opportunities.

Examples provided by current educator practitioners include the following:

- *Members of that _____ cultural group don't value education!*
- *I don't need to learn English language development strategies; I have a lifetime credential and don't need to learn another thing to teach in this state!*
- Physical abuse directed toward people due to their cultural group membership, such as gay bashing, misogyny, or bullying.

Cultural Incapacity—See the difference; make it wrong.

Another form of macroaggression, cultural incapacity, though less blatant than cultural destructiveness is no less extreme in effect. Cultural incapacity is the belief in the superiority of one's own culture and behavior that disempowers another's culture. It is any policy, practice, or behavior that subordinates all cultures to another. This point on the continuum describes organizational practices or individual behaviors that show extreme bias, belief in the superiority of a dominant group, or belief in the inferiority of subordinate groups. One example of cultural incapacity is having the belief that it is inherently better to be heterosexual than homosexual. Organizations or individuals exemplifying cultural incapacity are often characterized by ignorance, as well as either a dislike or an unrealistic fear of people who differ from the dominant group. Cultural incapacity virtually guarantees limited opportunities and can lead to *learned helplessness*, which is people's belief that they are powerless to help themselves because of their repeated experiences of disempowerment.

Historical examples include the Oriental Exclusion Acts, which were restrictive immigration laws targeting Asians and Pacific Islanders, and the Jim Crow laws that denied African Americans basic human rights. Other examples include discriminatory hiring practices, generally lower expectations of performance for dominated groups, and subtle messages to people who are not members of the dominant group conveying that they are not valued or welcomed.

Cultural incapacity is also exhibited by window dressing and tokenism, such as putting one or two members of a dominated group in highly visible positions to prove that the organization is open and inclusive. Individuals may respond to members of emerging majority groups based on stereotypic characteristics. Cultural incapacity assumes, for example, that all African American families are poor or that the Latina who has been hired recently will be a role model for Latinas, without recognizing that all children can profit from having role models from other cultural groups. Other examples include failing to hold accountable members of minority groups who are not performing well or making rules against hate speech instead of having a curriculum that teaches the cherishing of history, cultures, and languages that are different.

At Coolidge Middle School, Derek effectively teaches children from diverse ethnic and socioeconomic backgrounds, but down the hall, Brittney, a second-year teacher, is unsuccessful with and unhappy about having to teach "that kind of child," referring to various children from the local community. DeLois, Derek, and several other teachers at Coolidge Middle School organize their students by reading levels, continuously moving children to the next highest reading level as they progress through the year. By June, their top groups are quite large. On the other hand, Brittney is among the many other

> *teachers in the school who organize reading levels at the beginning of the year and keep the students in the same groups all year long, regardless of how much individual students progress.*

Examples provided by current educator practitioners include:

- *If their* _____ *[name the cultural group] had been important, I would have learned about it in school.*
- With regard to students with special needs, *I am very successful when working with normal kids.*
- Questioning the qualifications of women or persons of color but not doing the same for members of the dominant group.

Cultural Blindness—See the difference; dismiss it.

Cultural blindness is the least discernible form of macroaggression by those who perpetrate such behaviors. In truth, those who commit such macroaggressions believe they are acting "equitably." Cultural blindness is any policy, practice, or behavior that ignores existing cultural differences or that considers such differences inconsequential. This could include people acting as if the cultural differences they see do not matter or not recognizing that important differences exist among and between cultures. The third point on the Continuum, cultural blindness, is paradoxical for some people. Cultural blindness is the belief that color and culture make no difference and that all people are the same. For many educators, that is the goal of a diversity program. The values and behaviors of the dominant culture are presumed to be universally applicable and beneficial. The intention of the culturally blind educator is to avoid discriminating—that is, to avoid making an issue of the differences manifested among the students.

Culturally blind educators view students' cultural differences as indications of disobedience, noncompliance, or other deficiencies. They assume that members of dominated cultures do not meet the cultural expectations of the dominant group because they lack either the cultural traditions of the dominant culture (i.e., they're culturally deficient) or the desire to achieve (i.e., they're morally deficient). In reality, the system works only for the most highly assimilated groups. As a result of many educators' blindness to the differences among students, many students feel discounted or invisible in school.

In our conversations with educators who prize their own cultural blindness, they are always painfully unaware of how their behavior affects their students. It is difficult for well-intentioned people who are committed to fairness to believe that they sometimes hurt their students. It is important not to focus on intentions but to become aware of the effect that one's behavior can have on others.

Educators must recognize that students from dominated groups view their differences as important aspects of their identity. Their differences also affect how they are viewed both within their respective communities and in the larger society. These educators are surprised to learn that black children would not choose to be anything other than black, that Cambodian children are proud of their language, and that the child in the wheelchair does not feel disadvantaged.

Culturally blind educators may teach that Abraham Lincoln is a hero to all African Americans, assume that Cinco de Mayo is a holiday in all Spanish-speaking countries, and believe that girls are predisposed toward the arts rather than the sciences. Other examples of cultural blindness in schools include leadership training that fails to address issues of diversity and failure to articulate the school's cultural expectations to all students, staff, and faculty members.

Examples provided by current educator practitioners include the following:

- Believing that the achievement gap was uncovered when No Child Left Behind was enacted when, in truth, the National Assessment of Educational Practice (NAEP) has documented the achievement gap biannually since 1971
- *Really, I don't see color—I treat all kids alike!*
- Disassociating diversity training from other professional development

Cultural Precompetence—See the difference; recognize what you don't know.

Cultural precompetence is awareness of the limitations of one's skills or an organization's practices when interacting with other cultural groups. Cultural precompetence is reflected in people and organizations that are trying to use appropriate behaviors and practices while recognizing that they still have much to learn. In doing so, they may respond inadequately or become aware of what they don't know and commit to their own learning. Cultural precompetence is an awareness of limitations in one's intercultural interactions and is characterized by two distinct phases of development.

In the early phase of cultural precompetence, educators may engage proactively and effectively with cultures other than their own, but they are aware that they don't know enough and often are the victims of their own cultural faux pas. Thus, cultural precompetence often leads to forms of microaggression that, though not intended by the perpetrator, are nevertheless experienced by those who are the recipients of the behaviors. Educators might, for example, believe that the accomplishment of a single goal or activity fulfills any perceived obligation toward the dominated groups in their district; they may point with pride at the hiring of one disabled person or the serving of a soul food meal during Black History Month as proof of a school's cultural proficiency. Other examples include recruiting members of underrepresented groups, without providing support for them or making any adaptation to the differences they bring to the workplace, and dismissing as overly sensitive someone who complains about culturally inappropriate comments.

The latter phase of cultural precompetence is characterized by educators who engage proactively and effectively with cultures other than their own with the awareness that unlearning old, embedded assumptions about other cultural groups takes time and is achieved best by working with colleagues who provide substantive feedback. The educators who commit to longer-term learning about other cultural groups realize that they will be learning about the practices of cultures different from their own, about how they and their school may be perceived by groups within the community, about the limitations of the school's curriculum, and about a range of appropriate and useful teaching-learning styles. An example of the latter phase of precompetence is when schools begin to use accreditation processes to gather data from constituents and use the data to ensure that all demographic groups of students are academically successful.

Another example of cultural precompetence is developing multiyear professional development calendars that schedule opportunities to learn about cultures within the community, learning about the multiple perspectives that should be represented in the formal and nonformal curriculum, and learning how to use assessment data to inform instructional practice.

DeLois, Derek, and the other teachers who organize their reading groups in an ongoing fashion during the school year are always monitoring their students for clues to their motivation and to possible sources of impediments to their learning. Most recently, they were troubled that some of their students who had been doing quite well began to struggle and to exhibit misbehaviors that were somewhat unusual. In one of their grade-level meetings, they decided to share their concerns about the students and determine how they could be most helpful. In response to their concerns, Principal Díaz joined their meeting. He shared that upon further investigation, he had discovered that due to the recent economic downturn, all of the families of these particular students were experiencing extreme financial difficulties, ranging from job losses to potential foreclosure on their homes. The teachers and Díaz just sat for a moment and let this information soak in before they proceeded to consider ways in which they could be supportive of the students and keep them on track academically.

Examples provided by current educator practitioners include the following:

- *We are still trying to teach the students who used to go to school here and haven't adjusted practices to the new demographic groups of students here now.*
- *Through engaging in this cultural proficiency process, I am beginning to know what I don't know about cultural groups in our school community.*
- Folding short-term solutions, such as cultural events, into multiyear plans that involve being responsive to the students' educational needs

Cultural Competence—See the difference; understand the difference that difference makes.

Cultural competence is any policy, practice, or behavior that consistently uses the essential elements of cultural proficiency as the standards for interaction. At the point of cultural competence, schools and educators accept and respect differences; carefully attend to the dynamics of difference; continually assess their own cultural knowledge and beliefs; continuously expand their cultural knowledge and resources; and variously adapt their own belief systems, policies, and practices.

This is the first point on the Continuum that fully addresses the needs of diverse environments. Culturally competent educators incorporate culturally appropriate behavior in performance appraisals; advocate for changes in policies, practices, and procedures throughout the school and community; and speak on issues about persons with disabilities, Gay Men, Lesbians, and other underrepresented groups when no members of these groups are visibly present. An example of a culturally competent policy-level decision is the state of Montana's groundbreaking legislation, Indian Education for All (Montana Office of Public Instruction, 2008). Chapter 8 offers an expansive discussion of the essential elements of cultural competence.

Examples provided by current educator practitioners include the following:

- Students not formerly served well are engaged and are learning.
- Students can find themselves and people culturally different from them in the nonformal and formal curricula.
- *I regard our parent, Mrs. Cao, as a guest teacher partner, not as a guest presenter.*

Cultural Proficiency—See the differences; respond positively and affirmingly.

Cultural proficiency is the esteeming of culture—and it is more than that. A culturally competent educator functions effectively in several cultural contexts. The culturally proficient educator knows how to learn about culture. Confronted with the challenges of a new cultural setting, culturally proficient educators know how to find out what they need to know in an inoffensive manner, and they know what they need to teach about themselves. A culturally proficient educator has a palpable sense of his or her own culture and has the self-awareness to discern what about himself or herself may be offensive to others or what may be perceived as a barrier to others—especially if he or she is a member of an alpha or agent culture. The culturally proficient leader is forward-looking and seeks to add to the knowledge base of culturally proficient practices by conducting research, developing new culturally appropriate approaches, and taking advantage of opportunities to increase his or her awareness and knowledge of others.

Culturally proficient leaders unabashedly advocate for culturally proficient practices in all arenas. These educators have a strong sense of social justice, which is displayed by a readily apparent moral value for doing what is right for students, their families, and their communities. The culturally proficient educational leader is strategic in keeping apprised of demographic shifts in the community, in anticipating emerging educational issues and planning for them, and in using data to inform long-term professional development plans. As an example, in the current environment of mandated accountability, the culturally proficient educator would recognize the limitations of the legislation, would lead colleagues in developing an understanding of the "politics of education," and would also recognize the equity framework implicit in the accountability movement and use it to guide discussions about difficult and important issues.

Culturally proficient people may not know all there is to know about others who are different from them, but they know how to take advantage of teachable moments, how to ask questions without offending, and how to create an environment that is welcoming to diversity and to change. A culturally proficient organization is an open and inclusive learning organization that also has a strong core culture that is clearly articulated to all.

Examples provided by current educator practitioners include the following:

- *My role at this school is to make my learning even more important than our students' learning. That is the only way I can anticipate and respond to their educational needs. I regard it as the highest form of expectations.*
- A schoolwide focus on locating resources to enhance instruction
- A palpable sense of cultural proficiency being a process, not an event, and therefore elusive as something to achieve

GOING DEEPER

1. Read the teachers' statements in the vignette at the beginning of this chapter. Where would you plot each remark along the Continuum?

2. Reflect on your own life and think of situations or events that emerged because of the diversity—or absence of it—in that particular environment. Plot each event or situation along the Cultural Proficiency Continuum.

3. Complete the Diversity Lifeline drawing in the Resources section (Resource B, Activity B2) of this book. Where would you plot the various points of your lifeline along the Cultural Proficiency Continuum?

4. Think of a time when you did not respond well to the diversity in your environment. Where would you plot your own behavior in that situation?

REFLECTION

_____

_____

_____

_____

_____

_____

_____

_____

_____

_____

_____

_____

_____

_____

8

The Fourth Tool

The Essential Elements

Culture is a problem-solving resource we need to draw on, not a problem to be solved.

—Terry Cross (1989, p. 34)

At Rolling Meadows High School, the faculty curriculum committee has been charged with assessing the extent to which the school's curriculum was aligned with the emerging social studies standards. The committee is composed of new and experienced teachers, an administrator, the school counselor, and parents from the School Site Council. Dina Turner, the principal, is the chair of the task force studying the social science standards. Also on the task force are teachers, Celeste and Bobby, and a parent, Barbara Latimer. The diversity consultant, James Harris, had introduced the five essential elements early in the planning process and received enthusiastic support for using them to frame this planning.

"I see this as a very important task, one that is going to take considerable time and study," said Dina as they began the work of the task force.

"I couldn't agree more," said Celeste, "and as one of the old-timers here, I am pleased to have Bobby on our team. Bobby is a history teacher and a counselor. He knows the breadth and depth of our curriculum."

> *"It seems to me," said Mrs. Latimer, "that a place to begin is to get from Bobby a sense of how balanced he sees our curriculum. In other words, Bobby, what do you see as our strong points, and what are the points of omission?"*
>
> *After a moment of reflection, Bobby responded, "I'm comfortable with that as a starting point, but I want you to know that I don't know everything. For example, since the terrorists attacked the World Trade Center, I've realized how little I know about the Middle East, the Muslim religion, or our country's policies that affect these issues. One of the things I see coming from this study is that even though our school has no Middle Eastern or Muslim students that I know of, it will be important for our curriculum to be inclusive of them."*
>
> *"Yes, the new state standards for social studies," offered Dina, "are very explicit about our students being prepared to live and function in an interdependent, global world. I am sure, Bobby, that your concerns are shared by many of us. We need that kind of openness to do this work well."*

The Cultural Proficiency Continuum provides a broad look at the range of behaviors and attitudes that address the issues that emerge in a diverse environment. It gives you a common language for describing situations and encounters that you might experience or observe. The essential elements, located at the cultural competence point of the Continuum, enable you to go deeper to explore the values, behaviors, policies, and practices that describe positive and healthy responses to diversity. Take a moment to turn back to Table 4.2 and note the placement of the essential elements; note that cultural competence is on the "healthy" part of the Continuum.

To provide further context, the guiding principles provide the moral framework, or rationale, for doing what is right and responding to the barriers to cultural proficiency. Then, the Cultural Proficiency Continuum describes a range of unhealthy and healthy values, behaviors, policies, and practices. Finally, with those tools providing perspective, the essential elements guide the intentional selection and use of ethical educator behaviors and school practices that promote equitable outcomes for all students. As with the other tools of cultural proficiency, the essential elements can be used effectively with both the organization and the individual.

The essential elements serve as standards for educator values that are exhibited in our behavior and for organizational policies that inform school and district practices. Using the elements as standards, you can develop curricular standards for learners and performance standards for teachers, administrators, and staff. We have used the essential elements with our clients as the basis for developing rubrics for professional development, assessment and accountability, curriculum and instruction, and parent/community communications and outreach (Lindsey, Graham, Westphal Jr., & Jew, 2008). Once these approaches are in place, our clients have used the essential elements to guide performance appraisals and progress toward organizational goals.

The essential elements of cultural proficiency are standards that can be applied to the study of the culture of your school. When working in P–12 schools, we often ask our clients if they notice when grade-level meetings of elementary educators, such as meetings of the second- and fourth-grade teachers, or the department meetings of secondary educators, such as meetings of the English and mathematics departments, are different in traditions, rituals, and approaches to their work. The question is always met with amusement and an overwhelmingly positive response. It is important to remember that organizations have dynamic cultures that both influence and are influenced by the behaviors and values of the people within the organizations. It is important to observe the cultures and the practices of the organization, whether it be a school district, school, or the grade levels and departments within a school. It is often here that one will find apparently benign policies that unintentionally discriminate.

THE ESSENTIAL ELEMENTS OF CULTURAL PROFICIENCY

The essential elements are an interdependent set of standards to guide being intentional in your journey to cultural proficiency. With practiced use, they become second nature as you reflect on your behavior and the underlying values that support your behaviors. Similarly, they provide you with a metric by which you can examine classroom, school, and district practices and the policies that support them. Used this way, the essential elements guide you in the development of behaviors and practices that are congruent with the culturally proficient values and policies you profess to your colleagues, your students, and the community you serve.

Table 8.1 presents the essential elements with indicators to guide your thinking about each element and what it might look like in practice. Later in this chapter, we present a more detailed discussion of each element.

Table 8.1   The Essential Elements of Cultural Competence

Assess Culture: *Claim your differences.*

- Recognize how your culture affects others.
- Describe your own culture and the cultural norms of your organization.
- Understand how the culture of your organization affects those with different cultures.

Value Diversity: *Name the differences.*

- Celebrate and encourage the presence of a variety of people in all activities.
- Recognize differences as diversity rather than as inappropriate responses to the environment.
- Accept that each culture finds some values and behaviors more important than others.

Manage the Dynamics of Difference: *Frame the conflicts caused by differences.*

- Learn effective strategies for resolving conflict, particularly among people whose cultural backgrounds and values differ.
- Understand the effect that historic distrust has on present-day interactions.
- Realize that you may misjudge others' actions based on learned expectations.

Adapt to Diversity: *Change to make a difference.*

- Change the way things are done to acknowledge the differences that are present in the staff, clients, and community.
- Develop skills for intercultural communication.
- Institutionalize cultural interventions for conflicts and confusion caused by the dynamics of difference.

Institutionalize Cultural Knowledge: *Train about differences.*

- Incorporate cultural knowledge into the mainstream of the organization.
- Teach the origins of stereotypes and prejudices.
- For staff development and education, integrate into your systems information and skills that enable all to interact effectively in a variety of intercultural situations.

The Coolidge school board has not always supported cultural proficiency as its approach to diversity. It took several years of seeing the tools used successfully in individual classrooms and schools before the board members understood that cultural proficiency was applicable to their work as well. Two years ago, after middle school principal Richard Díaz heard that the board of education had voted to embrace cultural proficiency as a district policy, he decided to include the essential elements of cultural proficiency as standards for both his teachers and their students. He encouraged the teachers to meet regularly in cohort groups to offer one another support and encouragement for implementing their goals for cultural proficiency.

To move his school toward cultural proficiency, Richard carefully studied the essential elements, then decided to start with the element assessing culture, because many of his staff members fervently resisted any change and could not see how their behaviors prevented all children from learning. Their practices ranged from cultural incapacity to cultural blindness. At the same time, Richard had a couple of teachers, like Derek and

DeLois, who truly valued diversity and who were willing to chair committees to develop ideas for manifesting a value for diversity throughout the campus.

Initially, many of Richard's staff members resisted change because they didn't think they had done anything wrong. Given that resistance, Richard spent time allowing his teachers to grieve their perceived losses, and he gently, but persistently, pushed them toward new ways of doing things. He made a case for change by showing the resisters how some of their behaviors had damaged the students, the school's relationships with the community, and the school's reputation in the district. He then worked to convince his teachers that the proposed change was integral to the school program, not just a supplement to it.

He is pleased to report that despite several false starts, teachers began to recognize language and attitudes that were, at best, precompetent. To ensure long-term success, he created an environment where the faculty experienced some immediate success with a few "feel-good" cultural assemblies. He knew this was superficial, but it created momentum and got the resisters talking. After a discussion facilitated by James, the diversity consultant, the teachers have been seeking ways to address the issues of diversity in their classrooms.

Grace Ishmael, the principal at Coolidge High School, decided to focus on the element managing the dynamics of difference. Some of Grace's resisters declared that because they were not directly involved in any of the conflicts raised by the Citizen's Human Relations Council, they should not be punished by having to attend any workshops. Grace surmounted the resistance by reframing the situation. She pointed out that current activities were not punishment; they were simply a response to changes in the school's culture that heretofore had not been acknowledged well. This was an opportunity to show students and parents what good teachers they were and how well they could respond to their students' needs; otherwise, they were disempowering themselves and their students with behaviors that could only be described as cultural incapacity. They all needed to learn how to recognize conflicts caused by cultural differences, and they all needed to find appropriate ways to respond to them.

Assess Your Culture

Cultural proficiency is an inside-out response to the issues that emerge in a diverse environment. Rather than talking about "them," the culturally proficient leader starts with herself: *What do I bring to the school environment that may serve as a barrier to healthy interactions with our students and their parents/guardians? What do I bring that is manifested in the way I look, the language I speak, and the cultures with which I identify that will assist in creating a culturally proficient school climate?* The culturally proficient leader is cognizant of her own culture, in its broadest definition; the culture of her school and district; and the cultures of her students and their families. Assessment of culture results in knowledge that is deeper than the ability to name the various groups represented in the district. Culturally proficient leaders also understand how these groups affect one another and influence the culture of the schools and district.

Culturally proficient leaders analyze themselves and their environments so that they have a palpable sense of their own cultures and the cultures of their schools. As a culturally proficient educator, you start with yourself and your own school. You do not assume that everyone will share your values, nor do you assume that everyone knows what behaviors are expected and affirmed in a culturally proficient school; in fact, most people are simply unaware. Therefore, you understand how the cultures of your school and district affect those whose cultures are different. You will state and explain the cultural norms of each classroom, school, or district so that people whose cultural norms differ will know how they must adapt to the new environment. Also, by recognizing how the school's culture affects other people, you will gain the information you need to make adjustments in style or processes so that all people feel comfortable and welcomed.

Value Diversity

Many diversity programs use the word *tolerance* in their titles. Tolerance is a place to start; on the Cultural Proficiency Continuum, behaviors and policies that are tolerant of diverse groups fall around the point of cultural incapacity. Reflect on how you might respond to a baby. You *tolerate* that you have to clean up the baby's messes, you *accept* that the baby makes those messes, and you *value* the baby. Similarly, as a culturally proficient leader, you are *delighted* that you have such a heterogeneous mix of students, teachers, and staff. You *accept* that in such an environment, you must face many challenges. And you *tolerate* the fact that not everyone is as committed as you are to creating a positive learning experience for everyone.

Consequently, you are proactive in involving a wide variety of people from all areas of the school in creating programs, developing appropriate policies, and establishing standards for performance and learning. You demonstrate your value for diversity by openly addressing the need to serve all people effectively. As a culturally proficient school leader, you provide leadership in developing policy statements on diversity and ensuring that the school's and district's mission and goal statements address the issues that emerge in diverse environments. You take these statements and act on them by communicating in inclusive ways to marginalized groups and by directing human and financial resources into curriculum, training, and other school endeavors to address their needs proactively.

Your measure of success may be that you look at that mission statement that has been hanging on the wall above the administrative assistant's desk for all who enter the office to see and begin to see if it aligns with your emerging culturally proficient policy statements.

Manage the Dynamics of Difference

Human beings, in general, have difficulty with conflict; the humans in Canada and the United States are no exception. We are taught to deny, ignore, marginalize, and circumvent problems rather than confront and resolve them. In a diverse environment, the cultural lenses through which the situations are perceived compound the problems caused by conflicts. Consider the conflicts that you have with people you know—people with whom you have long-standing, personal, and intimate relationships. Most likely one of the characteristics of the enduring success of those relationships has been the manner in which you faced conflicts successfully. The same is true of cross-cultural relationships that occur within the school setting.

A school that values diversity is not without conflict. Imagine the increased level of complexity of the conflicts when you involve people who do not share your history, language, lifestyle, or worldview. Reflect on the difficulties faced by teachers and site administrators who are required to mediate conflicts daily without the necessary skills. This is where the culturally proficient leader starts: acknowledging the current situation and then providing information and skills to the people who must survive in these environments.

In fact, a culturally proficient leader wants more than survival for his colleagues and students. He wants them to thrive. As a culturally proficient leader, you acknowledge that conflict is a natural state of affairs, and you develop effective, culturally proficient strategies for managing the conflict that occurs. Once you have embraced the value of diversity and have begun to articulate the cultural expectations of your school or classroom, the differences among the school's community members become more apparent. As a leader, you provide training sessions and facilitate group discussions so that people understand the effect of historical distrust on present-day interactions. You realize that the actions of others may be misjudged based on learned expectations, and you implement programs and processes that create new cultural expectations for the culturally proficient community.

Adapt to Diversity

To move toward cultural proficiency is to honor relationships. The best dancers always adjust their styles to the movements of their partners. The dance of diversity requires the same kind of adjustment. When engaging in a long-term, committed relationship, the partners implicitly promise to change. They both know that the success of the relationship is tied to their ability to adjust and adapt to one another. Each partner retains what is most important, while also releasing habits and rituals that are no longer necessary or that are not productive in this relationship. In the best of relationships, the partners do not compromise—they are transformed. That is the goal of cultural proficiency. The organization examines its core culture, acknowledges what it will seek to retain, and then articulates the values and the cultural expectations to all who are in the organization. At the same time, when new people are invited into the organization, they are not invited to be guests but rather to become members of the community. This means that the community makes space for them and changes to adapt to their unique needs.

To adapt to diversity is first to recognize that everyone changes. With some approaches to diversity, the groups that are not a part of the dominant culture are expected to change and to adapt to the culture of the dominant group. The culturally proficient approach to diversity invites and encourages everyone to change. One of the more powerful experiences we have had was with a high school that was struggling to be successful with a growing immigrant population. After a few sessions on cultural proficiency a teacher exclaimed, *It is so clear now, we have been trying to educate the kids who used to go to school here! Our task is to learn how to be successful with the students who are in our classrooms now.*

Once you make the commitment to cultural proficiency, you help all aspects of the school community to adapt. You help the host groups change by becoming more conscious of cultural norms that deny the value of diversity and the goal of cultural proficiency. You encourage the newer or less dominant groups to change because they know clearly the cultural expectations of the school. You enable the school or district to change by using culturally proficient behaviors as the standards for performance appraisal and as the basis for analyzing and revising school and district policies.

Institutionalize Cultural Knowledge

When a school or district takes on a diversity initiative, it is marked by focus groups, interviews, training, and journeys into the surrounding community. As school members develop facility in responding to the issues that are found in diverse environments, culturally competent behaviors and practices are no longer seen as external or supplemental to the "real" work of the school. The processes for teaching, learning, and growing are institutionalized. The classrooms, the schools, and the district all become learning communities.

As a culturally proficient school leader, you prize ongoing professional development that promotes a commitment to lifelong learning. You understand that the exponential growth of information and technology dictates the need for continuous upgrading of knowledge and skills. You readily integrate into systems, learning the information and skills that enable educators and students to interact effectively in a variety of intercultural situations. You affirm the importance of cultural knowledge, not only for the climate of the school or district but also as a knowledge base on which all students will continue to build throughout their lives.

The three principals, Steve Petrossian, Richard Díaz, and Grace Ishmael, had attended one of James Harris's recent diversity sessions. Their interest was piqued by James's review of a recent study conducted by James Valadez (2008) regarding the need for educators and policymakers to focus on the cultural perspectives of Mexican immigrant youth.

Steve was first to comment, "Not being an immigrant myself, I had not considered that the path to higher education could be so bewildering for immigrant youth."

Richard nodded in agreement, "I have to confess, it had not occurred to me either on the need for our schools to be so much more proactive in reaching out to families in such a way that we listen to their cultural perspectives and answer their questions about the value of higher education."

There was a moment of quiet reflection, broken by Grace's comment, "Well, it is time for me to fess up. James's presentation touched me, too, because I keep hearing our colleagues make statements like, 'If parents were interested in their children's education, they would attend our College Forums.' Comments like that just swirl around me, and I had not taken time to consider the impact that going to college might have on family life, let alone the financial pressures of higher education."

Steve breathed deeply and addressed his colleagues. "I agree with both of you, and the part of James's comments about the Valadez study that still resonates with me is the cultural and ideological bind that these students and their families experience with our country's focus on individual achievement versus Mexican collaborative family life, which emphasizes group achievement. Whew, it must be max pressure!"

"Good point, Steve." Richard said. "Yes, James was very clear that the youth in Valadez's study valued education but not at the expense of remaining close to their families."

Grace listened intently and made a connection. "Precisely! Which means that we have to learn ways to interact with immigrant families that honor their traditional values and take into consideration their cultural perspectives. It all gets back to the essential element of 'institutionalizing cultural knowledge.' It is our responsibility—no, let me change that to 'it is our opportunity'—to move away from the school and get to know all members of our community in new ways."

Table 8.2 summarizes the roles and responsibilities of all leaders in the school community as they work to become culturally proficient. As a culturally proficient leader, you also realize that students need knowledge about both the cultural practices of different people and groups and the experiences that many of these people and groups have had with stereotyping and prejudice. With this awareness, you provide your school communities with an understanding of how prejudices and stereotypes are developed and maintained in the society. You also help students and colleagues develop skills for eliminating prejudices through various human interactions, curricula, and instructional programs in schools.

Table 8.2   Responsibilities of Culturally Proficient School Leaders

Roles	Essential Elements of Cultural Proficiency				
	Assess Culture	*Value Diversity*	*Manage the Dynamics of Difference*	*Adapt to Diversity*	*Institutionalize Cultural Knowledge*
Teachers *Observe and Instruct*	Assess own culture and its effect on students. Assess the culture of the classroom. Support students in discovering their own cultural identities.	Teach all subjects from a culturally inclusive perspective. Insist on and model classroom language and behaviors that value differences.	Use conflict as object lessons. Teach students a variety of ways to resolve conflict.	Learn own instructional and interpersonal styles. Develop processes to enhance them so that they meet the needs of all students. Help students to understand why things are done in a particular way.	Teach students appropriate language for asking questions about other people's cultures and telling other people about theirs.
School Site Administrators *Lead and Supervise*	Assess the culture of the school and articulate the cultural expectations to all who interact there.	Articulate a culturally proficient vision for the school. Work with educators and staff to establish standards for holding one another accountable for the vision.	Provide training and support systems for conflict management. Help faculty and staff learn to distinguish between behavioral problems and cultural differences.	Examine policies and practices for overt and intentional discrimination and change current practices when appropriate.	Model and monitor schoolwide and classroom practices.
District Administrators *Implement Policy*	Assess culture of the district and the administrator's role in maintaining or changing it.	Provide guidelines for culturally proficient practices and establish standards for appraisal.	Provide resources for developing and establishing new conflict management strategies, including culturally specific mediation techniques.	Assess policies and propose changes when appropriate.	Propose and implement culturally proficient policies.
Parents and Community *Articulate Expectations*	Share with school personnel parent and community perceptions of the school's culture and practices.	Elect board members who represent cultures in the community.	Discern and point out to school personnel the nature and source of conflict when it occurs.	Identify policies and practices that need changing.	Serve as resources to the formal school leaders.
School Board Members *Set Policy*	Assess the cultures of the district and the board and the effect of those cultures on the community.	Establish standards for culturally proficient practices.	Articulate the need and value for culturally specific conflict management and mediation.	Review and change policies as the student population changes to maintain culturally proficient environment.	Establish all policies from a culturally proficient perspective.

ANALYZING SCHOOL LEADERSHIP

As a culturally proficient school leader, it is important for you to understand what currently exists before you can begin to understand what *should* exist (Giroux, 1992b). Table 8.2 provides a matrix by which to examine schools. The first column lists the most typical roles of school leaders (i.e., school district administrators, site administrators, teachers, parents and other community members, and school board members) and identifies the function of each role in creating a culturally proficient school or district. The other columns represent the five essential elements of cultural proficiency and describe behaviors and practices related to each of the elements.

In constructing this table and the discussion that follows, we have drawn on the works of Argyris (1990), Banks (1994, 1999), Senge et al. (1994, 2000), and Wheatley (1992, 2002). Their combined works affirm this inside-out approach to culturally proficient leadership. Together, they provide two frameworks:

1. An *inwardly oriented framework* for examining assumptions about those who differ from one another, for understanding how schools function, and for seeing how each school's culture facilitates learning for some students and impedes others from learning

2. An *outwardly directed framework* for discovering how and why educators learn about others, engage in team learning, and examine data for the purpose of making informed changes in school practices

In culturally proficient schools, each participant has a definite role to play. The roles overlap in some instances, but they retain distinctive characteristics. Some people will be more proficient at executing their distinctive roles than will others. Barriers to culturally proficient leadership arise from myriad sources. For example, in school districts that have traditionally failed to involve parents and community members in school decision-making processes, part of the movement toward cultural proficiency will be to help parents and community members learn their roles. Some of them will be reticent to be involved, whereas others may manifest anger at having been excluded for so long. Still other parents and community members will clearly articulate their expectations of what they want the school to do for their children.

As a culturally proficient leader, you recognize that silence does not mean a lack of interest or concern, just as anger does not signify parents' irreverence for their children's educators. You will have to develop processes to involve these diverse people in school matters. In addition to responding to these differences, you must remain committed to listening for the messages of wanting to be involved and then providing support for involvement.

In other school districts, role conflicts may pose barriers to cultural proficiency. For example, the recent history between teachers and district administrators may have been so acrimonious that civility is rare. In this situation, too, the culturally proficient leader must listen for messages of wanting to be involved, remembering that the form of the message may not be what is expected from the dominant culture in the community. Leaders in various roles implement cultural proficiency in often divergent ways:

- *Community leaders and parents* communicate to educators what they want their children to gain from their education.
- *School board members* set school policy that represents the wishes of the community in serving the diverse needs of their children. They work with school leaders to determine policies that ensure the application of the essential elements of cultural proficiency.
- *District-level administrators* implement the policies of the board of education by acting as a conduit between the school board and the local schools. Not only do they interpret policy for those at the local schools, but they also carry data about local schools back to the district office to inform decision making about future changes in policies or procedures.
- *Site administrators* have the responsibility to provide formal leadership at the local school and to supervise for the purpose of providing support to classroom teachers.
- Classrooms are where the action is, and *teachers* have the responsibility to carry out curricular and instructional programs consistent with the district's cultural proficiency policies. Teachers also have the responsibility to observe their students, to raise questions about student needs, and to work with site administrators in gathering data about student achievement and social interactions for the purpose of continuing to improve the educational climate.

The cultural proficiency tools that you will use most often are the essential elements. To learn what they are and how they relate to everything you do as an educational leader, you will need to practice applying them to different aspects of your work. In our book *Culturally Proficient Instruction* (Nuri Robins et al., 2006), we devote an entire chapter to each of the elements. Our book *Culturally Proficient Inquiry* (Lindsey et al., 2008) provides rubrics that include applied use of the essential elements. In the context of expanding your skills as a culturally proficient leader, we suggest that you spend time with the activities in those books.

GOING DEEPER

1. Develop descriptions of the essential elements that relate to your classroom, school, or district.

2. Review each of the elements. For each, suggest three professional development topics that would help to reinforce understanding and application of that element.

REFLECTION

_____

_____

_____

_____

_____

_____

_____

_____

_____

_____

_____

_____

_____

_____

_____

_____

_____

_____

_____

_____

PART III

Making the Commitment to Cultural Proficiency

9

The Case

One Last Look

The ultimate test of a moral society is the kind of world that it leaves to its children.

—Dietrich Bonhoeffer (1906–1945),
German theologian and Nazi resister

The cases in this book are presented here in their entirety. In each chapter, you found a portion of the cases—at the beginning of the chapter and, sometimes, integrated into the chapter—to illustrate points that we made. The people and their stories in the cases are people we have met and have worked with in school districts across the country. Although none of what you have read is fiction, all of the names are fictionalized. So if you think you recognize your name or the name of someone you know, please be sure that it is purely coincidental. We present the cases here so that you can go further with your analysis of these two fictitious districts—comparing them to your own, identifying common responses to issues of diversity, honing your skills as you use the tools of cultural proficiency, and acknowledging that cultural proficiency is not an event but a process.

Rolling Meadows Unified School District has been getting some bad media coverage. In the past month, local newspaper feature articles about the school district have blared:

"RUSD Misses AYP Target for 2nd Straight Year"

"Local Attorney Alleges Racism at High School"

"Once Proud District, Now Troubled?"

Superintendent Hermon Watson is concerned and privately incensed. He has provided leadership for this district for the past 20 years, and he is not happy to have this kind of press coverage. One of the reasons people live in this bedroom community is that, historically, it has been a stable, safe, family-oriented neighborhood in which to raise kids. It has been a place where people move because the schools are good and people don't have to deal with the issues caused by integrated schools and neighborhoods.

At the same time, Superintendent Watson knows there is basis in fact for the news coverage. First, two of the schools in the district have missed their AYP targets. Second, one of the few black parents in the district, Barbara Latimer, an attorney, has accused some of the high school teachers of racism. However, he reacts strongly to any suggestion that the district is "troubled."

Although Rolling Meadows has its own business and civic center, the majority of the population makes a long commute into the urban center for work. The trade-off is a community that is not fraught with problems associated with larger, urban areas. Today, the paper is quoting parents as saying, "We came out here to get away from these people. Now all they are doing is moving here stirring up trouble and lowering the quality of education for our kids."

Hermon shudders as he imagines his board members reading such news articles over their morning coffee. "We have handled every single incident that has occurred in this district. We don't have racist teachers, we are working to be able to educate all students, and we certainly are not a racist district," Hermon says as he reviews the most recent Tribune article with his cabinet.

"No one is perfect, and we have had only a few isolated incidents of educators acting inappropriately. We handled them discreetly, involving as few people as we could, and once handled we don't speak of them again. Likewise, we are putting resources into schools so that we can be more successful with these kids from impoverished backgrounds. My goal is that when we look at the faces in a classroom, or out across the commons area at lunchtime, we don't see colors, we just see kids."

Later in the day at an emergency cabinet meeting, Winston Alexander, the assistant superintendent for business, clears his throat. "I'm not sure, Hermon, but do you think that we ought to hire a consultant? It might look good right now to bring in some outside experts so they can tell the press what a good job we are doing."

"That's a fabulous idea," exclaims Holly Kemp, the assistant superintendent for curriculum and instruction. "We just finished the Regional Association of Schools and Colleges (RASC) accreditation review, so the documents describing our programs and students are in order. We could hire consultants to provide a cultural accreditation of some sort. We are not bad people—surely they will know that."

His cabinet rarely lets him down, Hermon muses. That is why they have been honored as a nationally distinguished district three times in the past 10 years. Aloud he says, "A cultural audit. Good idea. Winston and Holly, can the two of you put *together a request for proposal (RFP) this week? Ask our attorney friend, Barbara Latimer, to give you a hand. That should quiet her down for a while, and it will also let her know that we really mean to do well by her people."*

"Winston, what kind of money can you find for this? We may need to dig deep to climb out of this hole."

Rolling Meadows Unified School District

Rolling Meadows is a bedroom community that has its own business and civic center. The majority of the population makes a long commute into the urban center for work. The district is growing; it currently has about 15,000 students in three high school clusters, a continuation high school, and an adult school. Ten years ago, 82 percent of the student population of the district was white with 4 percent Asian and Pacific Islanders, 6 percent Latino, 2 percent African American, and 1 percent First Nation students. Five years ago, the percentage of white students had declined to 52 percent, while the Asian and Pacific Islander, Latino, African American, and First Nation student populations had increased proportionately. In contrast to the changing student demographics, the teaching force has been relatively stable for the past 10 years. Ten years ago, 90 percent of the teachers were white; today, the percentage has decreased by only 5 percent.

Hermon Watson, the superintendent of the Rolling Meadows District, decides to hire consultants to conduct a cultural inquiry study of the district. As you read the text, you will meet his cabinet and some of the teachers as they respond to the idea of a cultural study.

Coolidge Unified School District

On the other side of the county, Coolidge Unified School District serves the families that live in the urban center where many Rolling Meadows parents work. Coolidge High School continues to be among the schools in the county that earn top academic honors. The advanced placement classes have fewer than 10 percent African American and Latino students. In the last five years, the Title I population has increased from 5 percent to 35 percent. In that same period, the English as a Second Language (ESL) classes have increased from serving less than 2 percent of the student population to serving slightly more than 35 percent of the student population.

These trends have had two results. The first has been decreased sections of honors classes and a dramatic increase in remedial and heterogeneous classes. The heterogeneous classes in English and social studies were created to overcome criticism about the negative effect of tracking; however, placement in mathematics and science classes has served to stratify the English and social studies classes, despite their alleged heterogeneity. The second effect of the demographic changes has been that the school's standardized test scores have steadily declined, giving local media the impression that the quality of education at the school has deteriorated. Teachers still have an interest in a traditional academic approach to curriculum. They also place a high value on a tracked system in which the highest achievers are allowed to move at an accelerated rate.

The extracurricular programs of the school, except for football and basketball, tend to be associated with cultural groups. Though the sports program is nominally integrated, swimming is perceived to be a European American sport, wrestling a Latino sport, track an African American sport, and tennis a sport for Asians and Pacific Islanders. Student government reflects the demographic profile of the school, but one ethnic group dominates most of the clubs and other organizations. Of the major ethnic groups at the school, Latino students participate least in clubs and other organizations. In recent years, there has been tension among ethnic groups. Some fights and retaliatory attacks have received wide coverage in the newspaper.

Bill Fayette, the superintendent of the Coolidge District, recently hired a diversity consultant, James Harris, to provide training for faculty on cultural proficiency. As you read, you will be able to eavesdrop on conversations among these characters.

As the demographics in Rolling Meadows changed, this very insular district, which rarely hired administrators from outside the district, hired the district's first woman and first African American high school principal, Dina Turner. She has served as an assistant principal in another state, but this was her first principalship.

In the first two years, there was little evidence that anyone mentored her or showed her the "Rolling Meadows way of doing business." Another pressure on Dina was that last year, Rolling Meadows was given only provisional accreditation from the regional accrediting agency, a blow to the egos in the district and the community. Only after a consultant spent six days on campus interviewing teachers, students, aides, administrators, and parents and issued a report of his findings did faculty confront the fact that the mission of the school had changed. It had been a school that "prepared students for college"; now it is a school that also has to prepare students to become citizens of this country.

The broad spectrum of opinions among faculty and administration at Rolling Meadows High School reflects the range of views in the community. Many believe that the school can be organized into learning communities to provide a high-quality education for all students. A smaller and very vocal group, however, continually decries any changes that appear to lower standards and accuses the school and district administration of not supporting the school by getting tough with

troublemakers. Members of this group believe that if the school returns to a well-defined tracking system that creates a vocational level for students who are not interested in learning, the needs of everyone will be served. They also believe that senior teachers should be given first choice for teaching courses. This vocal minority among the veteran faculty continues to protest loudly the many structural and curricular changes occurring at the high school.

Annoyed, Celeste, a teacher at Rolling Meadows High School, circled "sex" on the needs assessment form sent out from the district administrative offices. Beside it, she wrote, "Yes!" Then she wrote "gender" on the form, carefully drew a small box next to it, marked it, and wrote "female." Further down on the form, she was asked to indicate her race or ethnicity. "Ayy," she groaned and turned to her friend, Bobby, who was completing the same form. "I hate these forms. I am so tired of being forced into boxes that don't fit."

"Just fill out the form," Bobby chided. "It doesn't really matter. And besides, these are the categories that the U.S. Census uses."

"I don't care about the U.S. Census Bureau. They are wrong! Where is the box for me on this chart? I am not African American. My cultural identity is Brazilian. I am bicultural."

"Well, you are Black Hispanic, aren't you?"

"No. I am a U.S. citizen of African descent. I was born in Boston and moved with my parents to Brazil as a child. My first language is Portuguese. My father is Brazilian, and my mother is from Panama; they met when they were studying at Tufts University. I speak Spanish, but I am not Hispanic. I am black, and I relate most strongly to people from Central and South America."

Winston Alexander, Rolling Meadows's assistant superintendent for business, is reviewing the proposals he has received in response to the request for proposal (RFP) and is learning a lot. He gets some information from the specific responses to the questions the RFP team proposes, and the team gleans even more insight from the underlying values of the consultants. It is easy to discern what they believe from the way they present themselves and the extra materials they include. Right now, he muses over three ideas:

1. Our public schools work well for the students for whom they were designed.

2. No nation has ever sought to provide universal education for as broad a spectrum of social classes and ethnic or racial groups as does the United States.

3. We are more successful at education than any other nation in the world today, but our development of a de facto caste system has created great inequities. We are at a point in history where we must heed the warning to avoid creating "two societies, separate and unequal" (Riot Commission, 1968).

Superintendents Bill Fayette and Hermon Watson continue to have conversations about cultural proficiency. At one of their meetings, Bill shared this story with Hermon.

"My middle school and elementary school administrators had noticed for several years that large numbers of Mexican and Mexican American students regularly visit their families in Mexico around Christmas and Easter. What made this a problem was that the children were often gone for three or four weeks at a time. Consequently, they missed a lot of classroom work and lagged behind the other students.

"The teachers and the administrators at each school implored the parents to respect the school calendar and have their children back when school resumed, but most did not comply. The teachers even developed homework packets that the children could take with them, but those efforts had only mixed results.

"Finally it occurred to the leadership team that the school was organized around the living patterns of an agriculturally based community that had long ago become an urban center. The leadership team decided they needed to meet with parents and brainstorm ideas, share concerns, and see how best the school could respond to the educational needs of the children. From this meeting, the school people discovered that rather than demanding that the parents respect an anachronistic practice, they could demonstrate respect for the families by organizing the school calendar around their lifestyles, in much the same way as the school leaders' predecessors had done in generations earlier. So now, the schools are closed for four weeks in late December and early January and for two weeks during the observance of Passion Week and Easter. We make up the days in the summer.

"You see," Bill concluded, "once people understood that the school calendar wasn't etched in stone, and parents were engaged as active partners, it was pretty easy to get our priorities in order and decide how we could best meet the needs of our students and their families."

Rolling Meadows Superintendent Watson recognizes that during his tenure the demographics of the district have shifted from being almost totally white to increasingly multiethnic, and issues related to faith, ableness, and sexual orientation have emerged. He has gathered data on student achievement, noted the intercultural friction and fights at the high schools, and heard parents' complaints about the curriculum.

The request for proposal (RFP) that his staff prepares seeks consultants to conduct a year-long cultural inquiry study and needs assessment that tap into the views and beliefs of all sectors of the district—the educators, the staff, the students, and members of the community. Although he has not yet been introduced to the concept of cultural proficiency, Superintendent Watson knows intuitively to move in this comprehensive direction and to involve all district administrators in ways that support their understanding and share his vision for all students in the district. He uses his formal position to lead the district into this process.

Coolidge Middle School Principal Richard Díaz is also ready to conduct a needs assessment. This urban school's student demographics have changed from virtually all African American to about one-fourth Latino in fewer than five years. Among the many changes he has initiated at the middle school is to provide instruction in Spanish to all students. This not only provides those whose primary language is Spanish the opportunity to develop bilingual skills in both their native tongue and English, but it also offers native English speakers the chance to learn Spanish, which will prepare them to function in multilingual settings as teenagers and adults. His vision helps African American students learn about the lifestyles of the Spanish-speaking students, and it mitigates tensions that could result from having two language-based cultural groups in the school.

Leatha Harp, director of credentialing and certification in the Coolidge Unified School District, has gathered a small team of teachers and administrators who have agreed to serve on employment interview panels this school year to hire administrators for the district. They are reviewing anonymous comments written by other teachers and administrators when asked to discuss the type of leaders desired at Coolidge schools. The team has pulled out the comment sheets that reflect patterns or themes in the responses. About the formal leaders in the district, they read the following:

- That school needs a strict disciplinarian so the kids will know who is in charge.
- The Latino kids need a Latino administrator so they can have a positive role model.
- Principals come and go, but I will always be here.
- This school is entirely too tough for a woman administrator!
- I may not agree with her, but I know where she stands.
- One thing I will have to give the principal, he sure does relate well to the parents.
- She may be an expert in instruction and supervision, but how can she evaluate my physics lesson?

"I had no idea the comments would be so personal," exclaims Brittney. She is one of the middle school teachers, with a provisional teaching credential. "Some of them sound so jaded."

"Oh, they are not all bad," says Leatha. "They tell us a lot about what people want in their leaders. Look at this pile of comments. They tell us a lot about where the nonformal leadership is in this district."

"What do you mean by nonformal ?" asks Brittney.

"Nonformal leaders are not officially appointed or chosen but rather emerge from the group, based on the needs and aspirations of those who work in the environment," explains Leatha.

"Nonformal leaders are usually people like teachers, aides, students, or parents. People whose positions don't give them a lot of power but who have a lot of influence nonetheless. Barbara Latimer, who is on the board of the Citizens Human Relations Council, is a nonformal leader. She doesn't have a formal position of leadership, with a title, but everyone respects her and listens when she speaks. She is always at the district office and the board meetings, even though her daughter attends school in Rolling Meadows.

"Look at these comments; they acknowledge the nonformal leadership we have in this district."

- That secretary has trained seven principals!
- If you want to reach out to the parents, just tell Mrs. Latimer—Kim's mother—that woman is well respected in this community.
- To include more bilingual parents in school governance, you may want to use the services of the aide in Room 7; she knows all of the parents and they respect her highly.
- The union representative is a very important member of the leadership council, but DeLois Winters is the teacher to whom the others look for guidance.

"You can see from these comments that our job is very important. What is expected in a school administrator varies widely, which is why we have assembled this team to assist us in this search for new administrators. We fully realize that a prospective administrator has to be a technician and a visionary, one who knows the skills and artistry of formal and nonformal leadership. We are looking for leaders who display personal values and behaviors that enable them and others to engage in effective interactions among students, educators, and the communities they serve."

—◆◆◆—

The Rolling Meadows consultants are making a presentation to Superintendent Watson's cabinet, and Holly, the assistant superintendent of curriculum and instruction, is not so sure they really understand the situation at Rolling Meadows because she hasn't seen any of these problems. The consultants say, "Throughout U.S. educational history, students have been taught close to nothing about the caste system in this country and very little about U.S. citizens of lower castes. In recent decades, however, most textbooks and school curricula have inserted some materials and lessons mentioning women and people of color, although these insertions have generally been few and segregated from the sweep of U.S. history.

"Acknowledgment of African Americans is too often limited to brief lessons on slavery, the celebration of Dr. King's birthday, and observances of Black History Month in February. Lessons about People of the First Nations often range from highlighting their nobility to underscoring their savagery; usually, their only significant *role is to attend the first Thanksgiving. Lessons about Latinos are frequently relegated to music, dance, and a lesson about Cesar Chavez or Che Guevara, if they are mentioned at all outside of New York and the Southwestern United States. Students learn about Asians as the celebrants of Chinese New Year, the sneaky attackers at Pearl Harbor, and the reluctant recipients of our 'help' during the Korean and Vietnam Wars. Lessons about women often resort to the 'great woman' approach, focusing on a few heroic individuals rather than the historic and continuing role of women in the United States. These discrete lessons lead to the objectification and invisibility of females and people of color."*

During an inservice session on cultural proficiency at the Coolidge district, James Harris, the consultant, overhears this conversation between European American Principal Steve Petrossian and Puerto Rican Principal Richard Díaz:

Steve says, "You know, this activity in determining how prejudice differs from racism or sexism gives me some new ideas to work with. I had never considered the concept of power; it just never occurred to me. Let me ask you this: One of my African American teachers said that his student is 'a good athlete for a white boy.' Now isn't that racism?"

"Steve," Richard replies, "let me get this straight: You have been on this planet for decades, and you have never thought about the power that European American people have in this country?"

Steve is defensive. "Hey, why attack me? I'm being honest with you. Power is something I've just never considered. Just because I'm white doesn't mean that I have power. Besides, you haven't answered my question. Isn't my story an example of racism?"

James responds to Steve, "No, it isn't. Although your story illustrates an ethnocentric use of a stereotype and is definitely cultural incapacity, the teacher in your example lacks the power to institutionalize his beliefs. The term racism implies the power to act on one's bigotry. Or reflects the systems within our institutions that discriminate against people of color without the consent or the conscious participation of dominant group people in the system."

James continues, addressing the whole group, "Steve's story also shows his lack of awareness of—as well as his wish to deny—his own entitlement. The teacher in Steve's story was not reinforcing or perpetuating institutional racism, which affects every single person and has grave social consequences no matter whether it is recognized or acknowledged. More often than not, people who are not directly affected by oppression fail to understand when cultural groups speak out about their experiences. Members of the dominant group, whatever that group tends to be, usually fail to notice their power or entitlement."

Richard interrupts: "Yeah, they say, 'If I didn't experience the oppression, or witness it, then you must be overreacting.' Or they want to start talking about their own pain, like this was the oppression Olympics."

James goes on, "If we are to create an effectively functioning society—and, by extension, a school system that is culturally proficient—we must find ways to address issues of entitlement. By doing so, we can minimize gaps in the education of our educators that perpetuate their lack of awareness and their denial of their own empowerment."

The consultants at Rolling Meadows direct the cabinet's attention to a chart with these quotations from the focus groups they conducted during the cultural audit:

"If we are celebrating diversity, why don't we have celebrations like European American History Month?"

"The teacher wrote on my child's paper that she didn't understand the black inner-city experience and, therefore, couldn't grade her essay fairly. This child has never lived in the inner city! Her father is a chemist, and I am vice president of the Red Cross. Her teacher knows we are a middle-class family."

"These immigrant students don't even have magazines and books in their homes. They are at a tremendous disadvantage when compared to the other students."

"I don't believe we have to point out people who choose their sexual preference or orientation or whatever the politically correct term is! Does that mean we, then, need to identify George Washington as a heterosexual?"

After giving the cabinet a chance to reflect on the effect of these statements, the consultant remarks, "Each of these comments assumes that entitled students, the European American students and families of the dominant culture, are the standard of measure for other students. In the first comment, it is not recognized that most traditional school curricula celebrate the dominant culture daily. The second illustration shows the unawareness of the relationship of economic class to ethnic culture. The second to last quote reflects the assumption that the speaker knows what is in students' homes and that students with books and magazines read them. The final quote assumes that sexual orientation is chosen."

Derek is in his first year as a teacher-coach in the Coolidge district. He has been working to help his colleagues understand how much is communicated to children by the language and tone that is used by the teachers.

"Well, they are not going to do as well as the regular students," Harvey said of his Vietnamese students, "so I think it is a disservice to ask them to do as much as the others."

"No, no," said DeLois, "If they need more help, we give more help. That's our job! We don't lower our expectations for them."

Breathing deeply to calm himself, Derek opened the door of the next classroom in time to hear the teacher, Lane, say to his Latino students, "Your parents are poor and uneducated, so I know they won't be able to help you with your homework. I am going to have an afterschool homework session with all the needy kids like you. I really want to help you so you don't grow up to be like your parents."

At their staff development meeting with the diversity consultant, Richard Díaz, Coolidge Middle School principal, writes on the board, "That [women and] men do not learn very much from the lessons of history is the most important of all the lessons that history has to teach. Aldous Huxley, 1959."

"There he goes again," Harvey whispers to Lane. Richard has developed a mantra of change and a rallying cry for the new order of things he is trying to establish at Coolidge Middle School. He knows that one speech, one memo, or one staff meeting will not do it. Every time the faculty and staff see him, Richard talks about change and what it will mean for whomever he is addressing, as well as how it will affect the students and the school's community. He communicates regularly with the district's consultant, James Harris, so that each reinforces the work of the other when making presentations.

"These diversity staff development meetings are a waste of time," Harvey continues. "No one's going to change. I've been here for 17 years, and I've seen it all. I have tenure, so I'll just sit tight. These administrators are only here until they get a promotion. Each one brings his or her own program, and each program leaves with the administrator. If I wait long enough, I won't have to do a thing."

Across the room, DeLois and Derek are eagerly taking notes. "I wish I had taken more history courses when I was in college," DeLois sighs. "I'm sure that I could be more effective if I had a stronger historical foundation for what we are doing."

"We're not here to teach history, we're here to teach kids," Derek retorts. "I wish he would just tell us more about this cultural proficiency model so I can figure out what I need to change in my classroom."

"You're right," DeLois sighs. "Richard just needs to mandate what he wants done. Understanding history is not going to change some of the bigots in this room."

At Coolidge Middle School, consultant James Harris overhears this conversation in the parking lot:

Teacher DeLois says, "I am really enjoying these sessions on cultural proficiency. I can see where I can use a lot of this information to prepare the girls and Latinos in my classes to assume a responsible role in society."

Harvey, cynical as always, lashes back, "Are you for real? I would like you and this 'cultural expert' to spend a day in the vice principal's office. All day long, he deals with the scum of this school. If those kids were in your classroom, you would know why those people are so behind in school."

DeLois can't believe what she is hearing. "Let me tell you something," she hisses at him. "First, if you think the girls and the Mexicans are the ones who need help, you are in worse shape than you know. The true scum in this school are the educators who don't see students when they come to their office. All they see is the color of their skin . . . and you judge the kids and their families in the same way."

Harvey doesn't limit his discontent to his middle school colleagues. Consider a discussion that takes place among some teachers after a union meeting at Coolidge High School.

"I have been in this district for 17 years, and have I seen some changes!" says Harvey.

"Like what?" his friend Lane asks.

"Well, first of all," Harvey responds, "when I first came here, this was a nice, stable, working-class community where the parents wanted their children to have more than they did. Sure we had problems, but nothing like today. Then, 14 years ago, the school became all minority in no time at all!"

"And?" Lane challenges.

"What do you mean, 'And?'" Harvey was getting annoyed. "You know exactly 'and what.' That was when our test scores dropped, drug problems began, and the schools became one more ghetto nightmare. And I'm not a racist; these are just facts!"

Rolling Meadows High School Principal Dina Turner is conducting a meeting with her site council. "We are at the midpoint of our year, and our plan specifies that we are to assess our progress by examining our benchmarks. As you recall, our goals for this year were for schoolwide academic improvement in reading and for learning more about our interaction patterns with students."

Bobby, one of her consistently unhappy teachers, replies, "You know, I am all for academic improvement, but I still don't see how it is related to having a teacher observing me in my classroom."

Another teacher, Celeste, speaks up in Dina's defense. "I am not sure I agree with you. Since we have started the schoolwide focus on reading, it's easier for me to talk with my students about reading for fun."

Barbara Latimer, a very active parent in the district, adds, "That is a good point! Just this weekend, my daughter asked if I didn't think that we watched way too much television. I hated to admit it, but she is right. I was just wondering how parents who are not members of the site council are reacting."

Dina says, "Obviously, I am very supportive of our reading initiative. I am also deeply committed to our continued study of student-teacher interactions. Has anyone tried any of the teacher expectations behaviors in their classrooms?"

"I have," said Celeste. "You know, Bobby, even though I know I am a good teacher, those activities are helping me see some of my blind spots. I am beginning to see how my unintentional behaviors can keep kids from learning!"

"What occurs to me," adds Dina, "is that if these unintentional behaviors occur between teachers and students, they must occur among adults too. It scares me to think about the damage we do to one another without even realizing it."

Barbara has an idea. *"You know, we may want to consider some of that training for parents. From what you are saying, it may be very enlightening, possibly a little uncomfortable, but very worthwhile."*

"Most teachers are comfortable with the process," Dina replies. *"I believe if everyone sees oneself as a student and is willing to commit the energy it takes to walk this path to improvement, we will all grow, and our kids will really benefit. And, I agree, it would be good for this group too. It would be an excellent topic for training all our parents."*

Across town, neophyte teacher Brittney is looking at a framed list hanging on the wall near the desk of her mentor teacher, DeLois. *"What is this?"* Brittney asked.

"Oh," DeLois said, *"I am a quilter, and once, as I made a quilt of ribbon and lace, sewing one small strip after another, I thought about the life lessons that I was learning through quilt making. I try to remember these things whenever we are trying to implement some change in the district."* This is what was on DeLois's list:

- There is no rehearsal. It all counts.
- Sometimes you need the big picture before you can start.
- Don't skimp.
- Be patient with yourself.
- Do one square at a time.
- Try it out.
- Take it apart, start over.
- Nonconformity, although beautiful, is sometimes very disruptive.
- Stop when you are tired. It's better to have only three things to do when you are fresh than to have three things to do over when you are frustrated.
- Sometimes you won't know the best process to use until after you have finished.
- Good work is not always transferable. What works well in one setting may be totally wrong in another.
- Perfection is perception.

Perhaps you can put DeLois's list near your desk as well.

Bill Fayette, the superintendent of the Coolidge district, has hired a diversity consultant, James Harris, to provide training for faculty on cultural proficiency. At the first staff development session, James explains the underlying principles that inform his approach to dealing with the issues that emerge in a diverse environment. He also explains that the response to these issues usually falls within one of four categories:[1]

- *Right the wrongs:* Some people are angry or have a strong sense of justice. If something is wrong, they think that it should be fixed immediately and, if necessary, the wrongdoers should be punished.

---

[1]Thanks to our colleague Stephanie Graham for sharing this model with us.

- The golden rule: These people want everyone to get along. "If we all just treated everyone equally, with courtesy and kindness, there wouldn't be a problem," they say.
- My pain equals yours: Then there are those who say, "Everyone has been discriminated against about something. I got over it; so should they. We need to forget the past and move forward."
- Oppression Olympics: These people recognize that every group has suffered some form of discrimination. They are, however, certain that the group they are in has suffered the most and should not be minimized by discussing anyone else's alleged experiences of oppression.

"Each of these perspectives has some serious drawbacks," says James, "and each one also is useful. He presents the group with a list of comments he has collected from teachers and administrators in a number of districts:

Doesn't focusing on differences just make it harder for us to get along?

I don't have a culture. I'm just a generic person. Heinz 57 American.

He sure didn't sound black on the phone when we talked.

I didn't know there were Chinese people over six feet tall.

You are different, but we're comfortable with you.

We would have more of your kind around if they were just like you.

Why do they have to have a special program?

I think everyone should be given the same attention and information. That's fair.

It's the culture of that school that needs to be changed! After all, what can you expect from a school in that community?

James uses these comments to illustrate the need for the guiding principles of cultural proficiency.

The faculty at Rolling Meadows Middle School has heard that the district is going to hire consultants to evaluate their ability to teach and assess students in an effective cross-cultural manner. They are neither impressed nor pleased. Sitting in the staff lunchroom, they speak wistfully about when their own children attended the district, failing to acknowledge that the demographics have change dramatically. Their comments about the children and the impending work with the consultants range in attitude from culturally destructive to culturally proficient.

In one corner of the room we hear the following:

"This is America, everyone should speak English—they should be adapting to us. This is reverse discrimination. We didn't do anything to those people, so why do we have to change?"

"Our goal for examining our school policy on student grouping must be to enhance student achievement. If we get some quality consultants in here, they can help us to disaggregate these test data. Then we can really understand student needs."

"Why are we trying to fix something that's not broken? When I walk into a classroom, I do not see color or ability or gender—I only see children."

"I believe that conflict is natural and normal; I'm glad we will be learning how to do things differently when conflict occurs."

Across the room, some teachers are discussing their students:

"I didn't know his father was gay. He doesn't look gay to me."

"She catches well for a girl."

"I can't believe my Asian boys only scored in the 80th percentile!"

Over by the copier, some of the teachers are trying to be proactive:

"We need a Korean vice principal to help us with the Korean students."

"We celebrate Cinco de Mayo and Martin Luther King's birthday. What holiday can we use for American Indians?"

"Let's look at the school calendar to make sure we don't schedule our potlucks during Ramadan, Ridvan, or Yom Kippur."[2]

At Coolidge Middle School, Derek effectively teaches children from diverse ethnic and socioeconomic backgrounds, but down the hall, Brittney, a second-year teacher, is unsuccessful with and unhappy about having to teach "that kind of child," referring to various children from the local community. DeLois, Derek, and several other teachers at Coolidge Middle School organize their students by reading levels, continuously moving children to the next highest reading level as they progress through the year. By June, their top groups are quite large. On the other hand, Brittney is among the many other teachers in the school who organize reading levels at the beginning of the year and keep the students in the same groups all year long, regardless of how much individual students progress.

DeLois, Derek, and the other teachers who organize their reading groups in an ongoing fashion during the school year are always monitoring their students for clues to their motivation and to possible sources of impediments to their learning. Most recently, they were troubled that some of their students who had been doing quite well began to struggle and to exhibit misbehaviors that were somewhat unusual. In one of their grade-level meetings, they decided to share their concerns about the students and determine how they could be most helpful. In response to their concerns, Principal Díaz joined their meeting. He shared that upon further investigation, he had discovered that due to the recent economic downturn, all of the families of these particular students were experiencing extreme financial difficulties, ranging from job losses to potential foreclosure on their homes. The teachers and Díaz just sat for a moment and let this information soak in before they proceeded to consider ways in which they could be supportive of the students and keep them on track academically.

---

[2]These are the holidays of the Muslim, Baha'i, and Jewish faiths, respectively, that require the faithful to fast during the day. Ramadan and Ridvan last for several weeks, so your Muslim and Baha'i colleagues and students may be at school while fasting.

At Rolling Meadows High School, the faculty curriculum committee has been charged with assessing the extent to which the school's curriculum was aligned with the emerging social studies standards. The committee is composed of new and experienced teachers, an administrator, the school counselor, and parents from the School Site Council. Dina Turner, the principal, is the chair of the task force studying the social science standards. Also on the task force are teachers, Celeste and Bobby, and a parent, Barbara Latimer. The diversity consultant, James Harris, had introduced the five essential elements early in the planning process and received enthusiastic support for using them to frame this planning.

"I see this as a very important task, one that is going to take considerable time and study," said Dina as they began the work of the task force.

"I couldn't agree more," said Celeste, "and as one of the old-timers here, I am pleased to have Bobby on our team. Bobby is a history teacher and a counselor. He knows the breadth and depth of our curriculum."

"It seems to me," said Mrs. Latimer, "that a place to begin is to get from Bobby a sense of how balanced he sees our curriculum. In other words, Bobby, what do you see as our strong points and what are the points of omission?"

After a moment of reflection, Bobby responded, "I'm comfortable with that as a starting point, but I want you to know that I don't know everything. For example, since the terrorists attacked the World Trade Center, I've realized how little I know about the Middle East, the Muslim religion, or our country's policies that affect these issues. One of the things I see coming from this study is that even though our school has no Middle Eastern or Muslim students that I know of, it will be important for our curriculum to be inclusive of them."

"Yes, the new state standards for social studies," offered Dina, "are very explicit about our students being prepared to live and function in an interdependent, global world. I am sure, Bobby, that your concerns are shared by many of us. We need that kind of openness to do this work well."

The Coolidge school board has not always supported cultural proficiency as its approach to diversity. It took several years of seeing the tools used successfully in individual classrooms and schools before the board members understood that cultural proficiency was applicable to their work as well. Two years ago, after middle school principal Richard Díaz heard that the board of education had voted to embrace cultural proficiency as a district policy, he decided to include the essential elements of cultural proficiency as standards for both his teachers and their students. He encouraged the teachers to meet regularly in cohort groups to offer one another support and encouragement for implementing their goals for cultural proficiency.

To move his school toward cultural proficiency, Richard carefully studied the essential elements, then decided to start with the element assessing culture, because many of his staff members fervently resisted any change and could not see how their behaviors *prevented all children from learning. Their practices ranged from cultural incapacity to cultural blindness. At the same time, Richard had a couple of teachers like Derek and DeLois, who truly valued diversity and who were willing to chair committees, to develop ideas for manifesting a value for diversity throughout the campus.*

Initially, many of Richard's staff members resisted change because they didn't think they had done anything wrong. Given that resistance, Richard spent time allowing his teachers to grieve their perceived losses, and he gently, but persistently, pushed them toward new ways of doing things. He made a case for change by showing the resisters how some of their behaviors had damaged the students, the school's relationships with the community, and the school's reputation in the district. He then worked to convince his teachers that the proposed change was integral to the school program, not just a supplement to it.

He is pleased to report that despite several false starts, teachers began to recognize language and attitudes that were, at best, precompetent. To ensure long-term success, he created an environment where the faculty experienced some immediate success with a few "feel-good" cultural assemblies. He knew this was superficial, but it created momentum and got the resisters talking. After a discussion facilitated by James, the diversity consultant, the teachers have been seeking ways to address the issues of diversity in their classrooms.

Grace Ishmael, the principal at Coolidge High School, decided to focus on the element managing the dynamics of difference. Some of Grace's resisters declared that because they were not directly involved in any of the conflicts raised by the Citizen's Human Relations Council, they should not be punished by having to attend any workshops. Grace surmounted the resistance by reframing the situation. She pointed out that current activities were not punishment; they were simply a response to changes in the school's culture that heretofore had not been acknowledged well. This was an opportunity to show students and parents what good teachers they were and how well they could respond to their students' needs; otherwise, they were disempowering themselves and their students with behaviors that could only be described as cultural incapacity. They all needed to learn how to recognize conflicts caused by cultural differences, and they all needed to find appropriate ways to respond to them.

The three principals, Steve Petrossian, Richard Díaz, and Grace Ishmael, had attended one of James Harris's recent diversity sessions. Their interest was piqued by James's review of a recent study conducted by James Valadez (2008) regarding the need for educators and policymakers to focus on the cultural perspectives of Mexican immigrant youth.

Steve was first to comment, "Not being an immigrant myself, I had not considered that the path to higher education could be so bewildering for immigrant youth."

Richard nodded in agreement, "I have to confess, it had not occurred to me either that our schools need to be so much more proactive in reaching out to families in such a way that we listen to their cultural perspectives and answer their questions about the value of higher education."

There was a moment of quiet reflection, broken by Grace's comment. "Well, it is time for me to fess up. James's presentation touched me, too, because I keep hearing our colleagues make statements like, 'If parents were interested in their children's education, they would attend our College Forums.' Comments like that just swirl around me, and I had not taken time to consider the impact that going to college might have on family life, let alone the financial pressures of higher education."

Steve breathed deeply and addressed his colleagues. "I agree with both of you, and the part of James's comments about the Valadez study that still resonates with me is the cultural and ideological bind that these students and their families experience with our country's focus on individual achievement versus Mexican collaborative family life, which emphasizes group achievement. Whew, it must be max pressure!"

"Good point, Steve." Richard said. "Yes, James was very clear that the youth in Valadez's study valued education but not at the expense of remaining close to their families."

Grace listened intently and made a connection. "Precisely! Which means that we have to learn ways to interact with immigrant families that honor their traditional values and take into consideration their cultural perspectives. It all gets back to the essential element of 'institutionalizing cultural knowledge.' It our responsibility—no, let me change that to 'it is our opportunity'—to move away from the school and get to know all members of our community in new ways."

GOING DEEPER

Now that you have read the complete case, you may want to see how your analysis of it has changed from the portions of the case you read in each chapter. You may also want to use the case as a study tool. You and your colleagues may create new ways for using this case and those cases and vignettes that you develop. Let us hear from you so we can share your successes with others. Our e-mail is culturalproficiency@earthlink.net.

1. With which characters in the two cases do you identify most strongly? Why?

2. Does your school or district resemble either of the districts?

3. After reading the case, what lessons do you take with you?

4. What will be the first step you take toward becoming culturally proficient?

REFLECTION

Matrix

How to Use the Cultural Proficiency Books

Book	Authors	Focus
Cultural Proficiency: A Manual for School Leaders (3rd ed.), 2009	Randall B. Lindsey Kikanza Nuri Robins Raymond D. Terrell	This book is an introduction to cultural proficiency. It offers an extended discussion of each of the tools and the historical framework for diversity work.
Culturally Proficient Instruction: A Guide for People Who Teach (2nd ed.), 2002	Kikanza Nuri Robins Randall B. Lindsey Delores B. Lindsey Raymond D. Terrell	This book focuses on the five essential elements and can be directed to anyone in an instructional role. It can be used as a workbook for a study group.
The Culturally Proficient School: An Implementation Guide for School Leaders, 2005	Randall B. Lindsey Laraine M. Roberts Franklin CampbellJones	This book guides the reader to examine the school as a cultural organization and to design and implement approaches to dialogue and inquiry.
Culturally Proficient Coaching: Supporting Educators to Create Equitable Schools, 2007	Delores B. Lindsey Richard S. Martinez Randall B. Lindsey	This book aligns the essential elements with Costa and Garmston's cognitive coaching model. It provides coaches, teachers, and administrators with a personal guidebook; protocols and maps can be used for conducting conversations that shift thinking in support of all students achieving at levels higher than before.

(Continued)

(Continued)

Book	Authors	Focus
Culturally Proficient Inquiry: A Lens for Identifying and Examining Educational Gaps, 2008	Randall B. Lindsey Stephanie M. Graham R. Chris Westphal, Jr. Cynthia L. Jew	This book uses protocols for gathering and analyzing student achievement and access data, as well as rubrics for gathering and analyzing data about educator practices. A CD accompanies the book for easy downloading and use of the data protocols.
Culturally Proficient Leadership: The Personal Journey Begins Within, 2009	Raymond D. Terrell Randall B. Lindsey	This book guides the reader through the development of a cultural autobiography as a means to become an increasingly effective leader in our diverse society.
Culturally Proficient Learning Communities: Confronting Inequity Through Collaborative Curiosity (working title), 2009	Delores B. Lindsey Linda D. Jungwirth Jarvis V. N. C. Pahl Randall B. Lindsey	This book provides readers a lens through which to examine the purpose, the intentions, and the progress of the learning communities to which they belong or those they wish to develop. School and district leaders are provided protocols, activities, and rubrics to facilitate actions focused on the intersection of race, ethnicity, gender, social class, sexual orientation and identity, faith, and ableness with the disparities in student achievement.
The Cultural Proficiency Journey: Moving Beyond Ethical Barriers Toward Profound School Change (working title), 2009	Franklin CampbellJones Brenda CampbellJones Randall B. Lindsey	This book explores cultural proficiency as an ethical construct. It makes transparent the connection between values, assumptions, and beliefs and observable behavior, making change possible and sustainable.
Culturally Proficient Practices: An Assets-based Approach to Poverty (working title), 2009	Michelle S. Karns Keith Myatt Randall B. Lindsey	This book is designed for educators to learn how to identify and develop the strengths of students from low-income backgrounds.
Culturally Proficient Organizations: A Conversation with Colleagues About the Practice of Cultural Proficiency (working title), 2010	Kikanza Nuri Robins Raymond D. Terrell Delores B. Lindsey Randall B. Lindsey	This book answers the question "How do you do it?" It is directed to managers and organizational leaders who want to introduce cultural proficiency systemically.

Resources

Introduction to Resource Activities

We use the following activities in Resources A to G to reinforce the concepts presented in this book. The activities are organized by topic; however, an experienced facilitator can adapt or focus the debriefing of an activity to highlight other issues. The table at the beginning of each Resource summarizes the activities, giving the general category and the expertise of the facilitator, readiness of the group, and time needed to conduct the activity. It is our hope that you will use these activities with your colleagues and your students. The activities, however, do not substitute for reading, nor can they fix problems or change attitudes. It is tempting to use the activities as time fillers during professional development. We encourage you to make sure that you schedule the time so that you can debrief adequately, building upon the readings and past experiences and laying a foundation for future learning and change.

The guidelines below are hints to ensure your success. Read and consider each prior to using the activities in this Resources section.

DO YOUR OWN WORK

You need to know yourself well—including your biases, prejudices, and blind spots. This only comes from deep introspection, interaction with colleagues committed to telling you the truth, and hearing the truth about yourself. To be culturally proficient is to be a lifelong learner, committed to learning as much about yourself as about other things and other people. This includes modeling during the training by using yourself as an example when explaining how an activity is to be done. It also means that you will not ask the participants to engage in an activity that you have not already experienced.

BELIEVE IT

Unlike some academic subjects, which can be taught reasonably well regardless of how the teacher feels about the topic, issues of diversity can only be presented and processed well if the trainer truly believes in the importance of the work and the value of the particular activity.

BE ABLE TO WORK WITHOUT THE SCRIPT

Diversity-related training is not the kind of work that can be done well from a script or from an inauthentic place. Know your material so well that you have information, answers, and anecdotes that are not part of your lesson plan, which you can use as needed and appropriate.

SET THE TONE

Be clear about the message you want to communicate with the room arrangement. Think about issues of proximity and access. Set up the room for the comfort of the participants and to enhance their learning and inter-action. If your training is learner centered, make sure you are not in the center of the room. Take the time to have the participants introduce them-selves meaningfully. Make the time to discuss the expectations, learning goals, and agenda for the day. You may also want to establish guidelines for effective interaction among the participants.

TAKE TIME TO PROCESS

The learning is not in the experience; it is in the reflection upon the expe-rience. Trainers always struggle to balance the time between covering the material and processing the learning. It is better to give the participants an experience where they learn two things well than to send them off with a vague sense of four or five things that they really don't know. Debriefing is the most important part of the activity, because during that phase of the interaction, the participants will make meaning for themselves individu-ally and collectively.

USE SMALL GROUPS

Small groups allow participants more time to talk and tell their stories. In a small group, there is a greater sense of intimacy and safety. Often, with appropriate guidelines, a small group can help an individual work out issues or will discretely de-escalate someone who has chosen to make distracting comments in the large group.

In many training situations, it serves the agenda to mix the participants and move them from group to group. However, diversity training requires a high degree of safety to be effective, so it is best to allow people to self-select their small groups. If you have specific and necessary criteria for the group, state it clearly: *I'd like you to form diverse groups of four or five people. Make sure there is an aide and an administrator in each group.* Or, *make sure there are at least two schools represented in each group.* Unless it is necessary for the activity, allow people to remain in their small groups. Give people a chance to move if they choose to—they may have selected a group that does not fit for them; otherwise, allow them to bond and build trust and a sense of safety within their small groups.

WORK IN TEAMS

Teamwork is great because you can model your value for diversity in style, knowledge, approach, gender, and ethnicity. With two people, you can better meet the diverse needs of the participants in your group. Moreover, with a partner, you always have someone to step in and augment, explain, or take over for you if you are having difficulty getting a point across or responding to a participant. Remember that both team members are always on. Good training partners are not solo partners who work in tandem. They both work together. One may be presenting the content while the other is focusing on the process at the other end of the room.

DEVELOP YOUR OWN STYLE

No matter how good your mentors and idols are, you cannot be them or be like them in style. Find your own voice and rhythm. This will enhance your credibility as a facilitator, because otherwise people will experience you as inauthentic. This does not mean you should not try new things. It simply means that you should take your temperament and gifts into consideration when planning what and how you will present information and facilitate activities.

BE PREPARED FOR TROUBLE

Something unexpected is always going to happen. Be prepared to be surprised, challenged, or sideswiped. To prepare is to know what you plan to do very well, as well as to have alternative activities ready just in case what you have selected is inappropriate or in case you need to take an important detour to process something that has happened with your group.

HAVE FUN

Don't be afraid to use your sense of humor. If you are not having a good time, then you can be pretty sure that the participants in your session are not enjoying themselves either. Diversity work is hard and healthy laughter helps to ease people through the process.

Resource A

Understanding Diversity

Activity	Expertise of Facilitator	Readiness of the Group	Time Needed
A1. **A Few Definitions**	Low	Beginning	30 minutes
A2. **Telling Your Stories**	Moderate	Beginning	30–60 minutes
A3. **Diversity in Your Life**	Low	Beginning	20 minutes
A4. **Stand Up**	Moderate	Beginning	20 minutes
A5. **Line Up**	Moderate	Intermediate	30 minutes
A6. **Demographics**	Moderate	Intermediate	2 weeks
A7. **Starpower**	Moderate	Beginning	2 hours

Activity A1: A Few Definitions

Purpose

To clarify terms related to cultural proficiency

Expertise of Facilitator

Low

Readiness of Group

Beginning

Time Needed

30 minutes

Materials

Response Sheet: A Few Definitions

Briefing

We are going to take a look at words commonly used when doing this work so that we are using the same vocabulary.

Process

1. Organize the participants into groups of three to five people.

2. Give each group one or two words to discuss.

3. Ask the participants to read the definitions for these commonly used and misused terms. Reflect on the definition, comparing it to how you use the term. Note whether the definition affirms, helps to clarify, or challenges your thinking.

4. Ask each group to share the highlights of their discussion.

Debriefing

1. What surprised you?

2. What continues to challenge you?

3. About what do you still have questions?

Response Sheet: A Few Definitions

Read the definitions for these commonly used and misused terms. Reflect on the definition, comparing it to how you use the term. Note whether the definition affirms, helps to clarify, or challenges your thinking.

Culture. Everything you believe and everything you do that identifies you as a member of a group and distinguishes you from other groups. You may belong to more than one cultural group. Cultures reflect the belief systems and behaviors that are informed by race and ethnicity, as well as other sociological factors like gender, age, sexual orientation, and physical ability. Both individuals and organizations are defined by their cultures.

Diversity and Inclusion. The presence of diversity indicates generally that many people with many differences are present in an organization or group. Diversity refers to socioeconomics, power, privilege, class, ethnicity, language, gender, age, ability, and sexual orientation and all other aspects of culture. Inclusion in an organizational setting means that the diverse groups are represented and included in all sectors of the organization and organizational life.

Cultural Proficiency. This is the most ideal point on the cultural competence continuum developed by Terry Cross (1989). It is the policies and practices of an organization, or the values and behaviors of an individual, that enable that organization or person to interact effectively with clients, colleagues, and the community using the essential elements of cultural competence: assessing culture, valuing diversity, managing the dynamics of difference, adapting to diversity, and institutionalizing cultural knowledge.

Politically Correct. This term describes language that reflects sensitivity to the diversity of a group, often without an understanding or caring about why such sensitivity is important. The intention of using such language is to stay out of trouble. Politically correct responses are usually insincere and do not reflect an understanding of or concern for why a group makes a particular request.

Tolerance. This begrudging acceptance of differences with which one disagrees or is unfamiliar is the first in a progression of steps that may lead to cultural proficiency. Teaching tolerance is a good way to get beyond genocide or cultural destructiveness.

Praxis. This integration of one's theory about a particular field with one's practice in that field involves critical reflection about why one does what one does and conscious application of what one believes to one's professional practice.

Equity. This is the outcome of practices that result in the same outcomes for members of a group. Equitable programs may make accommodations for differences so that the outcomes are the same for all individuals. For example, women and men may receive equitable, not equal, treatment in regard to parental benefits at work.

Equality. Equal treatment, or inputs, in the name of fairness involves treating all people alike without acknowledging differences in age, gender, language, or ability. Though considered by some to be fair, it is in fact culturally blind and often results in very unfair and unequal outcomes.

Activity A2: Telling Your Stories

Purpose

To help people understand the emotional price of cultural incompetence

Expertise of Facilitator

Moderate

Readiness of Group

Beginning

Time Needed

30–60 minutes

Materials

Response Sheet: Telling Your Stories
Chart paper
Markers

Briefing

We are going to give you a chance to reflect on times when you have experienced these social phenomena. Take a look at the worksheet we have distributed. Do you have any questions about the definitions of these words?

Process

1. Organize the participants into groups of three to five people.

2. Select one of the words and model for the group by briefly telling a story that illustrates your experience.

3. Ask each group to go through the list, allowing whoever has a story to tell one. The goal is to tell a story about each word. However, participants may repeat a word to tell their own particular story.

4. After each person has told at least one story, call the groups together.

5. Check that a story was told about each word. For example, ask, "Who heard a story about *alienation*?"

6. Go through the list and about each word ask, "What feelings did you hear in the story about *alienation*." Chart the words and encourage participants to write the words on their worksheets. Expect words like *anger, frustration, fear, sadness,* and *loneliness*.

7. Complete the "Emotional Content" column on the worksheet in this manner.

Debriefing

1. After all of the emotions have been charted, ask participants to comment on the patterns of the words in the second column. Most of the words are negative; a lot of anger and frustration are associated with each of the social phenomenon except multicultural affirmation and cultural transformation.

2. Ask participants to talk about situations when they have experienced these emotions from others. Emphasize that these emotions are the reasons that we work to become culturally proficient.

3. Send participants back to their small groups and identify situations in their work environment when impatience, microaggressions, cultural blindness, or cultural precompetence causes problems for the students, their families, or your colleagues.

4. Discuss how participants might anticipate, respond to, and prevent such situations.

Telling Your Stories

Social Experience	Your Experience	Emotional Content	Situations at Your Work Site
Alienation Out of place; not fitting in; not belonging to any group			
Dissonance, Discordant, Disharmony Feeling out of sync, offbeat, out of tune with your surroundings			
Marginality Identifying with two groups but not fitting in either; being rejected by both groups and relegated to the margins			
Dualism Being involved in two cultures and having to hide that fact from one of the cultural groups			
Negotiation for Acceptance Having to prove that one deserves to be in a particular role or environment			
Multicultural Affirmation Belonging to two or more cultural groups, with both groups knowing and appreciating that you are part of the other			
Cultural Transformation People from different cultures interacting with one another over time, with all changed for the better because of the experience			

Activity A3: Diversity in Your Life

Purpose

To demonstrate the nature of diversity in the lives of the participants

Expertise of Facilitator

Low

Readiness of Group

Beginning

Time Needed

30 minutes

Materials

Clear plastic cups
Large, multicolored assortment of beads or marbles

Briefing

We are going to use these beads to demonstrate how much diversity there is in your life.

Process

1. For each prompt, put a bead of the appropriate color in your cup, using this list of options:

   White = European American

   Black = African/Black American

   Yellow = Asian/Pacific Islander

   Brown = Latino/Hispanic

   Beige = Biracial

   Red = Native/First Nation American

   Purple = Gay, Lesbian, Bisexual, Transgendered

   Green = Physically or Mentally Disabled

   - I am . . .
   - My teachers are mostly . . .
   - My children's teachers are mostly . . .

- My closest friend is . . .
- My dentist is . . .
- My spouse/partner is . . .
- My colleagues at work are mostly . . .
- My doctor is . . .
- My neighbors are mostly . . .
- People who visit my home are mostly . . .
- People whose homes I visit are mostly . . .
- My favorite actor is . . .
- My favorite musicians are . . .
- Artwork represented in my home is . . .
- I see on TV mostly . . .
- Authors that I read are mostly . . .
- People whom I see or read about in my newspaper are mostly . . .

Debriefing

1. What does this say about you? About your community?

2. What do you see when you look at your cup?

3. How do you feel about what you see in your cup?

4. What do you see in other people's cups?

5. How do you feel about what you see in other people's cups?

6. Do you want your cup to look different?

7. If so, what do you need to do to get your cup to look different?

Activity A4: Stand Up[1]

Purpose

To raise awareness of the diverse experiences people in a group may have had

Expertise of Facilitator

Moderate

Readiness of Group

Beginning

Time Needed

20 minutes

Materials

None

Briefing

I am going to ask you a series of questions. If your answer is yes to any questions, please stand up.

Process

Participants sit in a circle with space for them to stand and look at one another. Ask each question slowly. After each question, invite participants to look around the room to see who is standing or sitting. Invite them to notice what they think, feel, or wonder as they look around the room.

1. If you have ever eaten Chinese food, stand up.

2. If you have a tattoo, stand up.

3. If you have ever eaten Greek food, stand up.

4. If you have ever worshipped with people who are not of your faith tradition, stand up.

---

[1]Thanks to Stephanie Graham of Los Angeles, California, for this activity.

5. If you have ever traveled out of the country, stand up.

6. If you have lived outside of this country as an adult, stand up.

7. If you have ever made food from a different culture, stand up.

8. If you know anyone from a different ethnic or racial group, stand up.

9. If you speak more than one language, stand up.

10. If you are married to someone of a different ethnicity, stand up.

11. If you have ever been in the home of someone of a different ethnic or racial group as a guest, stand up.

12. If you live in a neighborhood where there are people who are not of your racial or ethnic group, stand up.

13. If you have ever taken part in a demonstration, stand up.

14. If you have ever participated in a worship service other than your own, stand up.

15. If you have changed your religion, stand up.

16. If you are a feminist, stand up.

17. If you have ever visited a prison, stand up.

18. Add other items as inspired and appropriate . . .

Debriefing

1. What did you notice as you were sitting and standing?

2. What surprised you?

3. What conclusions can you draw from the answers of the group?

4. What questions do you have for group members?

5. What other questions might have been asked?

6. What patterns did you notice in the questions? (These are all experiences of diversity about which people have choice.)

7. What was the purpose of this activity?

Variations

Allow participants to ask the questions to which people will stand or sit.

Activity A5: Line Up[1]

Purpose

To raise awareness of the entitled and stigmatized groups participants belong to or identify with

Expertise of Facilitator

Moderate

Readiness of Group

Intermediate

Time Needed

30 minutes

Materials

Room for participants to stand abreast in one line and cross from one side of the room to the other, as in preparing for "Mother, May I?" or "Red Rover." Or participants may sit in a circle as you ask participants to stand as appropriate.

Briefing

Everyone line up in the A line. You may not talk with one another during this exercise. I am going to make some statements to you, and you will move to the B line or return to the A line based on your responses.

Process

Make each statement slowly and without inflection. Insist on silence from the participants. After each statement, invite participants to make eye contact with the people who are in the same line they are in and to look across the room to see who is standing facing them. Invite them to notice what they think, feel, or wonder as they look around the room.

1. If you are a woman, move to line B. If not, stay in the A line.

2. If you are shorter than 5'2", move to line B. If not, return to or stay in the A line.

---

[1]Thanks to Stephanie Graham of Los Angeles, California, for this activity.

3. If you or a family member is Gay or Lesbian, move to line B.

4. If you are a person of color, move to line B.

5. If you have an invisible physical handicap, move to line B.

6. If you consider yourself a klutz, move to line B.

7. If you are not athletic, move to line B.

8. If you are over 50, move to line B.

9. If you are under 25, move to line B.

10. If you or a family member has a mental illness, move to line B.

11. If you were born in another country, move to line B.

12. If you are not a U.S. citizen, move to line B.

13. If your parents were born in another country, move to line B.

14. If your parents are not U.S. citizens, move to line B.

15. If you are perceived as fat, move to line B.

16. If you are perceived as old, move to line B.

17. If you depend on public transportation, move to line B.

18. If you are not married, move to line B.

19. If you are a woman, over 45, and not married, move to line B.

20. If you were not born into a Christian home, move to line B.

21. If you were not born into a Protestant home, move to line B.

22. If you or a family member has ever been on welfare or public assistance, . . .

23. If you ever shopped at a thrift store because you had to, . . .

24. If you do not have children, . . .

25. If you are a single woman with children, . . .

26. If you live with your parents, in their home, . . .

27. If neither of your parents graduated from college, . . .

28. If only one of your parents graduated from college, . . .

29. If you have never received a reward for an academic achievement, . . .

30. If you do not have an earned graduate degree, . . .

31. If you did not graduate from college, . . .

32. If you do not own your own home, . . .

33. If you or a family member have been incarcerated, . . .

34. If you or a family member have been held involuntarily in a mental institution, . . .

35. If as an adult, you have ever been involuntarily unemployed, . . .

36. Add others as inspired and appropriate . . .

Debriefing

1. What did you notice as you were crossing the room?

2. What surprised you?

3. What made this activity difficult or easy?

4. What conclusions can you draw from the answers of the group?

5. Did you react to any of the questions?

6. What patterns did you notice in the questions? (These questions are about aspects of diversity that are stigmatized in society.)

7. How were the questions phrased to ensure the safety and privacy of the participants?

8. What was the purpose of this activity?

Activity A6: Demographics

Purpose

To identify the demographic makeup of a community

Skill of Facilitator

Moderate

Readiness of Group

Intermediate

Time Needed

Two weeks; this activity will take place outside of a formal training room.

Materials

A list of appropriate Web sites—for example, those of your city and county and those of your local and county school district offices

A description of the process for gaining access to the following:
- Newspaper files and resources
- Census bureau data
- District demographic data

Briefing

This process will familiarize you with the demographic makeup of your school's community.

Process

1. Divide the group into teams of three to four people.

2. As a large group, identify the major and minor ethnic groups represented in the district.

3. Brainstorm how to gather information about a particular group of people: ideas might include churches, cultural centers, libraries, newspaper libraries, and specific social and civic organizations. Encourage the group also to consider nonformal techniques used by anthropologists, such as observation, participant observation, and use of a cultural informant.

4. Let each team select a group about which it will gather demographic information.

5. Provide a list of minimally acceptable data: total population in city, total population in district, area of the city that is most densely populated with this group, socioeconomic status, languages spoken, and resources for teachers about this group of people.

6. Challenge each team to find the most useful and interesting information about its group.

7. Discuss ethnically appropriate protocol and etiquette so that team members are not viewed as culturally incompetent intruders by other ethnic groups.

8. Describe the format in which the information should be presented.

Debriefing

Ask each team to present its information to the group in a way that is interesting and entertaining. Remind them to be nonjudgmental and to be aware of unintentional stereotyping. As part of or after the presentation, ask each team to respond to these questions, as well as others from members of the large group:

1. What did you learn about yourself in the process?

2. Did you have any serendipitous adventures?

3. What was the greatest challenge of this activity?

4. What was the greatest surprise?

5. How will you use what you have learned?

Activity A7: StarPower

Purpose

StarPower helps participants

- understand that power must have a legitimate basis to be effective.
- see and feel the effect of disempowerment.
- realize that sharing power can increase it, while hoarding or abusing power can diminish it.
- understand the effect that systems can have on power.
- be aware of how tempting it is for well-intentioned people to abuse power.
- understand that there are different kinds of power.
- personally experience and discuss the excitement of power and the despair of powerlessness.

Expertise of Facilitator

Moderate

Readiness of Group

Beginning

Time Needed

At least two hours

Materials

A copy of the *StarPower* simulation, which is available from Simulation Training Systems in Del Mar, California; 800-942-2900; www.stsintl.com/business/star_power.html.

A simulation is a relatively simple activity that recreates some aspect of society in a safe and controlled setting. During a simulation, participants experience the intense feelings that they might experience over a longer period of time in real life without the fear or vulnerability that might occur in real time or in a real situation. *StarPower* is a simple game played by exchanging poker chips, resulting in the creation of a three-tiered "society" and the privileges, misunderstandings, and abuses of power that are found in hierarchical systems.

This is one of our favorite activities. We have used it in every environment in which we have served since 1970 with participants from high school students through executive managers. It is a simple and powerful activity. We recommend it highly for helping participants to look at how power is distributed and shared in the United States and Canada and how it is distributed, shared, and abused within their own organizations.

Resource B

Getting to Know Myself

Activity	Expertise of Facilitator	Readiness of Group	Time Needed
B1. **Journaling**	Low	Beginning	At least 10 minutes
B2. **Diversity Lifeline**	Moderate	Intermediate	90 minutes
B3. **Name Five Things**	Low	Beginning	30 minutes
B4. **Who Are You?**	Low	Beginning	30 minutes
B5. **Who Am I?**	Low	Beginning	45 minutes
B6. **Cultural Portrait**	Moderate	Intermediate	45–60 minutes
B7. **Personal Stereotypes I**	Extensive	Intermediate	30 minutes
B8. **Personal Stereotypes II**	Extensive	Intermediate	90 minutes
B9. **The Process of Personal Change**	Moderate	Intermediate	20 minutes
B10. **Seven Dynamics of Change**	Low	Beginning	20 minutes
B11. **Paradigms**	Moderate	Intermediate	60 minutes
B12. **Strength Bombardment**	Moderate	Beginning	60–90 minutes

Activity B1: Journaling

Purpose

To record your thoughts and feelings during a change process. During any change process, it is useful to record, in a systematic way, one's feelings and reactions. We have found journaling to be a welcome activity during intense, multiday training sessions.

Skill of Facilitator

Low

Readiness of Group

Beginning

Time Needed

Ten minutes

Materials

A blank book or a special notebook for journaling; the book should be small enough for easy carrying. Invite participants to bring their own journals if they are already journalers.

Briefing

You are going to be hearing and experiencing things over the next few days, weeks, or months that will affect you profoundly. We want you to honor those feelings by reflecting on the experience in writing. This will give you an opportunity each day to give 100 percent attention to yourself.

Process

Give participants these guidelines for their writing:

Each day of the training, make an entry in your journal. This is a time for you to reflect on what has happened during the day and to think about how you will make use of the experience. You may want to organize your entry as follows:

- What happened today? Specify activities, exercises, or insights that stimulated new ways of thinking—"aha's."

- How do you feel about what happened? Based on what you say at first, what are your feelings about it? Was it a disturbing, energizing, positive, or negative experience?
- What are you going to do? Based on what you said happened and how you feel about it, what actions are you going to take? Consider both the short and the long term—tomorrow, in a few weeks, and several months from now—in your work environment.

Debriefing

1. At the beginning of each time the group meets, ask participants to share something (not everything) from their journal entries with one other person. They may choose a different person each time.

2. How did you feel about being given time to journal?

3. How many have journaled before?

4. Have you ever kept a journal on a work-related process?

5. What was it like to share portions of your writing?

6. In what other setting might journaling be useful?

Variations

1. Encourage people to journal but do not require that they share their thoughts with anyone.

2. Allow time at the end of each session for journaling.

Activity B2: Diversity Lifeline

Purpose

- To have participants analyze and share the significant events in their lives that have affected their perception of diversity
- To aid participants in understanding that diversity is a dynamic that has been and will be ever present in their lives

Skill of Facilitator

Moderate

Readiness of Group

Intermediate

Time Needed

90 minutes

Materials

Chart paper for each participant

Markers for each participant

Masking tape

Tables or floor space for participants to draw their lifelines

Enough wall space for all participants to hang their lifelines and discuss them in small groups

Briefing

Think about your life: How have you been affected by your diversity? When did you become aware of the diversity around you? On the chart paper, draw a graph of your life marking the significant points that reflect your awareness of diversity.

Process

1. Distribute markers and chart paper to each person.

2. Organize the participants into groups of two or three people. Encourage the participants to diversify their small groups. It is

important to keep the groups small so that each person can share extensively. It is also important that people in the small groups are comfortable with each other.

3. Allow about 20 minutes for participants to draw and post their lifelines.

4. Allow about 15 minutes per person to describe his or her lifeline.

5. Reorganize the small groups into one large group, allowing time for participants to view all of the lifelines.

Debriefing

1. What did you feel, think, or wonder as you started the assignment?

2. What did you notice about yourself as you drew?

3. What did you learn about yourself from this process?

4. What did you notice about your group members as they spoke or listened to the other members in the group?

5. What did you learn about your group members?

6. What did you learn about diversity?

7. How will you use what you have learned?

Variations

1. Use the lifeline process to have participants tell their stories without emphasizing any particular aspect of their lives.

2. Cover the wall with chart paper. As a group, draw a lifeline for the organization.

3. Allow participants to draw their personal lines to indicate where their lives intersect with the life of the school.

Activity B3: Name Five Things

Purpose

To help participants clarify how they define themselves. This activity will also demonstrate the effects of cultural blindness.

Expertise of Facilitator

Low

Readiness of Group

Beginning

Time Needed

30 minutes

Materials

Blank paper

Briefing

Think about who you are and how you describe yourself.

Process

1. Write five words or short phrases that describe the essence of who you are. These should be things that if they were taken away from you, you would not be the same person (5 minutes).

2. With a partner, share your list (15 minutes).

3. Now cross two items off of your list so that only the purest essence of who you are will be listed.

4. Participants may try to cooperate, but they will definitely struggle.

The point of this activity is to help you to see that when you seek to engage with only one aspect of someone, you are asking them to erase or deny the essence of who they are. It may be more difficult and take more time in a diverse environment, but if you don't engage fully, you won't be experiencing all of who each person is.

Debriefing

1. What did you notice as you wrote your list?

2. What did you notice as you shared your list?

3. What did it feel like to have to cross items off of your list?

4. What did you learn about your colleagues?

5. What did you learn about yourself?

6. What conclusions can you draw about the members of this group?

Variation

After the participants have written their lists, ask them to cross off one item, then another, until only two are left.

Discuss how it felt to cross off the items.

Consider not allowing the participants to share what was crossed off of their lists. This will demonstrate for them what it feels like to be in a group where they are only allowed to show a portion of themselves.

Activity B4: Who Are You?

Purpose

To help participants clarify how they define themselves. This activity is an effective follow-up to Name Five Things.

Expertise of Facilitator

Low

Readiness of Group

Beginning

Time Needed

30 minutes

Materials

Blank paper

Briefing

I am going to ask you 10 questions. Without talking, please write your answers.

Process

Read the questions slowly and solemnly. Do not respond to any comments the participants make. Do not allow them to speak to one another.

Question #1: Who are you?

Question #2: Who are you?

Question #3: Who are you?

Question #4: Who are you?

Question #5: Who are you?

Question #6: Who are you?

Question #7: Who are you?

Question #8: Who are you—really?

Question #9: Who are you?

Question #10: Who are you?

Debriefing

1. What did you notice as you wrote your list?

2. What did you learn about yourself?

3. Why do you think we did this exercise?

Variation

Ask participants to prioritize the items on their lists and share them.

Activity B5: Who Am I?

Purpose

To serve as a get-acquainted activity and to understand how others name themselves

Expertise of Facilitator

Low

Readiness of Group

Beginning

Time Needed

45 minutes

Materials

Chart paper

Markers

Paper and pencils for participants

Briefing

This activity will give you a chance to hear how others in your group define themselves and understand the relative importance of culture and ethnicity.

Process

As a group, develop a list of adjectives that describe the roles and groups with which the people in the group identify. Complete the sentence stem: "I am a(n) . . . ." For example, "I am a(n) . . .

- woman.
- educator.
- college graduate.
- teacher.
- administrator.

- European American.
- Hispanic American.
- Asian Pacific Islander.
- African American.
- husband.
- significant other.
- partner.
- Gay Man.
- Lesbian.
- daughter.
- brother.

Everyone takes the list of descriptors and ranks them individually according to how they define themselves, omitting words that do not apply.

Debriefing

1. What criteria did you use to rank the descriptors?

2. What surprised you about your list?

3. What surprised you about the list of the other members in your small group?

4. What have you learned about the members of this group?

5. What have you learned about labels, descriptors, and naming oneself?

6. How will you use this information?

Activity B6: Cultural Portrait

Purpose

To describe graphically one's cultural identity. This activity is a creative way for participants to consider the many cultural groups to which they belong and to see how many cultures are represented in the group.

Expertise of Facilitator

Moderate

Readiness of Group

Intermediate

Time Needed

45–60 minutes

Materials

Two or three markers for each person

One piece of chart paper for each person

Briefing

Each of us belongs to a number of cultural groups. These groups reflect our ethnicity, occupational and vocational cultures, and social groups that shape or reflect our values. Membership in a group is determined by how you identify with the group members, as well as how those group members perceive you. On the paper you have been given, depict the cultural groups with which you identify. *If you can,* show the relative importance and influence of each group by the size and placement of the icons you choose. You may use thinking maps, Venn diagrams, pictures, words—whatever is comfortable for you.

Process

1. Encourage each person to create a diagram that reflects the complexity of his or her cultural identity.

2. Have each person post his or her drawing on the wall.

3. Let members mill around the room, examining and discussing the drawings.

4. Have each person explain his or her drawing to the entire group or to a smaller group.

Debriefing

1. How did it feel to draw a diagram of your culture?

2. How well did you represent yourself?

3. What have you learned about your colleagues?

4. What did you learn about culture?

5. How can you apply this knowledge?

6. Given the diversity represented by the drawings in the room, how can you explain your ability to get along with one another?

7. How can you use this information in the work you are doing?

Activity B7: Personal Stereotypes I

Purpose

To identify the stereotypes associated with different kinds of people and to examine how stereotyping affects communication and self-esteem

Expertise of Facilitator

Extensive

Readiness of Group

Intermediate

Time Needed

30 minutes

Materials

Several large sticky notes for each person

Briefing

This activity will help you see how everyone is confronted with stereotypes.

Process

1. Ask each person to make of a list of the sociocultural groups to which they belong and with which they associate painful stereotypes.

2. On one sticky note, each person writes the name of one group—for example, "fat people"—and places it on his or her chest.

3. On another sticky, each person writes stereotypic comments associated with that group. For example, if on one sticky, "fat people" was written, the other sticky might have "stupid, lazy, and unhealthy."

4. Ask participants to walk *silently* around the room, reading the labels that have been written.

5. After everyone in the group has had a chance to read all the labels, ask them to organize themselves into small groups, based upon

what they have written on their labels. For example, if only one person wrote "fat people" but several wrote labels that were related to body size—"too thin," "skinny legs," "big butt"—they can sit together in a group.

6. Ask the participants to discuss their labels and the stereotypes associated with each of them.

Debriefing

1. How did you feel writing and wearing the stereotypic comments?

2. What was it like to talk to others who suffer from the same or similar stereotypes?

3. How did you feel reading the stereotypes of others?

4. How do stereotypes impede healthy human relations?

5. How do they affect self-esteem?

6. How are stereotypes helpful?

7. What was the most important thing you learned from this exercise?

8. How will you use the information?

Variations

Rather than wearing the sticky notes, participants sit in a semicircle. Ask each person to come to the front of the room and to state the sociocultural group and then the stereotypes associated with it. Move through the semicircle quickly and without comment until everyone has spoken. Then discuss the process, the feelings, and what was learned.

Activity B8: Personal Stereotypes II

Purpose

To identify the stereotypes associated with different racial/ethnic groups

Expertise of Facilitator

Extensive

Readiness of Group

Intermediate

Time Needed

90 minutes

Briefing

We are going to explore the stereotypes associated with the various ethnic groups to which we belong.

Process

1. Ask group members to sit with the people with whom they have the strongest ethnic identity. Trust the group to sort itself out. People may be uncomfortable at first, but if you give them time and no options, they will form appropriate groups. Be open to having a group that is comprised of people who are biracial or of mixed race heritage. Do *not* label the groups yourself; allow each group to label itself. You may also have a few people who choose not to be in a group; allow them to name themselves as "groups" of one and insist that they go through the same process as the other groups.

2. In the groups, ask members to make a list of the common stereotypes held about their group.

3. Then ask group members to discuss the truth that has been overgeneralized to create that stereotype and what they want others not in their group to know about the stereotype.

4. Ask group members to identify additional information that they want others to know about their group.

5. Ask small groups to share with the larger group the essence of their discussions and the information they wish to teach or that they feel is important for the other groups to hear.

Debriefing

1. How did you feel when you articulated the stereotypes about your group?

2. What was your response to the explanations of the stereotypes you heard?

3. Are there other stereotypes about which you have questions?

4. How do stereotypes impede healthy human relations?

5. How are stereotypes helpful?

6. What was the most important thing you learned from this exercise?

7. How will you use the information?

Variation

Separate participants by role—for example, classroom teachers, resource teachers, school administrators, district administrators; parents, teachers, students; or students, teachers, administrators—and conduct the activity.

Have groups creatively present their "findings."

Activity B9: The Process of Personal Change

Purpose

To raise awareness of how change takes place

Skill of Facilitator

Moderate

Readiness of Group

Intermediate

Time Needed

20 minutes

Materials

Copies of Response Sheet: The Process of Personal Change

Briefing

We have been talking about making change, and you are probably wondering why other people have not changed yet. Let's look at the process for personal change.

Process

1. Distribute Response Sheet.

2. Ask participants what they think of it.

3. Discuss the various points on the Response Sheet and the movement from one to another.

4. Elicit examples from the participants of personal changes they have experienced.

5. Discuss what the process would be for someone moving toward cultural proficiency.

6. Discuss the implications for the school's or district's learning process.

Debriefing

1. What did you learn or remember from this process?

2. How does this process differ from how children learn?

3. What are the differences between learning something as an adult and learning something as a child?

4. How should we adapt our expectations to one another as we grow?

5. How should we adapt our expectations for our district/school as we implement the cultural proficiency model?

Variation

Have participants write their personal examples on the Response Sheet as they analyze a specific change process situation they went through.

The Process of Personal Change

Unconscious Competence

Reinforcement

Practice

Change to Value Set B

Conscious Competence

Practice

Reinforcement

Feedback

Behavior Change

Conscious Incompetence

Attitudinal Shift

Awareness

Unconscious Incompetence

Inappropriate Behavior

Value Set A

Activity B10: Seven Dynamics of Change

Purpose

To help participants become aware of the normal responses to change

Skill of Facilitator

Low

Readiness of Participants

Beginning

Time Needed

20 minutes

Materials

Room for participants to stand and to pair off with a partner

Response Sheet: Seven Dynamics of Change

Briefing

We're going to see how well you and your partner pay attention to your environment. (This statement is intentionally ambiguous.)

Process

1. Have participants face their partners. Invite them to take a long, loving look at their partner and then turn around with their backs to one another.

2. Now ask each person to change five things about themselves. They will have many questions—don't answer them. Simply encourage them to quietly change five things. When both partners are ready, have them turn back around to face each other.

3. Ask the partners to notice what has been changed, sharing their observations with their partners. After they do that, tell the entire group to turn their backs to their partners and to change five more things.

4. They will grumble and complain. Ignore it. Encourage them to move more quickly and ask them to please just cooperate and to trust you.

5. When they are facing their partners once again, ask them to notice what has been changed. There will be much laughter and noise.

6. Quiet them down. Acknowledge how well they are cooperating. Ask them to now change 10 more things (or 15 or 20, whatever is plausible but at the same time a number that will be perceived as outrageous). The group will fall apart. Ask them to sit down.

7. Debrief the activity using the Seven Dynamics of Change Response Sheet.

8. Relate the dynamics of change to the changes the participants are experiencing in their lives, work, or organization.

Debriefing

Ask the group: How did you feel when you first heard the request to change things?

Reinforce this point: When changes are made in a relationship or in an organization,

1. people will feel awkward, uncomfortable, and ill at ease.

   Ask the group: What was the first thing that you did?

   Probable response: Remove something.

Reinforce this point: When changes are made in a relationship or in an organization,

2. people will think first about what they are going to lose.

   Ask the group: Did you feel embarrassed?

   Probable response: Yes.

   Ask the group: Did you notice what other people were doing?

   Probable response: Probably not.

Reinforce this point: When changes are made in a relationship or in an organization,

3. people will feel alone, even though everyone is going through the same thing.

   What did you think when I asked you to change 10 (or 15 or 20) more things?

Reinforce this point: When changes are made in a relationship or in an organization,

4. people can only handle so much.

   Ask the group: How many of you actually changed five things the first time and five more the second time?

   Probable response: Not everyone. Some people probably did not participate at all.

Reinforce this point: When changes are made in a relationship or in an organization,

5. people are at different levels of readiness for change.

   Ask the group: What were you thinking when I suggested you change even more things?

Reinforce this point: When changes are made in a relationship or in an organization,

6. people tend to be concerned that they will not have enough resources.

   Ask the group: What was the first thing you did when I invited you to sit down?

   Probable response: Put my clothes back on.

Reinforce this point: When changes are made in a relationship or in an organization,

7. then when the pressure is off, people revert back to old behavior.

Response Sheet: Seven Dynamics of Change

When changes are made in a relationship or in an organization,

1. people will feel awkward, uncomfortable, and ill at ease.

2. people will think first about what they are going to lose.

3. people will feel alone, even though everyone is going through the same thing.

4. people can only handle so much.

5. people are at different levels of readiness for change.

6. people tend to be concerned that they will not have enough resources.

7. then when the pressure is off, people revert back to old behavior.

Activity B11: Paradigms

Purpose

To develop common language and a new perspective for viewing the change process

Skill of Facilitator

Moderate

Readiness of Group

Intermediate

Time Needed

60 minutes

Materials

Copies of Response Sheet: Assessing Your Paradigms

Chart paper

Markers

Briefing

A paradigm is a set of rules or criteria that we use to judge the appropriateness or correctness of something. Let's talk about some of the paradigms in your life. (Refer to the discussion of paradigms in Chapter 5.) Now we will discuss the paradigms that affect the work we are doing in our school.

Process

Distribute Response Sheet: Assessing Your Paradigms. Assign the questions to small groups. Each group can answer one question, or, if you have time, each group can answer all seven questions.

1. What paradigms do you want to keep at our school [in our district]?

2. What paradigms do you want to reject?

3. What paradigms are changing or shifting?

4. What paradigms have been challenged unsuccessfully?

5. What new paradigms do you predict will develop in the next few years?

6. What is impossible today but, if it could be done, would fundamentally change the way we address issues of diversity?

7. What are the implications of the answers to these questions for your school?

As the groups present their responses, allow time for discussion, questions, and additions to each group's list by the other members in the class.

Debriefing

Discuss the answers to the questions.

Variation

Show the video by Joel Barker titled *The New Business of Paradigms* (available online at www.starthrower.com/barker.html). Discuss the film and then answer the paradigm questions.

We highly recommend this activity. The Joel Barker paradigm films are excellent.

Response Sheet: Assessing Your Paradigms

Think about the values, habits, processes, and policies that direct your activities at work. These are the paradigms. As you prepare for changes in your life or your organization, ask yourself these questions:

1. What paradigms do you want to keep?

2. What paradigms do you want to reject?

3. What paradigms are changing or shifting?

4. What paradigms have been challenged unsuccessfully?

5. What new paradigms do you predict for the organization?

6. What is impossible today but, if it could be done, would fundamentally change the way you live?

7. What are the implications for the answers to your questions?

Activity B12: Strength Bombardment

Purpose

To build a sense of team among participants through sharing personal stories and discovering similarities and differences. This is a good activity for team building. We have had success with it as an opening activity with a group whose members know one another well. We also have had success with it as a culminating activity for groups that have been working together on a project. This activity provides for a personal focus, allows for individual expression, and uses positive feedback as a communication tool.

Skill of Facilitator

Moderate

Readiness of Group

Beginning

Time Needed

60–90 minutes, depending on the size of the subgroups

Materials

Small adhesive labels, preferably colored circles about the size of a quarter; if large colored dots are not available, get labels that are large enough for writing one word. Each participant should have about 20–50 labels, depending on the size of the small group.

Briefing

In your small groups, you will be sharing stories about important aspects of your life.

Process

1. Distribute a plain sheet of 8 × 11½ inch paper to each participant.

2. Ask participants to write their names in the middle of the page.

3. Ask participants to turn the paper over. Divide your life into 10- or 15-year increments. For each of these periods, identify things that you have done that you are proud of. This does not necessarily

mean achievements from the perspective of society but accomplishments as you define them. Participants can make notes on the page.

4. Organize participants into groups of three to six participants. A group of three people will need about 30 minutes. Add 10 minutes of processing time for each additional member of the group.

5. In the small group, each person will take five minutes to share his or her accomplishments. The person is not to be interrupted during the telling of the story.

6. While the first person is telling his or her story, other group members are writing one-word adjectives on the labels that describe their assessment of his or her character in light of the accomplishments. In five minutes, each group member will write on several of the labels.

7. When the first person has completed his or her story, during which time colleagues have been recording their adjectives on the labels, he or she listens to the feedback from colleagues.

8. In turn, each colleague looks the storyteller in the eye and tells him or her what is written on each dot and alternately affixes it to the reverse side of the speaker's strength bombardment sheet. For example, "Mary, I see you as courageous because you stood up to your brother." In just a few minutes, Mary has many labels on her sheet that describe her character.

9. Repeat the process for each participant.

Debriefing

Ask the following questions:

1. What did you think, feel, or wonder while assessing your life?

2. What did you think, feel, or wonder while telling your story?

3. What was your reaction to the feedback you received in the two forms of communication: the verbal message with direct eye contact from your colleagues and the label dots affixed to the reverse side of your sheet?

4. (It never varies with this activity that someone will minimize the feedback from his or her colleagues. Some will indicate that their colleagues were generous. If this should occur, remind them that it was that person's story; the colleagues were only feeding back to that person what they were hearing.)

5. Let participants know that, yes, life is not always expressed in terms of positive feedback, but it sure does feel good when it occurs. Then continue with the following questions.

6. What did you think, feel, or wonder as you heard the stories of your group members?

7. What implications does this have for our work with students? With parents? With one another?

8. Invite participants to keep this sheet in a safe place so that someday in the future, they can pull it out and remind themselves of what people had to say to them on this day.

Resource C

Getting to Know Your Colleagues and Your Organization

Activity	Expertise of Facilitator	Readiness of Group	Time Needed
C1. **Introductory Grid**	Moderate	Intermediate	10–20 minutes
C2. **Cultural Perceptions**	Moderate	Beginning	20 minutes
C3. **What's Your Name**	Moderate	Beginning	20 minutes
C4. **Totems or Crests**	Low	Beginning	30 minutes
C5. **Family Portrait**	Moderate	Intermediate	60+ minutes
C6. **Group Stereotypes**	Extensive	Advanced	60 minutes
C7. **Circle of History**	Moderate	Beginning	1–3 hours
C8. **Storytelling**	Low	Beginning	60 minutes
C9. **Voices That Resonate**	Moderate	Beginning	15 minutes
C10. **Human Relations Needs Assessment**	Extensive	Beginning	3+ hours

Activity C1: Introductory Grid

Purpose

To help people get acquainted with each other. This is a very good "sponge" activity that orients participants to the differences and similarities of the other people in the room. As an opener or closer, a sponge activity soaks up extra people and extra time. People do not have to start at the same time to benefit from the activity.

Expertise of Facilitator

Moderate

Readiness of Group

Intermediate

Time Needed

Because this is a sponge activity to be used at the beginning of a session, 10–20 minutes for the activity and the debriefing is sufficient.

Materials

Chart paper on walls of room

Markers for participants

Masking tape

Briefing

As participants come in, ask them to fill in the blanks on the chart paper.

Process

1. Place a category at the top of each chart paper:
   a. Name
   b. City of birth
   c. Astrological sign
   d. City of residence
   e. Favorite restaurant or type of food
   f. Hobby or leisure activity
   g. Expectation for the session
   h. Other creative categories that will get people thinking and talking

2. Number the lines of Chart A with the number of participants.

3. Participants select a number on Chart A and then complete each chart using the same number so that their answers can be identified.

Debriefing

1. What do we have in common?

2. What are some differences we have?

3. What conclusions can you draw from the answers on the charts?

4. What questions do you have for group members?

Variation 1

Have members stand and introduce themselves by adding to the information on the charts, such as where they work and why they are in the program.

Variation 2

Divide the participants into random groups of four or five people. Have each group list the following:

a. What everyone in the group has in common

b. Something unique about each member

c. What they hope to achieve by the end of the program

d. A name for the group

Each small group makes a brief presentation to the larger group.

Variation 3

Add to the last page of the grid the category "Significant Family Value." Discuss the differences and similarities of family values and how, even when all the values appear to be positive and laudatory in a common workplace, those values may conflict with one another or cause conflicts within the individual. For example, the values for honesty and courtesy often conflict, because sometimes it is impossible to be honest and not hurt someone's feelings, which is considered discourteous.

Activity C2: Cultural Perceptions

Purpose

To be used as an opening warm-up activity, as a way to test assumptions, and to introduce the concept of stereotyping

Expertise of Facilitator

Moderate

Readiness of Group

Beginning

Time Needed

20 minutes

Materials

Copies of Response Sheet: Cultural Perceptions

Briefing

This activity will test your intuition and perceptions.

Process

1. Have participants select as a partner someone they don't know well or would like to get to know better.

2. Using Response Sheet: Cultural Perceptions, have the first partner share his or her perceptions of how the second partner would respond to each of the stems.

3. After the first partner shares his or her perceptions, the second partner gives his or her responses.

4. Switch roles and repeat the process.

Debriefing

1. Reassemble the group and ask for volunteers to share their experiences in learning about another person.

2. Which assumptions were accurate? Which were not accurate?

3. Ask how it felt to have the responsibility for making the perceptions, how it felt to be on the receiving end of the perceptions, and what insight this experience gives to the process of stereotyping.

4. Ask how this experience informs us about the stereotyping that may occur when we face new teachers, aides, students, and parents.

5. How are stereotypes helpful? How are they harmful?

6. If the school is large, how are these perceptions enacted with people we rarely see?

7. What was the most important thing you learned from this experience?

8. How will you use this information?

Response Sheet: Cultural Perceptions

Select for your partner someone whom you don't know well or would like to know better. Use the list below to share your perceptions. Ask your partner to give you his or her responses. Then switch roles and have your partner share his or her perceptions with you.

- Country of family origin and heritage

- Languages spoken

- Interests or hobbies

- Favorite foods

- Type of movies and TV programs preferred, if any

- Type of music preferred

- Pets, if any, or favorite animals

Activity C3: What's Your Name?

Purpose

To be used as an opening warm-up activity as a way to test assumptions

Expertise of Facilitator

Moderate

Readiness of Group

Beginning

Time Needed

20 minutes

Materials

Copies of Response Sheet: What's Your Name?

Briefing

This activity will give you a chance to get to know something new about your colleagues.

Process

Ask participants to sit in pairs (or small groups if you have the time) and share their responses to the questions in the response sheet.

Debriefing

1. What did you learn about yourself in the process of telling your story?

2. What did you learn about your colleagues as you listened to their stories?

3. Why is it important to acknowledge someone's name?

4. What stories do you think your clients would tell about how their names are used (or not) in this school?

5. What customer service standards might you set relating to the names of the students, their families, and others who visit this school?

Variation

Tell a story about your name.

Response Sheet: What's Your Name?

1. What is your name?

2. Have you had any other names?

3. What is the story of how you acquired your name?

4. What does your name mean?

5. How does your name reflect your culture?

6. How do people respond when they see or hear your name for the first time?

7. If you changed your name, what would it be?

Activity C4: Totems or Crests

Purpose

To help members of the group get to know one another in terms of cultural similarities and differences

Expertise of Facilitator

Low

Readiness of Group

Beginning

Time Needed

30 minutes

Materials

Blank paper (8 × 11½ inch or larger)

Masking tape

Colored markers

Briefing

We are going to engage in an activity so that you can get to know one another better and understand the diversity of your backgrounds.

Process

Talk about the use of culturally specific icons like totems or family crests. Indicate that these items are being adapted for this activity.

Distribute blank sheets. Allow participants to select the form they wish to use.

Ask participants to draw symbols on their papers to represent the following:

a. The group with which they most strongly identify

b. How they are like the members of that group

c. How they do not fit a stereotype of that group

d. An event when they felt very different

e. A person who has most influenced them in understanding or accepting diversity

Have each participant tape his paper to his chest and walk around the room, looking at the drawings of the other participants and asking questions as appropriate.

Debriefing

1. What did you see that surprised you?

2. What did you learn about your colleagues?

3. What did you learn about yourself?

4. What conclusions can we draw about the members of this group?

Variation

Change the theme from getting to know you to diversity or some other topic by changing the symbols you ask participants to draw. Symbols might represent the following:

1. Where they were born

2. A strong family value

3. Their present occupation

4. A dream or fantasy

5. A personal goal for this program

Activity C5: Family Portrait[1]

Purpose

To learn about participants' backgrounds and experiences while highlighting the unsuspected links among various participants

Skill of the Facilitator

Moderate

Readiness of the Group

Intermediate

Time Needed

10 minutes for explanation of activity plus 5–10 minutes per Family Portrait. The activity can be spread over several sessions.

Materials Needed

None

Briefing

This activity will provide you the opportunity to present yourself, your culture, and your history to colleagues in a novel manner. Constructing your Family Portrait with the assistance of colleagues provides for heightened mutual understanding. Likewise, as a participant, you have the opportunity to be a participant-observer in your colleagues' Family Portraits.

Process

1. Each participant has 5 to 10 minutes to present his or her Family Portrait.

2. The presenter chooses one or more person(s) from the group to represent each member of her family. The presenter decides which family members are in the "portrait."

---

1. Submitted by Jenni Taylor, Assistant Principal, and Mandy Breuer, Director of Student Services, Lawndale Charter High School, Lawndale, California.

3. The presenter invites each group member to the front of the room and introduces each "family member," using his name, his relationship, his story, and why this group member has been chosen to represent the family member.

4. The presenter may pose the members in the portrait or seat them in ways that demonstrate their interrelationships.

Debriefing

1. What did you learn about the presenter?

2. What surprised you about the presenter's background?

3. What assumptions did you have about the presenter that were supported by this activity? What assumptions were not supported?

4. What links are you discovering among those who have presented their Family Portraits?

5. What information have you learned that will help you work better with this person in the future?

Activity C6: Group Stereotypes

Purpose

To identify the stereotypes associated with different groups of people, to examine how stereotyping impacts one's perceptions of others, and to recognize how often negative stereotypes are applied to every cultural group

Skill of Facilitator

Extensive

Readiness of Group

Advanced

Time Needed

60 minutes

Materials

Several pieces of chart paper

Large sticky notes, about 20 for each participant

Briefing

This activity will help you to see how we stereotype other people.

Process

1. Label each piece of chart paper with one of these group categories: white women, white men, black women, black men, Hispanic women, Hispanic men, Gay Men, Lesbians, etc.

2. Hang the charts around the room.

3. Give each participant a small stack of large sticky notes.

4. Ask participants to write labels and stereotypes they have heard used about each group.

5. Silently have the participants affix the sticky notes to the appropriate chart.

6. Mill around and read what has been written.

Debriefing

1. How did you feel writing the stereotypes?

2. What did you think as you read what was written?

3. How did you feel as you read what was written?

4. What is your reaction to all these labels around the room?

5. What are the implications of this activity?

6. How will you use the information?

Variation

Instead of ethnic stereotypes, use the various roles in the school and district—for example, teacher, administrator, support staff, gifted student, average student, etc.

Activity C7: Circle of History

Purpose

To share the collective history of a group or an organization with all of its members. This activity will help participants to understand how far they have come or how certain norms and traditions in the organization were established. During this activity, more mature participants and skilled facilitators will also identify the cultural expectations of the group.

Expertise of Facilitator

Moderate

Readiness of Group

Beginning

Time Needed

1–3 hours, depending on the age of the organization and the number of participants

Materials

A room large enough for all participants to sit in one circle or a large horseshoe.

Four or five chairs in the middle of the circle or at the open end of the horseshoe.

Briefing

You are going to share the history of this group by telling your stories. Each person in turn will talk about the organization from the perspective of "when and where I entered."

Process

1. Ask participants to sit in the circle according to when each became a member of the group or organization. For most people, this will be the year they were hired. For volunteers or parents, it will be the date they first had an encounter with the school or district.

2. Notice any patterns as you look down the line. In some groups, for example, the people who have been there the longest will be white males, while those who have been in the organization the least

amount of time will be women or emerging majorities. Encourage the participants to articulate any other patterns they may observe.

3. Starting with those people who have been in the organization the longest, invite them to take the chairs in the middle of the circle or at the end of the horseshoe.

4. Ask participants to talk about the organization and tell what it was like when they joined, how they learned about it or decided to become a part of it, who was there, what the rules were, and other information. As the story progresses, new participants will take the seats in the center, and those who have spoken will sit in the circle.

5. If someone entered the organization, left, and then returned, he or she may take a speaker's seat a second time, when his or her story once again becomes part of the chronology.

6. If necessary, prompt the speakers so that they provide necessary details or redirect the speakers if they get off track or get more engrossed in their personal stories rather than in the organization's story.

Debriefing

1. What did you notice?

2. What surprised you?

3. What did you learn? About yourself? About others? About your organization?

4. What do you understand now that was puzzling before?

5. What shall we do now that we all know our collective history?

Variation 1

You may want to videotape this session.

Variation 2

1. Affix chart paper to the walls of a room.

2. Segment the charts into increments of time—years or decades as appropriate.

3. Provide markers, sticky notes, labels, and other materials and ask the participants to fill in the time line, noting the major events in the life of the organization.

Activity C8: Storytelling

Purpose

To demonstrate the power of storytelling, to get acquainted with each other, and to gain some insight into participants' leadership styles

Expertise of Facilitator

Low

Readiness of Group

Beginning

Time Needed

60 minutes

Materials

None

Briefing

This activity will give you a chance to get to know your colleagues in a deeper way.

Process

1. Divide the group into pairs, asking people to partner with the person whom they know least well.

2. Have each team member tell a story about himself or herself that reveals something about his or her personality or lifestyle that the partner may not know.

3. Have the pairs join with two other sets of partners so that they are in groups of six.

4. Have each person share his or her partner's story with the small group.

5. Have one member of the group synthesize the stories for the entire group.

Debriefing

1. What did you learn about yourself? Your partner? The other people in your group?

2. What conclusions can you draw about the members of your group?

3. What differences did you notice between the different groups?

4. What do the groups have in common?

5. How can you use this information in the work you will be doing?

Variation 1

Tell the story of when you

- became aware of your culture.
- first felt a need to serve the community.
- became an activist, pacifist, or something similar.
- decided to change your career.
- knew you were a leader.
- knew you didn't want to be a leader.

Variation 2

Think of a time when you did something that was hard for you and you were very proud of your accomplishment. This may be something that no one else knows about or that is easy for most people to do. Think of a time when you overcame a personal barrier. Prepare to tell this story to a member of your group.

Activity C9: Voices That Resonate

Purpose

To provide participants an opportunity to reflect on a meaningful professional development activity

Skill of Facilitator

Moderate

Readiness of Group

Beginning

Time Needed

15 minutes

Materials Needed

None

Briefing

This culminating activity provides for public reflection about a meaningful professional development experience. The activity is particularly powerful if the group has been together for several hours or days.

Process

1. Ask each participant to think of a comment spoken by another person during the professional development experience that was particularly meaningful.

2. Ask for a full minute of silent reflection.

3. Let participants know that they will have the opportunity to share publicly the meaningful comment but not to identify the speaker.

4. Invite participants to rise, if appropriate, in "popcorn fashion" (that is, one person responds and is reseated, followed by another person, and so forth). Provide for those who choose not to rise or for whom rising is challenging to raise their hands or otherwise indicate that they are speaking.

5. Be patient and let the activity runs its course. Don't be concerned about moments of silence.

6. When you think all who care to speak have done so, say something like, *I don't want to close the activity prematurely, but if someone wants to share their quote, please do so.* We find that a few more people will take the opportunity to share their quote.

7. Express your gratitude to everyone.

Debriefing

None

Activity C10: Needs Assessment

Purpose

The Needs Assessment Instrument surveys a respondent's opinion about cultural relations in a school or district

Expertise of Facilitator

Extensive

Readiness of Group

Beginning

Time Needed

At least three hours

Process

Arrange the items in random sequence for administration. For analysis purposes, organize the items according to the five essential elements of cultural proficiency: assessment of cultural knowledge, value for diversity, ability to manage the dynamics of difference, adaptability to diversity, and ability to institutionalize cultural knowledge.

The instrument can be used at least two ways. First, it can be administered to a group as a preintervention guide. Second, it can be used to contrast the opinions among groups—for example, educators, students, parents, and businesspeople in your community. However you choose to use the instrument, it should never be used as a diagnostic instrument but only to collect information to guide a school's planning.

We have used this instrument with an entire school district, combining the data from the instrument with other data collected. For example, you could audit district policies through document analyses and selected personnel interviews. We conducted a curriculum and instruction audit by reviewing documents, conducting interviews, and making school visits, and we analyzed newspaper and archival materials for the past 15 years. All data were analyzed using three sets of criteria: the district's core values, the five essential elements of cultural proficiency, and our posing the question "How are they doing?" These data then became the frame for commendations and recommendations regarding district policies and procedures, curriculum and instruction, school relationships, and community relationships.

Variation

Another use for the instrument is in combination with other data collection instruments and techniques to gauge the progress of university students in a teacher training program.

Human Relations Needs Assessment Instrument

1 = Rarely, 2= Occasionally, 3 = Sometimes, 4 = Often, 5 = Usually

School Districts Should . . .   This District Does . . .

Assessment of cultural knowledge.

1. Have a policy against racist and sexist jokes, slurs, and language
   1 2 3 4 5 NA   1 2 3 4 5 NA

2. Impose sanctions on those who use racist or sexist jokes, slurs, and language
   1 2 3 4 5 NA   1 2 3 4 5 NA

3. Provide opportunities for people to describe their cultural groups to others
   1 2 3 4 5 NA   1 2 3 4 5 NA

4. Teach people the effect that their ethnicity and gender have on those around them
   1 2 3 4 5 NA   1 2 3 4 5 NA

5. Examine organizational policies for unintentional discrimination
   1 2 3 4 5 NA   1 2 3 4 5 NA

6. Explicate clearly its norms, values, and cultural expectations
   1 2 3 4 5 NA   1 2 3 4 5 NA

Value for diversity

1. Have a formal selection process for materials that are inclusive
   1 2 3 4 5 NA   1 2 3 4 5 NA

2. Display materials that have culturally diverse images
   1 2 3 4 5 NA   1 2 3 4 5 NA

3. Sponsor activities to encourage making acquaintances with people of different cultural groups
   1 2 3 4 5 NA   1 2 3 4 5 NA

4. Take overt actions to hire people at all levels to represent a diverse workforce
   1 2 3 4 5 NA   1 2 3 4 5 NA

5. Establish policies that support diversity
   1 2 3 4 5 NA   1 2 3 4 5 NA

6. Promote activities that value the commonalities and differences among people
   1 2 3 4 5 NA   1 2 3 4 5 NA

7. Promote activities that recognize that there are differences within ethnic groups

    1 2 3 4 5 NA   1 2 3 4 5 NA

8. Promote activities that recognize that each ethnic group has its own strengths and needs

    1 2 3 4 5 NA   1 2 3 4 5 NA

Ability to manage the dynamics of difference

1. Teach people how to ask others appropriately about their cultural practices
    1 2 3 4 5 NA   1 2 3 4 5 NA

2. Acknowledge that conflict is a normal phenomenon
    1 2 3 4 5 NA   1 2 3 4 5 NA

3. Use effective strategies for intervening in conflict situations
    1 2 3 4 5 NA   1 2 3 4 5 NA

4. Teach collaborative problem-solving techniques
    1 2 3 4 5 NA   1 2 3 4 5 NA

5. Regularly review policies to ensure that there are no subtle discriminatory practices

    1 2 3 4 5 NA   1 2 3 4 5 NA

6. Hold educators accountable for demonstrating high expectations
    1 2 3 4 5 NA   1 2 3 4 5 NA

7. Hold all faculty and staff accountable for their performance
    1 2 3 4 5 NA   1 2 3 4 5 NA

Adaptability to diversity

1. Develop policies that promote inclusive, relational organization culture
    1 2 3 4 5 NA   1 2 3 4 5 NA

2. Have policies that prohibit discrimination
    1 2 3 4 5 NA   1 2 3 4 5 NA

3. Sanction, when appropriate, those whose behaviors conflict with practices that promote diversity
    1 2 3 4 5 NA   1 2 3 4 5 NA

4. Encourage students and school employees to talk about differences without making judgments
    1 2 3 4 5 NA   1 2 3 4 5 NA

5. Encourage cooperative learning strategies as a technique to get students to work and play together
    1 2 3 4 5 NA   1 2 3 4 5 NA

6. Teach students in their native language

    1 2 3 4 5 NA   1 2 3 4 5 NA

7. Employ and promote educators who reflect the ethnic and cultural makeup of the student body

    1 2 3 4 5 NA   1 2 3 4 5 NA

Ability to institutionalize cultural knowledge

1. Provide opportunities for learning about one's own culture

    1 2 3 4 5 NA   1 2 3 4 5 NA

2. Provide opportunities for learning about others' cultures

    1 2 3 4 5 NA   1 2 3 4 5 NA

3. Provide classes on different cultures for all students

    1 2 3 4 5 NA   1 2 3 4 5 NA

4. Provide workshops on different cultures for all employees

    1 2 3 4 5 NA   1 2 3 4 5 NA

5. Have policies that mandate learning about other ethnic groups

    1 2 3 4 5 NA   1 2 3 4 5 NA

6. Teach that ethnic groups often communicate in different ways

    1 2 3 4 5 NA   1 2 3 4 5 NA

7. Teach how to acknowledge the differences among people based on ethnicity

    1 2 3 4 5 NA   1 2 3 4 5 NA

8. Teach how to acknowledge the differences among people based on physical abilities and invisible differences

    1 2 3 4 5 NA   1 2 3 4 5 NA

9. Teach how to acknowledge the differences among people based on gender

    1 2 3 4 5 NA   1 2 3 4 5 NA

10. Provide a process for developing cultural understanding among all groups

    1 2 3 4 5 NA   1 2 3 4 5 NA

11. Ensure that the cultural groups within the community are represented on advisory groups (e.g., PTA)

    1 2 3 4 5 NA   1 2 3 4 5 NA

12. Ensure that the cultural groups within the community are represented in decision-making groups

    1 2 3 4 5 NA   1 2 3 4 5 NA

Resource D

Understanding Power and Privilege

Activity	Expertise of the Facilitator	Readiness of the Group	Time for the Activity
D1. **Barriers to Cultural Proficiency**	Moderate	Intermediate	60 minutes
D2. **Describe a Culturally Incompetent Organization**	Moderate	Beginning	45 minutes
D3. **A Survey of Privilege and Entitlement**	Extensive	Advanced	60 minutes
D4. **Listening and Hearing**	Extensive	Intermediate	2.5 hours
D5. **Seven-Minute Day**	Extensive	Intermediate	2 hours

Activity D1: Barriers to Cultural Proficiency

Purpose

To identify aspects of the organization's culture that may be barriers to cultural proficiency

Expertise of Facilitator

Moderate

Readiness of Group

Intermediate

Time Needed

60 minutes

Materials

Response Sheet: Barriers to Cultural Proficiency

Briefing

Let's see if we can identify some of the barriers to cultural proficiency in our school (or district).

Process

1. Distribute Response Sheet: Barriers to Cultural Proficiency.
2. Review the meaning of the terms to be sure that people understand them.
3. Organize participants into groups of three to five.
4. Ask each group to brainstorm examples for each term.
5. Invite each small group to share with the larger group.

Debriefing

1. What did you think, feel, or wonder as you completed this exercise?
2. What surprises you?
3. What made this activity difficult or easy?
4. What conclusions can you draw from the answers of the group?
5. What would you like to do with this information?

Response Sheet: Barrier to Cultural Proficiency

In your small groups, list examples within your organization of these barriers to cultural proficiency

Unawareness of the Need to Adapt

Not recognizing the need to make personal and organizational changes in response to the diversity of the people with whom you and your organization interact

Believing instead that only the others need to change and adapt to you

The Presumption of Entitlement and Unearned Privilege

Not recognizing that members of certain groups receive more privileges because of their position or because of the groups to which they belong

Assuming that you accrued all of your personal achievements and societal or organizational benefits because of your competence or your character and do not need to share or redistribute what you have or help others to acquire what you have

Systems of Entitlement and Privilege

Distributing power and privilege (consciously or unintentionally) only to members of dominant groups

Abusing power accrued through rules and roles within the organization

Throughout most organizations are systems of institutionalized racism, sexism, heterosexism, ageism, and ableism. Moreover, these systems are often supported and sustained without the permission of and at times without the knowledge of the people whom they benefit. These systems perpetuate domination and victimization of individuals and groups.

Activity D2: Describe a Culturally Incompetent Organization

Purpose

This activity is useful with resistant groups or with groups that find it hard to grasp the concepts of privilege and entitlement

Expertise of Facilitator

Moderate

Readiness of Group

Beginning

Time Needed

45 minutes

Materials

A copy of the Cultural Proficiency Continuum

Briefing

Use your imagination to describe the worst kind of school you can think of. Almost all of the behaviors and activities will fall along the left side of the continuum. Some may be characterized as culturally precompetent.

Process

1. Refer to the continuum.

2. Divide the participants into groups of four to six.

3. Encourage them to have fun as they develop their descriptions. Include the following:
   - Composition of the staff
   - Decision makers and their methods
   - How information is communicated to others
   - How resources are acquired
   - To whom are resources allocated
   - Symbols of privilege and entitlement

4. Let each group share their descriptions with the larger group.

5. After the groups have shared, identify those items on the group lists that exemplify barriers to cultural proficiency. Categorize the items listed as a manifestation of privilege, power, or entitlement or a reflection of the unawareness of the need to adapt.

Debriefing

1. What did you think, feel, or wonder as you completed this exercise?

2. What surprised you?

3. What made this activity difficult or easy?

4. What conclusions can you draw from the answers of the group?

5. Do you recognize any similarities between this imaginary organization and your organization?

6. How much of what you described is going on in the real-life organization?

7. What would you like to do with this information? Select one thing that you would like to address.

Activity D3: A Survey of Privilege and Entitlement

Purpose

To raise awareness of the distribution of societal privilege and power in a group

Expertise of Facilitator

Extensive

Readiness of Group

Advanced (This activity is particularly powerful if there are people of color in the group.)

Time Needed

60 minutes

Materials

A copy of the Response Sheet: A Survey of Privilege and Entitlement

Briefing

We have been talking about barriers to cultural proficiency. This survey will provide data so that we can examine our own power and privilege. Peggy McIntosh's (1988) article is the basis for this activity; it is based on her examination of her awareness of the societal privilege of being a European American. Take a few minutes to take this survey, answering from the perspective of your racial/ethnic group.

Process

1. Give participants about 15 minutes to complete the survey and total their points.

2. Invite participants to line up around the room according to their scores.

3. Ask participants what they notice about the patterns of who is in the line and their scores.

4. Encourage participants to ask questions of one another.

Debriefing

1. What did you think, feel, or wonder as you completed this exercise?

2. What surprised you?

3. What made this activity difficult or easy?

4. What conclusions can you draw from the answers of the group?

5. Do you recognize any similarities between the results of this activity and your organization?

6. How much of what you described is going on in the actual organization?

7. What would you like to do with this information? Select one thing that you would like to address.

Variations

1. Instead of taking the survey as a paper-and-pencil test, group the participants in the middle of a room the size of a classroom or larger. Starting in the middle of the room, ask the participants to take one step forward or one step backward based on a yes or no response to the questions.

2. Ask a small group to rewrite the survey focusing on sexual orientation or gender.

Response Sheet: A Survey of Privilege and Entitlement

Please respond to the following statements as candidly as possible, using the following scale:

1 = almost never, 2 = rarely, 3 = sometimes, 4 = usually, 5 = almost always

When you are finished, please total your points.

1. I can, if I wish, arrange to be in the company of people of my ethnic group most of the time.	1 2 3 4 5
2. If I should need to move, I can be pretty sure of renting or purchasing housing in an area that I can afford.	1 2 3 4 5
3. If I should need to move, I can be pretty sure of renting or purchasing housing in an area in which I would want to live.	1 2 3 4 5
4. I can be pretty sure that my neighbors in such a location will be neutral or pleasant to me.	1 2 3 4 5
5. I can go shopping alone most of the time, pretty well assured that I will not be followed or harassed.	1 2 3 4 5
6. I can turn on the television or open the front page of the paper and see people of my ethnicity widely represented.	1 2 3 4 5
7. When I am told about *our* national heritage or *civilization,* I know that the speaker assumes that people of my ethnicity are included.	1 2 3 4 5
8. I can be sure that my children will be given curricular materials that testify to the existence of their ethnic group.	1 2 3 4 5
9. I can go into any music shop and count on finding the music of my ethnic group represented.	1 2 3 4 5 1 2 3 4 5
10. I can go into any supermarket and find the staple foods that fit with my cultural traditions.	1 2 3 4 5
11. I can go into any hairdresser's shop and find someone who can deal with my hair.	1 2 3 4 5

12. Whether I use checks, credit cards, or cash, I am sure that the sales clerk will not use my skin color as a measure of my financial reliability.	1	2	3	4	5
13. I can arrange to protect my children most of the time from people who may not like them.	1	2	3	4	5
14. I can swear without having people attribute this choice to the bad morals, the poverty, or the illiteracy of my ethnic group.	1	2	3	4	5
15. I can dress in secondhand clothes without having people attribute this choice to the bad morals, the poverty, or the illiteracy of my ethnic group.	1	2	3	4	5
16. I can swear, dress in secondhand clothes, or not answer letters without having people attribute this choice to the bad morals, the poverty, or the illiteracy of my ethnic group.	1	2	3	4	5
17. I can speak in public to a powerful, predominantly male group without putting my ethnic group on trial.	1	2	3	4	5
18. I can do well in a challenging situation without being called a credit to my race.	1	2	3	4	5
19. I am never asked to speak for all the people of my ethnic group.	1	2	3	4	5
20. I can remain oblivious of the language and customs of people of color, who constitute the world's majority, without feeling any penalty for such oblivion.	1	2	3	4	5
21. I can criticize our government and talk about how much I fear its policies and behavior without being seen as a cultural outsider.	1	2	3	4	5
22. I can be pretty sure that if I ask to talk to "the person in charge," I will be facing a person of my ethnic group.	1	2	3	4	5
23. If a traffic cop pulls me over, I can be sure I haven't been singled out because of my ethnicity.	1	2	3	4	5
24. If the IRS audits my tax return, I can be sure I haven't been singled out because of my ethnicity.	1	2	3	4	5
25. I can easily buy posters, postcards, picture books, greeting cards, and children's magazines featuring people who look like me.	1	2	3	4	5

	1	2	3	4	5
26. I can easily buy dolls and toys featuring people who look like me.	1	2	3	4	5
27. I can go home from most meetings of organizations I belong to feeling somewhat tied in rather than isolated, out of place, outnumbered, unheard, held at a distance, or feared.	1	2	3	4	5
28. I can take a job with an affirmative action employer without having coworkers suspect that I got it because of my ethnicity.	1	2	3	4	5
29. I can choose public accommodations without fearing that people of my ethnicity cannot get into the places I have chosen.	1	2	3	4	5
30. I can choose public accommodations without fearing that people of my ethnicity will be mistreated in the places I have chosen.	1	2	3	4	5
31. I can be sure that if I need legal help, my ethnicity will not work against me.	1	2	3	4	5
32. I can be sure that if I need medical help, my ethnicity will not work against me.	1	2	3	4	5
33. If my day, week, or year is going badly, I need not ask of each negative episode or situation whether it has racial overtones.	1	2	3	4	5
34. I can choose blemish cover or bandages in a "flesh" color that more or less matches my skin.	1	2	3	4	5

Total Score:

SOURCE: Adapted from Peggy McIntosh, Unpacking the Knapsack of Privilege, *Peace and Freedom*, July/August 1989.

Activity D4: Listening and Hearing

Purpose

To engage participants in a data collection activity to help identify underlying values operating within the school

Skill of Facilitator

Extensive

Readiness of Group

Intermediate

Time Needed

30 minutes for explanation of activity. Several days for data collection. Two hours for analysis of the data.

Materials Needed

One copy of the Response Sheet: Listening and Hearing Data Analysis and Response Sheet: Listening and Hearing Data Follow-up for each participant

Four 3 × 5 inch cards for each interview. For example, if you plan to interview 15 people, you will need 4 cards × 15 participants = 60 cards.

Briefing

This activity will allow you to identify underlying assumptions. Once the data are collected, you will be able to determine the extent to which expressed values and policies align with behaviors and practices.

Process

1. Though this activity can be performed by individuals acting alone, it is more effective when learning teams undertake it to foster group learning.

2. As a team, identify the groups of students who are underperforming academically at the school (e.g., English-language learners or boys).

3. Each team member selects one demographic group of students who are underperforming, or underserved, as the focus of data collection.

4. Each member of the team is to interview at least 10 adults who are employees of the school or school district (or, if doing this alone, conduct 40 interviews) and ask the same four questions:

   a. How do you describe students from this demographic group?
   b. How do you describe their parents/guardians?
   c. How do you describe the neighborhoods where they live?
   d. How do you describe the language the students and their families use at home?

5. Record the adjectives spoken by the interviewee and use one card per question for a total four cards per interviewee.

6. Bring all cards to the next session.

7. In the next session, begin by laying the cards on the table and arranging them into groups of similar adjectives.

8. Keep sorting and resorting the cards until you are comfortable that you have them into similarly themed stacks.

9. Have one of your colleagues review your stacks and ask you probing questions that guide you into thinking more deeply about the rationale for your groupings.

10. Using the Listening and Hearing Data Analysis Response Sheet, enter the words from each stack into the cells in the "Common Words" column.

11. If you have three stacks of cards, you will use three of the cells in the first column; if you have four stacks, you will use four of the cells; and so on.

12. Look at the common words in the first cell and ask yourself, *What theme emerges from these common words?* Enter the description of the theme into the middle column, "Themes."

13. Repeat the process for the remaining "Common Words" cells.

14. Take a few moments and record any comments or reactions that emerge for you as the themes become clear.

15. Respond to the prompts in the Listening and Hearing Data Follow-up Response Sheet.

Debriefing

1. How did you feel conducting the interviews?

2. How did interviewees respond to the questions?

3. What assumptions surfaced about the demographic group of students you were studying?

4. In what ways are your findings similar to or different from the findings of your colleagues?

5. What insights does this activity provide for you?

6. How will you use this information?

7. What implication does this information have for professional development?

Listening and Hearing Data Analysis

Guidelines:

- Arrange your 3 × 5 inch cards into stacks of words with common themes.
- Sort the cards into stacks according to common themes.
- Consult with colleagues to test your devised themes.

Response Sheet: Listening and Hearing Data Analysis

Common Words	Themes	Your Comments/Reactions

Response Sheet: Listening and Hearing Data Follow-up

The difference between what we do, and what we are capable of doing, would suffice to solve most of the world's problems.

—Mahatma Gandhi (1869–1948), leader of Indian independence movement and pioneer of civil disobedience

1. What sources can you consult to determine the school's, district's, or agency's expressed value for student achievement?

2. What additional data might you collect to shed light on organizational responses to achievement differences?

   • Externally required data:

   • Internally required data:

3. Which of these data can you bring to a professional development meeting?

Activity D5: Seven-Minute Day

Purpose

To use role-playing to practice mediating the conflict that arises from cultural misunderstandings. This activity invites participants to use their problem-solving and decision-making skills when working with parents and other community members in stressful situations. Although it can be used with only educators, this activity is designed for use with mixed groups of teachers, administrators, and parents.

Skill of Facilitator

Extensive

Readiness of Group

Intermediate

Time Needed

2 hours

Materials

Chart paper

Marking pens

Copies of role descriptions for each of the three role groups

Copies of general instructions for all participants

Copies of Seven-Minute Day Data Sheet for all participants

One room to serve as a communications center

Three breakout rooms

Briefing

You will be engaged in a simulated role-playing situation in which you will have the opportunity to play roles other than your current school-related roles. This activity will give you the opportunity to experience how it feels to be a member of another group. You will also practice decision-making, conflict resolution, and problem-solving skills.

Process

1. To the extent possible, have teachers role-play administrators, board members, or parents of this school. Likewise, have parents play roles other than parents and board members; have administrators do the same.

2. Distribute and read aloud the general instructions. Respond to questions of clarification.

3. Distribute and read aloud the Seven-Minute Day Data Sheet.

4. Divide the group into the three role groups and situate them in separate rooms—parents, teachers, and administrators/board members. Distribute their role descriptions and respond to questions of clarification.

5. Provide the groups 20 minutes to do their initial planning.

6. At the end of the 20 minutes, announce, "This is the beginning of Day 1." (You may want to designate it as a specific date or day of the week, such as Monday, October 14.)

7. Have one room serve as the communications center and receive and distribute messages as appropriate. You may just have to step aside and let the process unfold.

8. Announce every seven minutes, "It is now Day 2," or, "It is now Tuesday, October 15," and so on. Repeat this process until you have enough information to have a productive discussion. Usually it takes only four to six "days" to provide enough information for a very informed discussion.

Debriefing

You can begin the debriefing process in either of two ways:

1. You can ask each group in turn to respond to the questions that follow.

2. You can have each group return to its breakout room, spend a few minutes charting answers to the questions, and then return in 15–20 minutes and post responses.

Then ask the following questions:

1. What did you think, feel, or wonder when I first described this activity?

2. What did you notice as a member of your role group during the planning phase of the activity?

3. What did you think, feel, or wonder about being a member of your role group during the conduct of the seven-minute days?

4. What did you think, feel, or wonder about other two role groups? During the planning phase? During the seven-minute day phase?

5. What insights does this provide for the way we do business in schools?

6. What did you learn about your role group? What did you learn about the other role groups?

7. In what ways will you be able to use the information learned in this session?

8. In looking at the outcomes of your meeting, where do you judge them to be on the Cultural Proficiency Continuum? What evidence do you have for your judgment?

9. How could you improve the process of your meeting as well as the outcome of the meeting?

Variations

1. Add role groups—for example, students, business leaders, activist groups, and other interest groups.

2. Select other issues that have more immediate relevance to your school.

Seven-Minute Day Roles

Administrators and board members: From your group, select participants to serve as board members, the superintendent, the business manager, the public information officer, the principal of the high school where the fight took place, a middle school principal, and an elementary school principal.

Teachers: Select officers for your local association. Designate your group members to be 70 percent European American, 10 percent Latino, 15 percent African American, and 5 percent Asian and Pacific Islander.

Parents: Designate your group members to be 40 percent Latino, 33 percent European American, 20 percent Asian and Pacific Islander, 5 percent African American, and 2 percent other.

General Instructions

1. Use the initial 20-minute strategy session to develop your course of action. Record it on chart paper.

2. Select a message carrier. All communications are to be delivered to the communications center.

3. Develop responses to the other groups' messages and record them on newsprint during each seven-minute day.

4. Any group may move time ahead and skip a day by informing the other groups in writing.

5. Plan your strategies well.

Seven-Minute Day Data Sheet

1. Your district has had a diversity plan in effect for three years. The plan had broad community support when it was first implemented.

2. Parents have recently expressed a concern that violence and vandalism are increasing in the schools.

3. Teachers have filed grievances over the administration's lack of effective action in handling three recent assaults on teachers.

4. African American and Latino parents have charged the board of education and administration with unfair treatment of their children, predicated on the high rate of suspensions and expulsions and their underrepresentation in honors classes.

5. The current student population is 40 percent Latino, 23 percent European American, 20 percent African American, and 15 percent Asian and Pacific Islander.

6. The current faculty population is 70 percent European American, 15 percent African American, 10 percent Latino, and 5 percent Asian and Pacific Islander.

7. A fight that occurred two days ago resulted in the suspension of three African American students, two European American students, and two Latino students. They may be recommended for expulsion.

8. A small group of parents went to the school to protest the suspensions, and a heated interchange led to some pushing and shoving. This action led to the arrest of one European American and one African American parent.

A group of angry parents are demanding the following:

a. The board of education and the administration eliminate the racist practices in the school.

b. The suspended students be readmitted and their records cleared.

c. All charges be dropped against the parents who were arrested.

If the demands are not met, the parents will withdraw their students from the school, causing the district to lose finances because of the reduced average daily attendance allotment.

Resource E

Going Deeper With the Principles

Activity	Expertise of Facilitator	Readiness of Group	Time Needed
E1. **Guiding Principles Discussion Starters**	Extensive	Intermediate	60 minutes
E2. **Family Values**	Low	Beginning	30–60 minutes
E3. **My Work Values**	Moderate	Beginning	60–90 minutes
E4. **Managing Conflict With Our Core Values**	Extensive	Advanced	60–90 minutes
E5. **Examining Your Organizational Values**	Extensive	Advanced	90–120 minutes

Activity E1: Guiding Principles Discussion Starters

Purpose

To reinforce the guiding principles of cultural proficiency

To identify how the principles of cultural proficiency can be translated into school behavior

Skill of Facilitator

Extensive

Readiness of Group

Intermediate

Time Needed

60 minutes

Materials

Response Sheet: The Guiding Principles of Cultural Proficiency

Briefing

Let's look at the principles of cultural proficiency to make sure we know what they mean in relationship to how we do things at this school.

Process

1. Distribute Response Sheet: The Guiding Principles of Cultural Proficiency. Divide the group into small groups, assigning one question to each group.

2. Ask the small groups to discuss the principle and to make meaning for their group discussion. What does it mean? How does it relate to my life? How does it relate to my work? How does it relate to what we are trying to do as a professional community? What examples might we cite to illustrate this principle?

3. Reconvene the large group and share the responses, encouraging critical reflection and review.

Debriefing

1. What happened in your small groups? How easy or difficult was it to answer the questions?

2. How do you feel about your responses?

3. Have you ever thought of parents, community, students, or one another as customers?

4. How does thinking in terms of customer or client relations alter the way you respond to these groups?

5. What are the implications for your responses?

6. How will you use this information?

Variations

Examine the principles from the perspective of a classroom or the district. Conduct this activity with one large group, inviting discussion and responses of everyone to all the questions. Answer these questions for each of the principles:

1. What would your classroom look like if this principle were acknowledged?

2. What would be strategies for responding to this principle in your classroom?

3. What issues might arise when this principle is not acknowledged?

4. Give examples of the types of conflicts that might arise.

Response Sheet: The Guiding Principles
of Cultural Proficiency

Culture Is a Predominant Force.

Acknowledge culture as a predominant force in shaping behaviors, values, and institutions. Although you may be inclined to take offense at behaviors that differ from yours, remind yourself that they may not be personal; they may be cultural.

People Are Served in Varying Degrees by the Dominant Culture.

What works well in organizations and in the community for you and others who are like you may work against members of other cultural groups. Failure to make such an acknowledgment puts the burden for change on one group.

The Group Identity of Individuals Is as Important as Their Individual Identities.

Although it is important to treat all people as individuals, it is also important to acknowledge their group identity. Actions must be taken with the awareness that the dignity of a person is not guaranteed unless the dignity of his or her people is also preserved.

Diversity Within Cultures Is Vast and Significant.

Since diversity within cultures is as important as diversity between cultures, it is important to learn about cultural groups not as monoliths—for example, Asians, Hispanics, Gay Men, and Women—but as the complex and diverse groups that they are. Often, because of the class differences in the United States, people have more in common across cultural lines than within them.

Each Group Has Unique Cultural Needs.

Each cultural group has unique needs that cannot be met within the boundaries of the dominant culture. Expressions of one group's cultural identity does not imply disrespect for yours. Make room in your organization for several paths that lead to the same goal.

The Family, as Defined by Each Culture, Is the Primary System of Support in the Education of Children.

The traditional relationship between home and school is to place most of the responsibility for involvement directly with parents. While that holds true for most cultural groups, cultural proficiency provides a different frame by which teachers, parents, and education leaders assume greater responsibility for finding authentic ways to engage in culturally proficient practices to support student achievement.

People Who Are Not a Part of the Dominant Culture Have to Be at Least Bicultural.

Parents have to be fluent in the communication patterns of the school, as well as the communication patterns that exist in their communities. They also have to know the cultural norms and expectations of schools, which may conflict with or be different from those in their communities, their countries of origin, or their cultural groups. In ideal conditions, their children are developing bicultural skills, learning to code switch appropriately as the cultural expectations of their environments change, yet parents may not have these skills. They are then penalized because they do not respond as expected to the norms set by educators, nor do they negotiate well the educational systems of the public schools.

Inherent in Cross-Cultural Interactions Are Social and Communication Dynamics That Must Be Acknowledged, Adjusted to, and Accepted.

People who belong to groups that have histories of systemic oppression have heightened sensitivities regarding the societal privileges they do not receive and to the many unacknowledged slights and putdowns that they receive daily. These microaggressions are usually unnoticed by dominant group members and, when brought to their attention, are often dismissed as inconsequential.

The School System Must Incorporate Cultural Knowledge Into Practice and Policymaking.

Culturally proficient educators are self-consciously aware of their own cultures and the culture of their schools. This is crucial knowledge, because in addition to the cognitive curriculum, the cultural norms and expectations of the school must be taught as well. First, culturally proficient educators must assess and raise consciousness about their own individual and organizational cultures. Then, as they teach the cultural expectations of the school and classroom to all students and their families, educators must learn about the cultures of their students.

Activity E2: Family Values

Purpose

To allow participants to compare the values they learned in their families of origin

To help participants realize how they are influenced by these values

Expertise of Facilitator

Low

Readiness of Group

Beginning

Time Needed

30–60 minutes

Materials

Chart paper

Markers

Masking tape

Briefing

Think about lessons you learned in your family of origin. What were the values on which those lessons were based? Identify three values that you learned at home and that you bring to the workplace.

Process

1. Organize the participants into groups of three to five.

2. Model for the group three values you learned from your family of origin. These can be positive or negative things that you learned.

3. Each person in the groups will have a turn sharing their family values.

4. Clarify for the participants that they do not need to agree with all of the values shared. Encourage them to go beyond a word like *education* to the value about the word—for example, *education is a privilege.*

5. After the participants have shared the values and the stories that explain them in their small groups, ask them to discuss how these values influence their behavior and expectations of others at school.

6. Ask them to chart the values discussed in their groups. Hang the charts around the room.

Debriefing

1. Each group highlights the values they discussed.

2. Discuss the apparent similarity of the values despite cultural, generational, or other differences.

3. Point out the obvious and then the subtle differences in values.

4. Identify how values that, in isolation, may be perceived as positive might clash and cause conflicts with the values of other people. Take, for example, *get an education* and *education is a privilege.* Both are positive values, but they will result in different expectations and attitudes about learning in the workplace.

5. Discuss how families of origin influence behavior.

6. Discuss how family cultures influence the culture of the school.

7. Point out the need for a strong, clearly articulated core culture at the school. Discuss what happens when there is no strong school culture.

Activity E3: My Work Values

Purpose

To identify individual values that affect the workplace

To increase awareness of how apparently positive values may cause conflict in the workplace

Expertise of Facilitator

Moderate

Readiness of Group

Beginning

Time Needed

60–90 minutes

Materials

Chart paper

Markers

Masking tape

Briefing

Think about lessons you learned in your home growing up. What were the values on which those lessons were based? Identify three values that you learned at home that you now bring to the workplace. Share how these values affect your perceptions and relationships at work.

Process

1. Organize the participants into groups of three to five. Encourage the participants to diversify their groups.

2. Model for the group three values that you learned from your parents or the family in which you grew up and still use in the workplace—for example: *My father always told me to get an education, be nice to your siblings, and don't get pregnant. This translates today into my expectation that everyone will want to learn and be glad to go to*

training, that people will be especially courteous to the people they work with, and that they will be responsible for the consequences of their actions.

3. Clarify for the participants that in the small groups they do not need to agree with all the values shared.

4. After participants have shared in the small groups, ask them to chart their values. Hang the charts around the room.

Debriefing

1. Each group shares the values and the some of the stories that explain them to the large group.

2. Discuss the apparent and subtle similarities and differences of the values.

3. Identify how values that in isolation are perceived as positive may clash and cause conflicts with the values of other people. For example, *get an education* and *education is a privilege* are two positive yet potentially conflicting values. They will result in very different expectations and attitudes about learning.

Activity E4: Managing Conflict With Our Core Values

Purpose

To discuss the relationship of your school's core values, the elements of cultural proficiency, and managing conflict

Skill of Facilitator

Extensive

Readiness of Group

Advanced

Time Needed

60–90 minutes

Materials

Copies of Response Sheet: Managing Conflict With Our Core Values

A grid that has the same three-column headings but is otherwise blank. This can be on paper or on transparencies.

Chart paper and marking pens or an overhead projector and markers

A list of the school's core values or shared values

Briefing

We are going to talk about the relationship of our core values to managing conflict.

Process

1. Distribute a list of the school's shared or core values.

2. Distribute the Response Sheets. Complete one row of the blank chart as a large group.

3. Ask each person to spend 15 minutes making notes that reflect his or her individual views and perspectives regarding the organizational responses to its stated core values.

4. Organize participants into diverse groups of four to six.

5. Give participants 30–60 minutes to discuss each core value as it relates to managing conflict and to complete the blank Response Sheet.

6. Ask participants to post their work on chart paper or on the transparencies.

7. Invite critical review of each group's contribution.

8. Note the similarities and differences in the groups' products.

Debriefing

1. What did you think, feel, or wonder when you first received the Response Sheet?

2. What did you think, feel, or wonder during the discussion in your group?

3. How can you incorporate your new understanding of conflict into your daily practice?

4. What did you learn about yourself? Your colleagues? Your school?

5. What is the implication of this activity for you in your role at school?

6. What information or skills do you believe you need to do an even better job?

7. How can we use this information?

Variations

1. Step 5 in the process can be done within culturally defined groups, and the information can be shared among cultural groups.

2. Use this activity at the classroom or district level.

Response Sheet: Managing Conflict
With Our Core Values—*Example*

Core Values	Relationship of Core Values to Managing Conflict	What I Can Say or Do to Reduce Tension and Conflict
Quality	Unresolved conflict reduces the quality of your efforts.	"I am concerned about the quality of the work we are doing here. Can we talk about how it can be improved?"
People	Without the people, we would have not have a job.	Involve the people who are having the conflicts in resolving them: "I think we need to clear the air. Let's sit down and talk about what the real issues are."
Integrity	Acknowledge your contribution to the conflicts that arise around you.	"It was not my intention to offend you. I was trying to say . . . ."
Caring	Demonstrate that you care about your colleagues by taking the time to reduce tension and solve the problem together.	"I am on my way to a meeting, but I do want to address these issues. Let's plan to talk at . . . ."

Response Sheet: Managing Conflict
With Our Core Values

Core Values	Relationship of Core Values to Managing Conflict	What I Can Say or Do to Reduce Tension and Conflict

Activity E5: Examining Your Organizational Values

Purpose

To identify the barriers to cultural proficiency that are evidenced in the covert values of your school or district

Skill of Facilitator

Extensive

Readiness of Group

Advanced

Time Needed

90–120 minutes

Materials

Copies of Response Sheet: Examining Your Organizational Values

Copies of the school's core values or shared values for diversity

Chart paper and marking pens or overhead projector and transparency markers

Briefing

This activity will provide you with the opportunity to apply your understanding of (a) the sense of entitlement concept and (b) unawareness of the need to adapt. You will also examine the relationship between our stated and unarticulated values and the implication that this has for creating change in our school. The activity will be a mix of personal and group viewpoints and experiences.

Process

1. Distribute the school's shared values, or core values, for diversity.

2. Review the meaning of *covert value* or *unarticulated value*. Remind participants that it is the hidden curriculum.

3. Add your school's core values in the first column. You may do this ahead of time.

4. Ask each person to spend 15 minutes making notes on the Response Sheet that reflect his or her individual views and perspectives.

5. Have participants form into diverse groups of four to six.

6. Give participants 30–60 minutes to discuss each core value and complete the Response Sheet.

7. Request that participants post their work on a chart or onto transparencies.

8. Encourage critical review of and reflection on the responses.

Debriefing

1. What were your feelings when you first received the Response Sheet?

2. What did you think, feel, or wonder about the discussion in your small group?

3. How do you feel about the levels of congruence between the stated and unarticulated values?

4. What observations do you have about the columns "Consequences" and "Implications for Change"?

5. What did you learn about your school? Your colleagues? Yourself?

6. What is the implication of this activity for you in your role at school?

7. What information or skills do you believe you need to do an even better job?

8. How will you use this information?

Variations

Divide the participants into culturally specific small groups.

Response Sheet: Examining Your Organizational Values—Example

Value	Overt or Covert	Unarticulated Information	Consequences	Implications for Change
Organizational value	*Is this an overt or a covert value?*	*Is there an unarticulated contradiction or addendum to this value?*	*What behaviors or practices do you see as a result of this value?*	*Given this value, what are the implications for culturally proficient behavior or practices?*
Excellence in all things	Overt	If it goes to the director, it is perfect; otherwise, just make it good.	The work is inconsistent in quality. Some people get praised for good work; others are chastised for "perfectionism."	We need to state publicly that there are two sets of standards and teach people how to use them.
Caring	Covert	We care about people as long as they meet our expectations.	Everyone does not receive fair and equitable treatment.	I need to examine my own personal prejudices before I take an action.

Response Sheet: Examining Your Organizational Values

Value	Overt or Covert	Unarticulated Information	Consequences	Implications for Change
Organizational value	Is this an overt or a covert value?	Is there an unarticulated contradiction or addendum to this value?	What behaviors or practices do you see as a result of this value?	Given this value, what are the implications for culturally proficient behavior or practices?

Resource F

Going Deeper With the Continuum

Activity	Expertise of Facilitator	Readiness of the Group	Time for the Activity
F1. **The Cultural Proficiency Continuum**	Moderate	Intermediate	30 minutes
F2. **Exploring Behaviors Along the Continuum**	Moderate	Intermediate	90–120 minutes

Activity F1: The Cultural Proficiency Continuum

Purpose

To identify examples of the points on the Continuum

Expertise of Facilitator

Moderate

Readiness of Group

Intermediate

Time Needed

30 minutes

Materials

Response Sheet: The Cultural Proficiency Continuum

Chart paper

Marking pens

Masking tape

Briefing

Let's look at the Cultural Proficiency Continuum presented in this chapter and on the Response Sheet to see what meaning it has in our lives. We are going to develop some examples of the points on the Cultural Proficiency Continuum.

Process

1. Label six pieces of chart paper with the six points on the Continuum. Put one point at the top of each chart. Hang the chart paper on the wall.

2. Distribute a marker and about 10 sheets of 4 × 6 inch sticky notes to each participant.

3. Ask the groups to generate examples for the points along the Continuum. Think about negative and positive comments about

students that you have heard from other educators. Write one comment on each of your sticky notes.

4. After people have written comments on their sticky notes, invite them to place the notes on the appropriate charts.

5. As you, the facilitator, read the comments, you may need to move some of the sticky notes to more appropriate charts. Participants tend to place their comments higher on the Continuum than they deserve to be.

6. Encourage participants to mill around, reading all of the comments.

Debriefing

1. What did you notice as you wrote the comments?

2. What did you notice as you read the other comments?

3. What did you feel, think, or wonder about the comments or the process?

4. What does this say about you?

5. What does this say about your school or district?

Variation

Focus the discussion on classroom behavior instead of on district or school behavior.

Response Sheet: The Cultural Proficiency Continuum

Looking at Differences

Cultural proficiency is a set of values and behaviors in an individual or the set of policies and practices in an organization that creates the appropriate mind-set and approach to respond effectively to the issues caused by diversity. A culturally proficient organization interacts effectively with its employees, its clients, and its community. Culturally proficient people may not know all there is to know about others who are different from them, but they know how to take advantage of teachable moments, how to ask questions without offending, and how to create an environment that is welcoming to diversity and to change. There are six points along the Continuum.

Cultural ▼ Destructiveness	Cultural ▼ Blindness	Cultural ▼ Competence
▲ Cultural Incapacity	▲ Cultural Precompetence	▲ Cultural Proficiency

Cultural Destructiveness: *See the difference; stomp it out.*

Cultural destructiveness comprises any policy, practice, or behavior that effectively eliminates all vestiges of other people's cultures. It may be manifested through an organization's policies and practices or through an individual's values and behaviors. Sometimes these destructive actions occur intentionally:

- Social reproduction—One group re-creates itself, resulting in the exclusion of most other groups
- Discrimination against observable manifestations of ethnicity (e.g., accent, hair, and adornments)
- No institutional support for people whose socioeconomic class affects their work

Cultural Incapacity: *See the difference; make it wrong.*

Members of dominated groups receive treatment based on stereotypes and the belief that the dominant group is inherently superior. Cultural incapacity includes any policy, practice, or behavior that disempowers people who differ from the dominant group. Examples include the disproportionate allocation of resources, discrimination against people on the basis of whether they "know their place," and belief in the supremacy of the dominant culture. Other examples are discriminatory hiring practices, subtle messages to people who are not members of the dominant group that they are not valued or welcome, and generally lower expectations of performance for minority group members. Yet more examples include the following:

- Questioning the qualifications of people of color
- Assuming that affirmative action appointees are not proficient
- Not perceiving people of color as successful unless they are bicultural
- Establishing committees for compliance with, not for commitment to, a goal

Cultural Blindness:
See the difference; act like you don't.

Failure to see or to acknowledge that differences among and between groups often do make a difference to the groups and the individuals who are members of those groups. This is the belief that color and culture make no difference and that all people are the same. Values and behaviors of the dominant culture are presumed to be universally applicable and beneficial. It is also assumed that members of minority cultures do not meet the cultural expectations of the dominant group because of some cultural deficiency or lack of desire to achieve, rather than the fact that the system works only for the most assimilated of the minority groups. Following are some examples:

- Using the behavior of a "model minority" as the criteria for judging all minority groups
- Management training that does not address diversity
- Not articulating the cultural expectations of the organization to all of its members

Cultural Precompetence:
See the difference; respond inappropriately.

People and organizations that are culturally precompetent recognize that their skills and practices are limited when interacting with other cultural groups. They may have made some changes in their approaches to the issues arising from diversity, but they are aware that they need assistance and more information. They may also do the following:

- Recruit people who are not part of the mainstream culture but not provide them with any support or make any adaptation to their differences.
- Show discomfort and unwillingness to confront or hold accountable people from dominated groups who are not performing well.
- Make rules instead of teaching appropriate behavior (e.g., rules against hate speech).

Cultural Competence: *See the difference; understand the difference that difference makes.*

Cultural competence involves the use of the essential elements as the standards for individual behavior and organizational practice. This includes acceptance and respect for difference; continuing self-assessment regarding culture; careful attention to the dynamics of difference; continuous expansion of cultural knowledge and resources; and a variety of adaptations to belief systems, policies, and practices. Other forms of cultural competence are as follows:

- Performance standards for culturally appropriate behavior
- Modeling appropriate behaviors
- Risk taking (e.g., speaking against injustice, even when doing so may cause tension and conflict)

Cultural Proficiency: *See the difference; respond positively and affirmingly.*

Cultural proficiency involves knowing how to learn and teach about different groups; having the capacity to teach and to learn about differences in ways that acknowledge and honor all the people and the groups they represent; holding culture in high esteem; and seeking to add to the knowledge base of culturally proficient practice by conducting research, developing new approaches based on culture, and increasing the knowledge of others about culture and the dynamics of difference.

The Cultural Proficiency Continuum

Cultural Destructiveness	Cultural Incapacity	Cultural Blindness	Cultural Precompetence	Cultural Competence	Cultural Proficiency
Reactive >>> Tolerance			Proactive >>> Transformative		

280

Activity F2: Exploring Behaviors Along the Continuum

Purpose

To reinforce the relationship of behaviors along the Cultural Proficiency Continuum

Expertise of Facilitator

Moderate

Readiness of Group

Intermediate

Time Needed

90–120 minutes

Materials

Response Sheet: Behaviors Along the Continuum

Briefing

Now that you have been introduced to the Continuum and the essential elements of cultural competence, let's see how you would describe the behaviors at points along the Continuum.

Process

1. Divide the participants into groups of three to five.

2. Distribute the Response Sheet: Behaviors Along the Continuum.

3. Discuss how the sample shows both effective and dysfunctional behaviors along the Continuum.

4. Assign each group one aspect of their positions to work on.

5. Ask each group to develop a continuum of behavior for that aspect of work. This continuum could be used by their colleagues to assess the appropriateness of their behaviors.

6. After each small group has finished, ask it to share its responses with the entire group and have the other participants refine their contributions.

7. The first attempt at this activity will miss the mark in many ways. Spend 5–10 minutes per group giving feedback and redirection.

8. Ask the groups either to select another behavior or continue working on their first choice.

9. Allow the groups to develop descriptions for the six points on the Continuum.

Debriefing

1. How does this activity add to your understanding of the Continuum or the elements?

2. How does this activity help you to understand what it means to do your job in a culturally proficient manner?

3. How might you use the chart you created?

4. How might you use this activity with your colleagues?

Behaviors Along the Continuum

		Parent-Community Involvement ("parent" includes parent/community in all cases)			
Destructiveness	*"See the difference; stomp it out."*	Prevent diverse parent group involvement.	Block, prevent, and sabotage meaningful communication with some parent groups.	Ignore, intimidate, sabotage, or punish expression of needs of diverse parents.	Block, prevent, or sabotage discussion of allocating or decisions to allocate resources to meet the needs of diverse parent groups.
Incapacity	*"See the difference; make it wrong."*	Discourage meaningful involvement from diverse parent groups.	Communication is predominantly one way, in English, and in writing. Communication focuses on school rules and policies and may contain jargon, terms, or acronyms not understood by parents. Specific home-school communication is often reserved for disciplinary or other school compliance issues.	Intentionally assimilate diverse parents or co-opt their needs to the school/district, believing this to be of greatest value for all.	Intentionally/ unintentionally instigate competition for resources among diverse parent groups.
Blindness	*"See the difference; act like you don't."*	Do not offer specific opportunities for or support to involve diverse parent groups, believing that doing so may promote divisiveness.	Disseminate newsletters/ bulletins about school policies, calendar events, and volunteer opportunities to all. Translation may only be offered in one language other than English, often resulting in one-way communication between school and diverse parents.	Promote/support parent agendas that represent the status quo or align with school district needs without acknowledging diverse needs.	Promote equal sharing of resources among all groups, regardless of need or expression of need.

(Continued)

(Continued)

		Parent-Community Involvement ("parent" includes parent/community in all cases)			
Precompetence	*"See the difference; respond inappropriately."*	Facilitate ability of diverse parent groups to navigate the educational system.	School newsletters, bulletins, and meetings are translated for some parent groups but not others. Promoting agendas of some parents groups but not others results in inconsistent or uneven parent participation.	Learn about diverse parents and some of their needs, sometimes in indirect or inauthentic ways.	Identify and promote resources to meet the needs of some diverse parent groups, perhaps inconsistently.
Competence	*"See the difference; value it."*	Evidence exists of ongoing opportunities for meaningful interaction and participation of diverse parent groups in school programs and decisions.	Evidence exists of translating and interpreting all school communications and meetings for all language groups in the parent community, allowing all diverse parent groups to share meaningful information and collaborate with the school to improve the education of their children.	Evidence exists of learning about diverse parent groups and their needs in authentic ways and of increased involvement and collaboration with parents.	Evidence exists of promoting resources to help parents become successful partners in educating their children.

	Parent-Community Involvement ("parent" includes parent/community in all cases)		
Proficiency	"Seek difference; esteem it; advocate for equity."	All parents and community members participate as partners in important school and district discussions and decisions.	Encourage and facilitate opportunities for diverse parent groups to meet on their own, in affinity groups, between and within cultures, and with school district partners to identify and eliminate barriers to meaningful parent communication and encourage involvement in school/district discussions and decisions.
		Identify and address the needs of all parent groups in school/district meetings, communications, and decisions.	Identify and allocate resources needed for all diverse parents to help narrow and close educational gaps for their children, as well as for other underserved groups in the educational community.

Resource G

Going Deeper With the Essential Elements

Activity	Expertise of Facilitator	Readiness of Group	Time Needed
G1. **Understanding the Essential Elements**	Moderate	Beginning	40 minutes
G2. **Essential Elements of Culturally Proficient Leaders**	Moderate	Intermediate	30 minutes
G3. **Cultural Competence Self-Assessment**	Moderate	Beginning	60 minutes

Activity G1: Understanding the Essential Elements

Purpose

To reinforce the essential elements of cultural competence

To begin the process of translating the concepts into individual behaviors and organizational practices

Expertise of Facilitator

Moderate

Readiness of Group

Beginning

Time Needed

40 minutes

Materials

A copy of the Response Sheet: Culturally Proficient Practices

Briefing

Now that you have been introduced to the essential elements, let's see what cultural proficiency would look like at this school.

Process

1. Introduce or review the essential elements of cultural proficiency on the Response Sheet: Culturally Proficient Practices.

2. Divide the participants into groups of three to five.

3. Assign each group one element to work on.

4. Ask each group to describe the behaviors of an individual or the practices of the school by discussion of the Response Sheet: Culturally Proficient Practices. Encourage groups to be as specific as possible.

5. After each group has finished, ask it to share its responses with the entire group and have the other participants add to the list of behaviors and practices.

Debriefing

1. How difficult was it to describe what each element would look like in our school?

2. Was it easier to describe individual behavior or organizational practices?

3. Did you notice whether people set standards for others or for themselves?

4. How would you like to use these lists?

Variations

1. Focus on a work group, a department, or a classroom.

2. Save the lists for use during schoolwide planning.

3. As you increase your understanding of the elements, add to the lists.

Response Sheet: Culturally Proficient Practices

Essential Element	Current Practices	Proposed Practices
Assessing Culture *Naming the Differences* Guiding questions: • What are the unwritten rules in your school? • How do you describe your own culture? • How does your school provide for a variety of learning styles?		
Valuing Diversity *Claiming the Differences* Guiding questions: • How would you describe the diversity in your current professional setting? • How do you react to the term *valuing diversity*? • How do you and your colleagues frame conversations about the learners?		
Managing the Dynamics of Difference *Reframing the Differences* Guiding questions: • How do you handle conflict in the classroom? • What skills do you possess to handle conflict? • Describe situations of cross-cultural conflict that may be based on historic distrust.		

(Continued)

Essential Element	Current Practices	Proposed Practices
Adapting to Diversity *Changing for the Differences* Guiding questions: • How have you recently adapted to the needs of a new member? • How has your organization recently adapted to the needs of new members? • Describe examples of inclusive language and of inclusive materials. • How do you teach your clients about the organization's need to adapt to cultures?		
Institutionalizing Cultural Knowledge *Training About Differences* Guiding questions: • What do you currently know about the cultural groups in your organization and among your clients? • What more would you like to know about those cultures? • How do you and your colleagues learn about these cultural groups?		

Activity G2: Essential Elements of Culturally Proficient Leaders

Purpose

To identify leadership behaviors associated with each of the elements of cultural proficiency

Skill of Facilitator

Moderate

Readiness of Group

Intermediate

Time Needed

30 minutes

Materials

A copy of the five essential elements of cultural proficiency

Chart paper

Markers

Briefing

Now that we know what the five essential elements are, let's discuss what they look like as specific behaviors for leaders and classroom teachers.

Process

1. Distribute or post a copy of the essential elements of cultural proficiency.

2. Divide the participants into at least five small groups.

3. Assign one element to each group.

4. Ask the participants to brainstorm specific leader actions.

5. When the lists are completed, have each group share its work and invite the other participants to respond to the lists with additions and critical comments.

6. Reinforce the different elements by asking participants to indicate whether they agree that an activity is related to the specific element being discussed.

Debriefing

1. Ask participants to discuss their level of comfort with the process of brainstorming activities.

2. Then ask them to discuss what it would take to implement the activities.

3. Decide as a group what you will do with the lists of activities.

Variations

1. Reproduce and distribute the lists. Ask the group to refine them.

2. Assign committees to implement particular activities.

3. Repeat the activity, focusing on the school or district culture.

4. Repeat the activity with different audiences (e.g., students, parents, teachers, and staff).

5. Compare the lists to the self-assessment in the next activity.

6. Ask participants to create their own self-assessments.

Activity G3: Cultural Competence Self-Assessment

Purpose

To provide a baseline of information and a starting point for conversation about becoming culturally proficient. This checklist will *not* certify anyone. It simply provides some key questions for exploration.

Expertise of Facilitator

Moderate

Readiness of Group

Intermediate

Time Needed

20 minutes to complete the assessment and an additional 20–40 minutes to discuss the results

Materials Needed

Response Sheet: Cultural Competence Self-Assessment

Briefing

This instrument will ask you questions that will help you to determine where to start as you develop your cultural competence.

Process

1. Distribute Response Sheet: Cultural Competence Self-Assessment.

2. Encourage participants to be candid in their responses.

Debriefing

1. How do you think you did?

2. Was there any pattern to your responses?

3. What would you like to know, do, and learn as a result of your answers?

4. What additional questions would you add to this self-assessment?

5. Where shall we go as a group?

Variations

1. Organize the participants into cohort groups. Have them share their responses with one another and decide as a group what they would like to do next.

2. Organize the participants into five groups, one for each element. Have each group brainstorm ideas for developing skills and knowledge that will increase their competence for that particular element.

Cultural Competence Self-Assessment

Circle the numbers that best reflect your responses to the questions:

rarely = 1, seldom = 2, sometimes = 3, often = 4, usually = 5

Assesses Culture					
1. I am aware of my own culture and ethnicity.	1	2	3	4	5
2. I am comfortable talking about my culture and ethnicity.	1	2	3	4	5
3. I know the effect that my culture and ethnicity may have on the people in my work setting.	1	2	3	4	5
4. I seek to learn about the culture of this organization.	1	2	3	4	5
5. I seek to learn about the cultures of this organization's employees.	1	2	3	4	5
6. I seek to learn about the cultures of this organization's clients.	1	2	3	4	5
7. I anticipate how this organization's clients and employees will interact with, conflict with, and enhance one another.	1	2	3	4	5
Values Diversity					
8. I welcome a diverse group of clients and colleagues into the work setting.	1	2	3	4	5
9. I create opportunities at work for us to be more inclusive and more diverse.	1	2	3	4	5
10. I appreciate both the challenges and opportunities that diversity brings.	1	2	3	4	5
11. I share my appreciation of diversity with my coworkers.	1	2	3	4	5
12. I share my appreciation of diversity with other clients.	1	2	3	4	5
13. I work to develop a learning community with the clients (internal or external) I serve.	1	2	3	4	5
14. I make a conscious effort to teach the cultural expectations of my organization or department to those who are new or who may be unfamiliar with the organization's culture.	1	2	3	4	5
15. I proactively seek to interact with people from diverse backgrounds in my personal and professional life.	1	2	3	4	5
Manages the Dynamics of Difference					
16. I recognize that conflict is a normal part of life.	1	2	3	4	5
17. I work to develop skills to manage conflict in a positive way.	1	2	3	4	5

18. I help my colleagues to understand that what appear to be clashes in personalities may in fact be conflicts in culture.	1	2	3	4	5
19. I help the clients I serve to understand that what appear to be clashes in personalities may in fact be conflicts in personal or organizational culture.	1	2	3	4	5
20. I check myself to see if an assumption I am making about a person is based upon facts or upon stereotypes about a group.	1	2	3	4	5
21. I accept that the more diverse our group becomes, the more we will change and grow.	1	2	3	4	5

Adapts to Diversity

22. I realize that once I embrace the principles of cultural proficiency, I, too, must change.	1	2	3	4	5
23. I am committed to the continuous learning that is necessary to deal with the issues caused by differences.	1	2	3	4	5
24. I seek to enhance the substance and structure of the work I do so that it is informed by the guiding principles of cultural proficiency.	1	2	3	4	5
25. I recognize the unsolicited privileges I might enjoy because of my title, gender, age, sexual orientation, physical ability, or ethnicity.	1	2	3	4	5
26. I know how to learn about people and cultures unfamiliar to me without giving offense.	1	2	3	4	5

Institutionalizes Cultural Knowledge

27. I work to influence the culture of this organization so that its policies and practices are informed by the guiding principles of cultural proficiency.	1	2	3	4	5
28. I speak up if I notice that a policy or practice unintentionally discriminates against or causes an unnecessary hardship for a particular group in this organization's community.	1	2	3	4	5
29. I take advantage of teachable moments to share cultural knowledge or to learn from my colleagues.	1	2	3	4	5
30. I take advantage of teachable moments to share cultural knowledge with this organization's clients.	1	2	3	4	5
31. I seek to create opportunities for my colleagues, managers, clients, and the communities we serve to learn about one another.	1	2	3	4	5

References

Adams, David Wallace. (1996). Fundamental considerations: The deep meaning of Native American schooling, 1880–1900. In Tamara Beauboeuf-Lafontant & D. Smith Augustine (Eds.), *Facing racism in education* (2nd ed., pp. 153–184). Cambridge, MA: Harvard University Press.

Argyris, Chris. (1990). *Overcoming organizational defenses: Facilitating organizational learning.* Englewood Cliffs, NJ: Prentice Hall.

Baca, Leonard, & Almanza, Estella. (1991). *Language minority students with disabilities.* Reston, VA: Council for Exceptional Children.

Ball, Edward. (1998). *Slaves in the family.* New York: Ballantine.

Banks, James. (1994). *Multiethnic education: Theory and practice.* Needham, MA: Allyn & Bacon.

Banks, James. (1999). *An introduction to multicultural education* (3rd ed.). Needham, MA: Allyn & Bacon.

Barker, Joel. (1989). *Discovering the future: The business of paradigms.* Lake Elmo, MN: Ili Press.

Barker, Joel. (Producer). (1996). *Paradigm principles* [Motion picture]. (Available from Charthouse International Learning Corporation, Burnsville, MN).

Bass, Bernard M. (1997). Does the transactional/transformational leadership paradigm transcend organizational and national boundaries? *American Psychologist, 52*(2), 130–139.

Begley, Sharon. (1995, February 13). Three is not enough: Surprising new lessons from the controversial science of race. *Newsweek,* 68.

Blankstein, Alan M. (2004). Failure is not an option: Six principles that guide student achievement in high-performing schools. Thousand Oaks, CA: Corwin.

Bochenek, Michael, & Brown, A. Widney. (2001). *Hatred in the hallways: Violence and discrimination against lesbian, gay, bisexual and transgender students in U.S. schools.* New York: Human Rights Watch.

Boyd, Malcolm. (1984). *Take off the masks.* Philadelphia: New Society.

Bridges, William. (1980). *Transitions: Making sense of life's changes.* Reading, MA: Addison Wesley.

Burris, Carol Corbett, & Garrity, Delia T. (2008). *Detracking for excellence and equity.* Alexandria, VA: Association for Supervision and Curriculum Development.

Collins, James, & Porras, Jerry. (1997). *Built to last: Successful habits of visionary companies.* New York: Harper.

Collins, Jim. (2001). *Good to great.* New York: HarperCollins.

Comer, James P. (1988). Educating poor and minority children. *Scientific American, 259*(5), 42–48.

Cose, Ellis. (1998). *Color-blind: Seeing beyond race in a race-obsessed world.* New York: Harper Perennial.

Cross, Terry L. (1989). *Toward a culturally competent system of care.* Washington, DC: Georgetown University Child Development Program, Child and Adolescent Service System Program.

Cross, Terry L., Bazron, Barbara J., Dennis, Karl W., & Isaacs, Mareasa R. (1993). *Toward a culturally competent system of care: Vol. 2.* Washington, DC: Georgetown University Child Development Program, Child and Adolescent Service System Program.

Cummins, Jim. (1990). Empowering minority students. In Nitza M. Hidalgo, Caesar L. McDowell, & Vanessa Siddle Walker (Eds.), *Facing racism in education* (pp. 50–68). Cambridge, MA: Harvard University Press.

Delpit, Lisa. (1988). The silenced dialogue: Power and pedagogy in educating other people's children. *Harvard Educational Review, 58*(3), 280–298.

Delpit, Lisa. (1993). Silenced dialogue. In Lois Weis & Michelle Fine (Eds.), *Beyond silenced voices: Class, race, and gender in United States schools.* Albany: State University of New York Press.

Duchene, Marlys. (1990). Giant law, giant education, and ant: A story about racism and Native Americans. In Nitza M. Hidalgo, Caesar L. McDowell, & Vanessa Siddle Walker (Eds.), *Facing racism in education* (pp. 20–27). Cambridge, MA: Harvard University Press.

DuFour, Richard, & Eaker, Robert. (1998). *Professional learning communities at work: Best practices for enhancing student achievement.* Alexandria, VA: Association for Supervision and Curriculum Development.

Ellison, Ralph. (1952). *Invisible man.* New York: Random House.

Fine, Michelle. (1993). Missing discourse of desire. In Lois Weis & Michelle Fine (Eds.), *Beyond silenced voices: Class, race, and gender in United States schools.* Albany: State University of New York Press.

Franklin, John Hope, & Moss Jr., Alfred A. (1988). *From slavery to freedom: A history of Negro Americans.* New York: Knopf.

Freire, Paolo. (1970). *Pedagogy of the oppressed* (Nyra Bergman Ramos, Trans.). New York: Seabury.

Freire, Paolo. (1997). *Democracy and ethics.* New York: Continuum.

Fullan, Michael. (1991). *The new meaning of educational change.* New York: Teachers College Press.

Fullan, Michael. (2003). *The moral imperative of school leadership.* Thousand Oaks, CA: Corwin.

Gay, Geneva. (2000). *Culturally responsive teaching: Theory, research, and practice.* New York: Teachers College Press.

Gilligan, Carol. (1983). *In a different voice.* Cambridge, MA: Harvard University Press.

Giroux, Henry A. (1992a). *Border crossings: Cultural workers and the politics of education.* New York: Routledge.

Giroux, Henry A. (1992b). Educational leadership and the crisis of democratic government. *Educational Researcher, 21*(4), 411.

Harrison, Barbara Schmidt. (1992). *Managing change in organizations.* Los Angeles: Baskin-Robbins International.

Hawley, Willis. (1983). *Strategies for effective desegregation: Lessons from research.* Lexington, MA: Lexington Books.

Heifetz, Ron, & Linsky, Martin. (2002). *Leadership on the line: Staying alive through the dangers of leadership.* Cambridge, MA: Harvard Business School Press.

Hooks, Bell. (1990). *Yearning: Race, gender and cultural politics.* Boston: South End Press.

Hord, Shirley M., Rutherford, William L., Huling-Austin, Leslie, & Hall, Gene E. (1987). *Taking charge of change.* Alexandria, VA: Association for Supervision and Curriculum Development.

Hord, Shirley M., & Sommers, William A. (2008). *Leading professional learning communities: Voices from research and practice.* Thousand Oaks, CA: Corwin, National Association of Secondary School Principals, & National Staff Development Council.

Howard, Gary R. (1993). Whites in multicultural education: Rethinking our role. *Phi Delta Kappan, 75*(1), 36–41.

Hudson, J. Blaine. (1999). Affirmative action and American racism in historical perspective. *The Journal of Negro History, 84*(3), 260–274.

Ibarra, Luis. (2008). *Transforming a school culture: Examining the leadership behavior of successful principals.* Unpublished doctoral dissertation, University of California—San Diego and California State University—San Marcos.

Kovel, Joel. (1984). *White racism: A psychohistory.* New York: Columbia University Press.

Kozol, Jonathan. (1991). *Savage inequalities: Children in America's schools.* New York: Harper Perennial.

Kozol, Jonathan. (2007). *Letters to a young teacher.* New York: Crown.

Kruse, Sharon D., & Seashore Louis, Karen. (1995). *Professionalism in community: Perspectives on reforming urban schools.* Thousand Oaks, CA: Corwin.

Ladson-Billings, Gloria. (2005). *Beyond the big house: African American educators on teacher education.* New York: Teachers College Press.

Lawson, Michael A. (2003). School-family relations in context: Parent and teacher perceptions of parent involvement. *Urban Education, 38*(1), 77–133.

Levin, Henry M. (1988). *Accelerated schools for at-risk students.* New Brunswick, NJ: Center for Policy Research in Education.

Lindsey, Delores B., Daly, Alan J., & Ibarra, Luis. (2009). *From systems of failure to systems of support: A qualitative study of principals whose schools exited program improvement.* Unpublished manuscript.

Lindsey, Delores B., Jungwirth, Linda D., Pahl, Jarvis V. N. C., & Lindsey, Randall B. (in press). *Culturally proficient learning communities: Confronting inequities through collaborative curiosity.* Thousand Oaks, CA: Corwin.

Lindsey, Randall B., Graham, Stephanie M., Westphal Jr., R. Chris, & Jew, Cynthia L. (2008). *Culturally proficient inquiry: A lens for identifying and examining educational gaps.* Thousand Oaks, CA: Corwin.

Lindsey, Randall B., Roberts, Laraine M., & CampbellJones, Franklin. (2005). *The culturally proficient school: An implementation guide for school leaders.* Thousand Oaks, CA: Corwin.

Locust, Carol. (1996). Wounding the spirit: Discrimination and traditional American Indian beliefs. In Tamara Beauboeuf-Lafontant & D. Smith Augustine (Eds.), *Facing racism in education* (2nd ed.). Cambridge, MA: Harvard University Press.

Marzano, Robert, J. (2003). *What works in schools: Translating research into action.* Alexandria, VA: Association of Supervision and Curriculum Development.

McCarthy, Cameron. (1993). After the canon: Knowledge and ideological representation in the multicultural discourse on curriculum reform. In Cameron McCarthy & Warren Crichlow (Eds.), *Race identity and representation in education* (pp. 289–305). New York: Routledge.

McIntosh, Peggy. (1988). *White privilege and male privilege: A personal account of coming to see correspondences through work in women's studies.* Wellesley, MA: Wellesley College.

Miller, Neil. (2006). *Out of the past: Gay and lesbian history from 1869 to the present.* New York: Alyson Books.

Milner IV, H. Richard. (2007). Race, culture, and researcher positionality: Working through dangers seen, unseen, and unforeseen. *Educational Researcher, 36,* 388–400.

Montana Office of Public Instruction. (2008). *Indian education for all.* Retrieved February 4, 2009, from http://www.opi.mt.gov/IndianEd2/Index.html

Nieto, Sonia. (2004). *Affirming diversity: The sociopolitical context of multicultural education* (4th ed.). Boston: Pearson.

Nuri Robins, Kikanza, Lindsey, Randall B., Lindsey, Delores B., & Terrell, Raymond D. (2006). *Culturally proficient instruction: A guide for people who teach* (2nd ed.). Thousand Oaks, CA: Corwin.

Oakes, Jeannie. (1985). *Keeping track: How schools structure inequality.* New Haven, CT: Yale University Press.

Oakes, Jeannie, & Lipton, Martin. (1990). *Making the best of school.* New Haven, CT: Yale University Press.

Ogbu, John U. (1978). *Minority education and caste: The American system in cross-cultural perspective.* New York: Academic Press.

Ogbu, John U., & Matute-Bianchi, María Eugenia. (1990). Understanding sociocultural factors: Knowledge, identity, and school adjustment. In Bilingual Education Office, California State Department of Education, *Beyond language: Social and cultural factors in schooling language minority students* (pp. 73–142). Los Angeles: California State University. (ERIC Document Reproduction Service No. ED304241)

Orfield, Gary, & Frankenberg, Elizabeth. (2007). *Lessons in integration: Realizing the promise of racial diversity in America's public schools.* Charlottesville: University of Virginia Press.

Owens, Robert G. (1991). *Organizational behavior in education.* Englewood Cliffs, NJ: Prentice Hall.

Owens, Robert G. (1995). *Organizational behavior in education* (5th ed.). Boston: Allyn & Bacon.

Oxley, Diana. (2004). *Small learning communities: A review of the research.* Philadelphia: The Laboratory for Student Success, The Mid-Atlantic Regional Educational Laboratory, Temple University Center for Research in Human Development and Education. Retrieved February 4, 2009, from http://www.temple.edu/lss/pdf/ReviewOfTheResearchOxley.pdf

Perie, Marianne, Moran, Rebecca, & Lutkus, Anthony D. (2005). *NAEP 2004 trends in academic progress: Three decades of student performance in reading and mathematics* (NCES 2005-464). Washington, DC: U.S. Department of Education, Institute of Education Sciences, National Center for Education Statistics.

Reeves, Douglas B. (2008). *The leader's guide to standards: A blueprint for educational equity and excellence.* San Francisco: Jossey-Bass.

Riot Commission. (1968). *Report of the National Advisory Commission on Civil Disorders.* Washington, DC: Government Printing Office.

Rosenthal, Robert, & Jacobson, Lenore. (1966). Teachers' expectancies: Determinants of pupils' IQ gains. *Psychological Reports, 19,* 115–118. Available February 4, 2009, at http://www.indiana.edu/~educy520/readings/rosenthal66.pdf

Sadker, Myra, & Sadker, David. (1994). *Failing at fairness: How America's schools cheat girls.* New York: Charles Scribner's Sons.

Sapon-Shevin, Mara. (1993). Gifted education. In Lois Weis & Michelle Fine (Eds.), *Beyond silenced voices: Class, race, and gender in United States schools.* Albany: State University of New York Press.

Schein, Edgar H. (1985). *Organizational culture and leadership: A dynamic view.* New York: Jossey-Bass.

Senge, Peter M. (1990). *The fifth discipline. The art and practice of the learning organization.* London: Random House.

Senge, Peter M., Cambron-McCabe, Nelda H., Lucas, Timothy, Kleiner, Art, Dutton, Janis, et al. (Eds.). (2000). *Schools that learn: A fifth discipline fieldbook for educators, parents, and everyone who cares about education.* New York: Doubleday.

Senge, Peter M., Roberts, Charlotte, Ross, Richard, Smith, Bryan, & Kleiner, Art. (1994). *The fifth discipline fieldbook: Strategies and tools for building a learning organization.* New York: Doubleday.

Shirts, R. Garry. (1969). *StarPower.* Del Mar, CA: Simile II.

Singleton, Glen E., & Linton, Curtis. (2006). *Courageous conversations about race: A field guide for achieving equity in schools.* Thousand Oaks, CA: Corwin.

Sizer, Theodore. R. (1985). *Horace's compromise: The dilemma of the American high school.* Boston: Houghton Mifflin.

Slavin, Robert. (1996). *Every child, every school: Success for all.* Thousand Oaks, CA: Corwin.

Sleeter, Christine E., & Grant, Carl A. (2007). *Making choices for multicultural education: Five approaches to race, class, and gender* (2nd ed.). New York: Macmillan.

Tappan, Mark. (2006). Reframing internalized oppression and internalized domination: From the psychological to the sociocultural. *Teachers College Record, 108*(10), 2115–2144. Retrieved February 4, 2009, from http://www.tcrecord.org

Terry, Robert W. (1970). *For whites only.* Grand Rapids, MI: Eerdmans.

Tochluk, Shelly. (2008). *Witnessing whiteness: First steps toward an antiracist practice and culture.* Lanham, MD: Rowman & Littlefield Education.

Townley, Arthur J., & Schmeider-Ramirez, June H. (2007). *School law: A California perspective* (3rd ed.). Dubuque, IA: Kendall-Hunt.

Valadez, James R. (2008). Shaping the educational decisions of Mexican immigrant high school students. *American Educational Research Journal, 45*(4), 834–860.

Weiss, Andrea, & Schiller, Greta. (1988). *Before Stonewall: The making of a gay and lesbian community.* Tallahassee, FL: Naiad.

Wenger, Etienne. (1998). *Communities of practice: Learning, meaning, and identity.* New York: Cambridge University.

West, Cornel. (1993). *Race matters.* New York: Vintage Books.

Wheatley, Margaret J. (1994). *Leadership and the new science: Learning about organization from an orderly universe* (new ed.). San Francisco: Berrett-Koehler.

Wheatley, Margaret J. (2002). *Turning to one another: Simple conversations to restore hope to the future.* San Francisco: Berrett-Koehler.

Wheelock, Anne. (1992). *Crossing the tracks: How "untracking" can save America's schools.* New York: New Press.

Willis, Arlette Ingram. (1996). Reading the world of school literacy: Contextualizing the experience of a young African American male. In Tamara Beauboeuf-Lafontant & D. Smith Augustine (Eds.), *Facing racism in education* (2nd ed.; pp. 287–308). Cambridge, MA: Harvard University Press.

Wright, Richard. (1940). *Native son.* New York: Harper & Row.

Zadra, Dan. (Ed.). (2008). *Be the difference.* Seattle: Compendium.

Additional Suggested Readings

Alvesson, Mats, & Berg, Per-Olof. (1992). *Corporate culture and organizational symbolism.* New York: De Gruyter.

Armstrong, Thomas. (1994). *Multiple intelligences in the classroom.* Alexandria, VA: Association for Supervision and Curriculum Development.

Baldwin, James. (1986). Blood, bread and poetry. In Adrienne Rich (Ed.), *Blood, bread and poetry: Selected prose 1979–1985.* New York: W. W. Norton.

Banks, James, & Banks, Cheryl McGee. (2001). *Multicultural education: Issues & perspectives; Strategies, issues and ideas for today's increasingly diverse classrooms* (4th ed.). New York: Wiley/Jossey-Bass.

Barth, F. (Ed.). (1991). *Ethnic groups and boundaries.* Boston: Little, Brown.

Beckhard, Richard, & Harris, Rueben. (1987). *Organizational transitions: Managing complex change.* Reading, MA: Addison Wesley.

Beckhard, Richard, & Pritchard, Wendy. (1992). *Changing the essence: The art of creating and leading fundamental change in organizations.* San Francisco: Jossey-Bass.

Bennis, Warren, & Nanus, Bert. (1985). *Leaders: The strategies for taking charge.* New York: Harper & Row.

Berliner, David C. (1992, February). *Educational reform in an era of disinformation.* Paper presented to the Annual Meeting of the American Association of Colleges for Teacher Education, San Antonio, TX.

Blank, Renee, & Slipp, Sandra. (1994). *Voices of diversity: Real people talk about problems and solutions in a workplace where everyone is not alike.* New York: American Management Association.

Block, Peter. (1989). *The empowered manager: Positive political skills at work.* San Francisco: Jossey-Bass.

Boaz, David, & Crane, Edward (Eds.). (1985). *Beyond the status quo: Policy proposals for America.* Washington, DC: Cato Institute.

Bolman, Lee G., & Deal, Terrence E. (2001). *Leading with soul: An uncommon journey of spirit* (Rev. ed.). New York: Wiley.

Bolman, Lee G., & Deal, Terrence E. (2002). *Reframing the path to school leadership.* Thousand Oaks, CA: Corwin.

Bothwell, Lin. (1983). *The art of leadership.* New York: Prentice Hall.

Boutte, Gloria S. (2001). *Resounding voices: School experiences of people from diverse backgrounds.* Boston: Allyn & Bacon.

Boyer, Ernest L. (1983). *High school: A report on secondary education in America.* New York: Harper & Row.

Boyer, Ernest L. (1995). *The basic school: A community for learning.* Menlo Park, CA: Carnegie Foundation.

Bracey, Gerald R. (1991). Why can't they be like we were? *Phi Delta Kappan, 73*(2), 104–117.

Branding, Ronice. (1998). *Fulfilling the dream.* St. Louis, MO: Chalice Press.

Bridges, William. (1991). *Managing transitions: Making the most of change.* Reading, MA: Addison Wesley.

Bridges, William. (2001). *The way of transition: Embracing life's most difficult moments.* Cambridge, MA: Perseus.

Brookover, W. (1982). Creating effective schools: An inservice program for enhancing school learning climate and achievement. Holmes Beach, FL: Learning.

Brown, Susan C., & Kysilka, Marcella L. (2001). *Applying multicultural and global concepts in the classroom and beyond.* Boston: Allyn & Bacon.

Bureau of the Census. (1997). *Census updates, 1997.* Washington, DC: Author.

California Commission on Teacher Credentialing. (1995). *Standards of quality and effectiveness for administrative services credential programs.* Sacramento, CA: Author.

Callahan, Raymond E. (1962). *Education and the cult of efficiency.* Chicago: University of Chicago Press.

Campbell, David. (1984). *If I'm in charge here, why is everybody laughing?* Greensboro, NC: Center for Creative Leadership.

Capper, Coleen (Ed.). (1993). *Educational administration in a pluralistic society.* Albany: State University of New York Press.

Carson, Charles C., Huelskamp, Robert M., & Woodall, Thomas D. (1991). *Perspectives on education in America, annotated briefing—third draft.* Alamogordo, NM: Sandia National Laboratories, Systems Analysis Department.

Carter, Thomas P. (1971). *Mexican Americans in school: A history of educational neglect.* Princeton, NJ: College Entrance Examination Board.

Cheek, Robert. (1976). *Assertive black puzzled white.* San Luis Obispo, CA: Impact.

Chinn, Phillip, & Gollnick, Donna. (2002). *Multicultural education in a pluralistic society* (6th ed.). Upper Saddle River, NJ: Merrill Education/Prentice Hall.

Comer, James P., & Haynes, N. M. (1991). Parent involvement in schools: An ecological approach. *Elementary School Journal, 3,* 271–277.

Cross, Elsie. (2000). *Managing diversity: The courage to lead.* Westport, CT: Quorum.

Cross, Terry L., Bazron, Barbara J., Dennis, Karl W., & Isaacs, Mareasa R. (1989). *Toward a culturally competent system of care: Vol 1.* Washington, DC: Georgetown

University Child Development Program, Child and Adolescent Service System Program.

Culbertson, James. A. (1988). A century's quest for a knowledge base. In Norman J. Boyan (Ed.), *Handbook of research on educational administration* (pp. 3–26). White Plains, NY: Longman.

Cummins, Jim. (1988). From multicultural to anti-racist education: An analysis of programmes and practices in Ontario. In Tove Skutnabb-Kangas & Jim Cummins (Eds.), *Minority education* (pp. 127–157). Philadelphia: Multilingual Matters.

Davidman, Leonard, & Davidman, Patricia. (2000). *Teaching with a multicultural perspective* (3rd ed.). New York: Longman.

Davis, G., & Watson, C. (1985). *Black life in corporate America: Swimming in midstream.* Garden City, NY: Anchor.

Deal, Terence, & Kennedy, Allen. (1982). *Corporate cultures: The rites and rituals of corporate life.* Reading, MA: Addison Wesley.

Deal, Terence, & Peterson, Kent D. (1998). *Shaping school culture: The heart of leadership.* San Francisco: Jossey-Bass.

Deming, C. Edwards. (1986). *Out of the crisis: Productivity and competitive position.* Cambridge, England: Cambridge University Press.

De Pree, Max. (1997). *Leading without power: Finding hope in serving community.* San Francisco: Jossey-Bass.

Derman-Sparks, Louise, Phillips, Carol Brunson, & Hilliard III, Asa G. (1997). *Teaching/learning anti-racism: A developmental approach.* New York: Teachers College Press.

Dinnerstein, Leonard, Nichols, Roger L., & Reimers, David M. (1979). *Natives and strangers: Ethnic groups and the building of America.* New York: Oxford University Press.

Doyle, Denis P., & Pimentel, Susan. (1998). *Raising the standard: An eight-step action guide for schools and communities.* Thousand Oaks, CA: Corwin.

Drucker, Peter F. (1954). *The practice of management.* New York: Harper & Row.

Eakin, Sybil, & Backler, Alan. (1993). *Every child can succeed: Readings for school improvement.* Bloomington, IN: Agency for Instructional Technology.

Edmonds, Ronald. (1979). Some schools work and more can. *Social Policy, 9*(5), 3.

Educational Testing Service. (2001). *A framework for school leaders: Linking standards to practice.* Princeton, NJ: Author.

El Sadat, Anwar. (1978). *In search of identity: An autobiography.* New York: HarperCollins.

Espinosa, Ruben W., & Ochoa, Alberto M. (1992). *The educational attainment of California youth: A public equity crisis.* San Diego, CA: San Diego State University, Department of Policy Studies in Language and Cross-Cultural Education.

Fanon, Frantz. (1963). *The wretched of the earth.* New York: Grove.

Feldstein, Stanley, & Costello, Lawrence. (1974). *The ordeal of assimilation: A documentary history of the white working class 1830s to the 1970s.* Garden City, NY: Anchor.

Flamholtz, Eric G., & Randle, Yvonne. (1987). *The inner game of management.* New York: American Management Association.

Foriska, Terry J. (1998). *Restructuring around standards: A practitioner's guide to design and implementation.* Thousand Oaks, CA: Corwin.

Francis, Dave, & Woodcock, Mike. (1990). *Unblocking organizational values.* Glenview, IL: Scott Foresman.

Franklin, John Hope. (1968). *Color and race.* Boston: Beacon.

Fullan, Michael. (2001). *Leading in a culture of change.* New York: Wiley.

Galbraith, John Kenneth. (1977). *The age of uncertainty.* New York: Houghton Mifflin.

García, Eugene E. (2001). *Hispanic education in the United States.* Lanham, MD: Rowman & Littlefield.

Gardner, Neely D. (1974). *Group leadership.* Washington, DC: National Training and Development Service Press.

Gladwell, Malcolm. (2000). *The tipping point: How little things can make a big difference.* Boston: Little, Brown.

Goffman, Erving. (1959). *The presentation of self in everyday life.* New York: Doubleday.

Goodlad, John. (1983). *A place called school: Prospects for the future.* St. Louis, MO: McGraw-Hill.

Gordon, Milton M. (1964). *Assimilation in American life: The role of race, religion, and national origins.* New York: Oxford University Press.

Greer, Colin. (1972). *The great school legend: A revisionist interpretation of American public education.* New York: Viking.

Griffiths, Daniel E. (1988). Administrative theory. In Norman J. Boyan (Ed.), *Handbook of research on educational administration* (pp. 27–51). White Plains, NY: Longman.

Guild, P., & Garger, S. (1985). *Marching to different drummers.* Alexandria, VA: Association for Supervision and Curriculum Development.

Hall, Edward T. (1959). *The silent language.* New York: Doubleday.

Hall, Edward T. (1966). *The hidden dimension.* New York: Anchor.

Hall, Edward T. (1981). *Beyond culture.* New York: Anchor.

Hall, Edward T. (1983). *The dance of life: The other dimension of time.* New York: Anchor Doubleday.

Hamada, Tomoko. (1994). *Anthropology and organizational culture.* New York: University Press of America.

Hanson, Marci J., Lynch, Eleanor W., & Wayman, Karen I. (1990). Honoring the cultural diversity of families when gathering data. *Topics in Early Childhood Special Education, 10*(1), 112–131.

Harragan, Betty L. (1977). *Games mother never taught you: Corporate gamesmanship for women.* New York: Warner.

Harrison, Roger, & Stokes, Herb. (1992). *Diagnosing organizational culture.* San Diego, CA: Pfeiffer.

Henry, Jules. (1963). *Culture against man.* New York: Vintage.

Henze, Rosemary, Katz, Anne, Norte, Edmundo, Sather, Susan, Walker, Earnest, & Tsang, Sam-Lim. (2002). *Leading for diversity: How school leaders promote positive interethnic relations.* Thousand Oaks, CA: Corwin.

Hersey, Paul. (1984). *The situational leader.* Escondido, CA: Center for Leadership Studies.

Hilliard, Asa. (1991). Do we have the will to educate all children? *Educational Leadership, 40*(1), 31–36.

Hodgkinson, Harold. (1991). Reform versus reality. *Phi Delta Kappan, 73*(1), 8–16.

Hofstede, G. (1980). *Culture's consequences: International differences in work-related values.* Beverly Hills, CA: Sage.

Howe, Harold. (1991). America 2000: A bumpy ride on four trains. *Phi Delta Kappan, 73*(3), 193–203.

Immegart, Gerald L. (1988). Leadership and leader behavior. In Norman J. Boyan (Ed.), *Handbook of research on educational administration* (pp. 259–278). White Plains, NY: Longman.

Kanter, Rosabeth Moss. (1977). *Men and women of the corporation.* New York: Basic Books.

Katz, Michael B. (1973). *Education in American history: Readings on the social issues.* New York: Praeger.

Keyes Jr., Ken. (1985). *The 100th monkey.* Coos Bay, OR: Vision Books.

Knowles, Louis L., & Prewitt, Kenneth. (1969). *Institutional racism in America.* Englewood Cliffs, NJ: Prentice Hall.

Kohn, Alfie. (1998). Only for my kid: How privileged parents undermine school reform. *Phi Delta Kappan, 79,* 568–579.

Ladson-Billings, Gloria. (1994). *Dreamkeepers: Successful teachers of African American children.* San Francisco: Jossey-Bass.

Lewis, Anthony. (1994, 19 December). Abroad at home; Leading from behind. *New York Times.* (Available February 4, 2009, at http://www.nytimes.com)

Lightfoot, Sara Lawrence. (1983). *The good high school: Portraits of character and culture.* New York: Basic Books.

Loewen, James W. (1995). *Lies my teacher told me: Everything your American history textbook got wrong.* New York: New Press.

Maccoby, Michael. (1981). *The leader.* New York: Simon & Schuster.

Machiavelli, Niccolò. (1940). *The prince and the discourses* (Trans. Luigi Ricci & Christian E. Detmold). New York: Modern Library.

Malinowski, Bronislaw. (1933). *A scientific theory of culture.* Chapel Hill: University of North Carolina Press.

Massey, Morris. (1979). *The people puzzle: Understanding yourself and others.* Reston, VA: Reston.

Massey, Morris (Producer). (1979). *What you are is where you were when . . .* [Motion picture]. (Available from Morris Massey Associates, Boulder, CO)

McDermott, Diane, & Stadler, Holly A. (1988). Attitudes of counseling students in the United States toward minority clients. *International Journal for the Advancement of Counseling, 11*(1), 61–69.

McGregor, Douglas M. (1960). *The human side of enterprise.* New York: McGraw-Hill.

Miner, Barbara. (1995). Teachers, culture and power: An interview with Lisa Delpit. In David Levine, Robert Lowe, Bob Peterson, & Rita Tenorio (Eds.), *Rethinking schools: An agenda for change* (pp. 136–147). New York: New Press.

Moore, Alexander. (1992). *Cultural anthropology: The field study of human beings*. San Diego, CA: Collegiate.

Naisbitt, John. (1984). *Megatrends: Ten new directions transforming our lives*. New York: Warner.

Naisbitt, John, & Aburdene, Patricia. (1990). *Megatrends 2000: Ten new directions for the 1990's*. New York: William Morrow.

National Association of Elementary School Principals. (2001). *Leading learning communities: Standards for what principals should know and be able to do*. Alexandria, VA: Author.

National Commission on Excellence in Education. (1983). *A nation at risk: The imperative for educational reform*. Washington, DC: Government Printing Office.

Nieto, Sonia. (2000). *Affirming diversity: The sociopolitical context of multicultural education* (3rd ed.). Reading, MA: Addison Wesley.

Obiakor, Festus. (2001). *It even happens in "good" schools: Responding to cultural diversity in today's classrooms*. Thousand Oaks, CA: Corwin.

Ogbu, John U. (1992). Understanding cultural diversity and learning. *Educational Researcher, 21*(8), 5–14.

Ouchi, William G., & Wilkins, Alan L. (1985). Organizational culture. *Annual Review of Sociology, 11*, 457–483.

Pate, Gerald S. (1988). Research on reducing prejudice. *Social Education, 52*(4), 287–289.

Peters, Thomas J., & Waterman, R. H. (1982). *In search of excellence: Lessons from America's best-run companies*. New York: Harper & Row.

Peterson, Kent, & Deal, Terrence. (1998). *Shaping school culture*. San Francisco: Jossey-Bass.

Pfeiffer, J. William. (1987–1994). *Annuals: Developing human resources*. San Diego, CA: University Associates.

Pfeiffer, J. William, & Goodstein, Leonard D. (1982–1986). *Annuals for facilitators, trainers, and consultants*. San Diego, CA: University Associates.

Pfeiffer, J. William, & Jones, John E. (1972–1981). *Annual handbooks for group facilitators*. San Diego, CA: University Associates.

Pignatelli, Frank, & Pflaum, Susanna W. (1994). *Experiencing diversity: Toward educational equity*. Thousand Oaks, CA: Corwin.

Ponterotto, Joseph G. (1988). Racial consciousness development among white counselor trainees: A stage model. *Journal of Multicultural Counseling, 16*, 146–156.

Pritchett, Price. (1994). *The employee handbook of new work habits for a radically changing world: Thirteen ground rules for job success in the information age*. Dallas, TX: Pritchett & Associates.

Pritchett, Price. (1995). *Culture shift: The employee handbook for changing corporate culture*. Dallas, TX: Pritchett & Associates.

Pritchett, Price, & Pound, Ron. (1990). *The employee handbook for organizational change*. Dallas, TX: Pritchett & Associates.

Pritchett, Price, & Pound, Ron. (1991). *High-velocity culture change: A handbook for managers*. Dallas, TX: Pritchett & Associates.

Pritchett, Price, & Pound, Ron. (1995). *A survival guide to the stress of organizational change*. Dallas, TX: Pritchett & Associates.

Reddin, William J. (1970). *Managerial effectiveness*. New York: McGraw-Hill.

Rendon, Laura I., & Hope, Richard O. (Eds.). (1995). *Educating a new majority: Transforming America's educational system for diversity*. San Francisco: Jossey-Bass.

Richardson, Ken, & Spears, David. (1972). *Race and intelligence: The fallacies behind the race-IQ controversy*. Baltimore: Penguin.

Roberts, Wess. (1987). *Leadership secrets of Attila the Hun*. New York: Warner.

Roosevelt Jr., R. Thomas. (1992). *Beyond gender and race: Unleashing the power of your total workforce managing diversity*. New York: American Management Association.

Rosenfeld, Gerry. (1976). Shut those thick lips! Can't you behave like a human being? In Joan I. Roberts & Sherrie K. Akinsanya (Eds.), *Schooling in the cultural context* (pp. 226–238). New York: David McKay.

Ryan, William. (1976). *Blaming the victim*. New York: Vintage.

Sargent, Alice G. (1983). *The androgynous manager*. New York: American Management Association.

Sashkin, Marshal. (1981). An overview of ten management and organizational theorists. In William Pfeiffer & John E. Jones (Eds.), *The 1981 annual handbook for group facilitators* (pp. 206–221). San Diego, CA: University Associates.

Scott, Cynthia D., & Jaffe, Dennis T. (1995). *Managing change at work*. Menlo Park, CA: Crisp Learning.

Senge, Peter M., Kleiner, Art, Roberts, Charlotte, Roth, George, Ross, Rick, & Smith, Bryan. (1999). *The dance of change: The challenges to sustaining momentum in learning organizations*. New York: Doubleday.

Sergiovanni, Thomas J. (1991). *The principalship: A reflective practice perspective*. Boston: Allyn & Bacon.

Sergiovanni, Thomas J., & Corbally, John E. (Eds.). (1984). *Leadership and organizational culture: New perspectives on administrative theory and practice*. Urbana: University of Illinois Press.

Sheive, Linda T., & Schoenheit, Marian B. (Eds.). (1987). *Leadership: Examining the elusive; 1987 yearbook of the association for supervision and curriculum development*. Alexandria, VA: Association for Supervision and Curriculum Development.

Sizemore, Barbara A., Brossard, Carlos A., & Harrigan, Birney. (1983). *An abashing anomaly: The high achieving predominately black elementary school*. Pittsburgh, PA: Department of Black Community Education, Research and Development, University of Pittsburgh. (ERIC Document Reproduction Service No. ED236274)

Slavin, Robert. (1990). *Cooperative learning: theory, research and practice*. Englewood Cliffs, NJ: Prentice Hall.

Sleeter, Christine E. (Ed.). (1991). *Empowerment through multicultural education*. Albany: State University of New York Press.

Sleeter, Christine E., & Grant, Carl A. (1991). Mapping terrains of power: Student cultural knowledge versus classroom knowledge. In Christine E. Sleeter (Ed.), *Empowerment through multicultural education* (pp. 49–67). Albany: State University of New York Press.

Smitherman, Geneva. (1977). *Talkin and testifyin: The language of Black America.* Boston: Houghton-Mifflin.

Snyder, Thomas D., Tan, Alexandra G., & Hoffman, Charlene M. (2005). *Digest of education statistics 2005* (NCES 2006-030). Washington, DC: U.S. Department of Education, National Center for Education Statistics. (ERIC Document Reproduction Service No. ED492945)

Sparks, Dennis. (1997). Maintaining the faith in teachers' ability to grow: An interview with Asa Hilliard. *Journal of Staff Development, 18,* 24–25.

Spring, Joel H. (2000). *Deculturalization and the struggle for equality: A brief history of the education of dominated cultures in the United States* (3rd ed.). New York: McGraw-Hill.

Sue, Derald Wing, Capodilupo, Christina M., & Holder, Aisha M. B. (2008). Racial microaggressions in the life experience of Black Americans. *Professional Psychology: Research and Practice, 39*(3), 329–336.

Suzuki, Bob H. (1987, October). *Cultural diversity: Achieving equity through equity.* Keynote address presented at the Los Angeles Multicultural Conference, Los Angeles. (ERIC Document Reproduction Service No. ED303527)

Testimony of Michael A. Wartell & Robert M. Huelskamp: Hearings before the Subcommittee on Elementary, Secondary, and Vocational Education of the House Committee on Education and Labor, 102nd Cong. (1991, July 18) (testimony of Michael A. Wartell & Robert M. Huelskamp, Sandia National Laboratories, Albuquerque, NM).

Tiedt, Iris, & Tiedt, Pam. (2001). *Multicultural teaching: A handbook of activities, information, and resources* (6th ed.). Boston: Allyn & Bacon.

Tyack, David B. (1974). *The one best system: A history of American urban education.* Cambridge, MA: Harvard University Press.

Valverde, Leonard A., & Brown, Frank. (1988). Influences on leadership development among racial and ethnic minorities. In Norman J. Boyan (Ed.), *Handbook of research on educational administration.* White Plains, NY: Longman.

Vigil, James Diego. (1980). *From Indians to Chicanos: A sociocultural history.* St. Louis, MO: Mosby.

Vroom, Victor H., & Yetton, Philip W. (1973). *Leadership and decision-making.* Pittsburgh, PA: University of Pittsburgh Press.

Warren, David R. (1978). *History, education, and public policy.* Berkeley, CA: McCutchan.

West, Cornel. (1993). The new cultural politics of difference. In C. McCarthy & W. Crichlow (Eds.), *Race identity and representation in education* (pp. 11–23). New York: Routledge.

Wiggins, Grant. (1989). A true test: Toward more authentic and equitable assessment. *Phi Delta Kappan, 71,* 703–719.

Index

CORWIN

A SAGE Company

The Corwin logo—a raven striding across an open book—represents the union of courage and learning. Corwin is committed to improving education for all learners by publishing books and other professional development resources for those serving the field of PreK–12 education. By providing practical, hands-on materials, Corwin continues to carry out the promise of its motto: **"Helping Educators Do Their Work Better."**